60
MINUTE
ESTATE
PLANNER

SANDY F. KRAEMER

Titles also in this series:

60 Minute Financial Planner

60 Minute Tax Planner

60 Minute Investment Planner (forthcoming)

60 MINUTE ESTATE PLANNER

SANDY F. KRAEMER

PRENTICE HALL PRESS

Library of Congress Cataloging-in-Publication Data

Kraemer, Sandy F.
    60 minute estate planner : fast and easy illustrated plans to save
taxes, avoid probate, and maximize inheritance / by Sandy F. Kraemer.
  -Rev. and expanded.
       p. cm.
   Includes bibliographical references and index.
   ISBN 0-13-081033-9. — ISBN 0-7352-0060-2 (pbk.) — ISBN 0-13-020432-3 (with CD ROM)
   1. Estate planning—United States—Popular works.   I. Title.
KF750.Z9K73 1999
346.7305'2—dc21

98-28696
CIP

Printed in the United States of America
10 9 8 7 6 5 4 3 2 1

60 Minute Estate Planner is sold with the understanding that the author and publisher
are not engaged in rendering legal, accounting, estate planning, or other professional
services. The information is intended to present a comprehensive overview of estate
planning advantages and alternatives. While every attempt has been made to provide
accurate information, neither the author nor the publisher can be held accountable for
any error or admission. Ultimately, you must seek and rely on qualified counsel in your
state residence in completing your estate plan.

Sixty-Minute Estate Plans™ and 60-Minute Estate Plans™ are trademarks of Sandy F.
Kraemer. All graphic illustrations are the exclusive property of Sandy F. Kraemer.

ISBN 0-7352-0060-2 (pbk.)

ATTENTION: CORPORATIONS AND SCHOOLS
Prentice Hall books are available at quantity discounts with bulk purchase for educational, business, or sales promotional use. For information, please write to:
Prentice Hall Special Sales, 240 Frisch Court, Paramus, New Jersey 07652. Please
supply: title of book, ISBN, quantity, how the book will be used, date needed.

PRENTICE HALL PRESS
Paramus, NJ 07652

A Simon & Schuster Company

On the World Wide Web at http://www.phdirect.com

Prentice Hall International (UK) Limited, *London*
Prentice Hall of Australia Pty. Limited, *Sydney*
Prentice Hall Canada, Inc., *Toronto*
Prentice Hall Hispanoamericana, S.A., *Mexico*
Prentice Hall of India Private Limited, *New Delhi*
Prentice Hall of Japan, Inc., *Tokyo*
Simon & Schuster Asia Pte. Ltd., *Singapore*

PRAISE FOR THE
60 MINUTE ESTATE PLANNER
◆ ◆ ◆

"Sandy Kraemer, who wrote the 60 Minute Estate Planner, warns that up to eight federal and state taxes can take more than 55% of a persons's wealth."

NBC Nightly News with Tom Brokaw

"If [you] have time to read only one book on estate planning, this is it. Sandy Kraemer's guide unravels the complexities of this important subject in a clear and entertaining style."

Charles R. Schwab
Charles Schwab & Company, Inc.

"*60 Minute Estate Planner* is a home run for the consumer. Sandy Kraemer has taken a complex subject and made it very understandable. A practical hands-on book I will use often."

Marvin Strait, C.P.A.
Past Chairman,
American Institute of Certified Public Accountants (AICPA)

"With $10 trillion of inheritance in the balance, this book is a must."

William J. Hybl,
President, United States Olympic Committee,
Chairman and CEO of Charitable Foundation, and Attorney

"Give a copy of this book to every client. Talk about it. This may be the best investment advice you ever give."

Benjaman C. Glidden,
Financial Consultant and Stockbroker,
Smith Barney Shearson

"*60 Minute Estate Planner* includes everything you need to know on estate planning—and it's so easy to understand."

Johnnie Long Finance Show
WJR Radio, Detroit

"The *60 Minute Estate Planner* will help my clients and me as well as reduce attorney's fees."

Barton L. Enoch,
Estate Planning Attorney

"I predict Kraemer's *60 Minute Estate Planner* will become the most widely used third party resource tool for the estate planner and for those solving estate planning problems."

Journal of the American Society of CLU and CHFC

"...since the cost of the *60 Minute Estate Planner* by Sandy F. Kraemer is roughly 7.5 minutes of lawyer time, it's money well spent. If you read this book with care and follow its instructions, you'll be money ahead. (You'll also know more about estate planning than most lawyers.)"

Jim Flynn,
"Expert Advice" Newspaper columnist

"*60 Minute Estate Planner* is the most important book I have ever read on this complex subject. Every life underwriter should own a copy and share its messages with clients."

Daniel Teas II, CLU, ChFC, MSFS
The New England

"This is the best book I've ever read on this important subject."

Life Association News

"I saved time and money using the new illustrated charts and examples in the *60 Minute Estate Planner.* It was also most helpful in family discussions and decisions."

David C. Martz, M.D.
President, Colorado Medical Society

"In my own estate planning practice, I have reduced time spent with clients by 50%...and greatly increased client satisfaction by using the 60 Minute Estate Planner."

Gregory John Hock,
General Practice Attorney

"*60 Minute Estate Planner* will lead you through the maze of complex legal and tax issues. Sandy Kraemer's book has all the solutions and simplifies decision making. I recommend it to everyone interested in estate planning."

James A. Shambo, CPA, Chairman,
Personal Financial Planning Division, AICPA

"Absolutely the best estate planning book available. The terrific graphics have saved hours of time for my clients and me."

John N. Yates, CLU, ChFC, MSFS
The New England

"We are using *60 Minute Estate Planner* as a training tool for our new associates."

James R. Fredrick, CLU
New York Life Insurance Company Agency Manager

"The most informative and user-friendly book ever published on estate planning."

Public Radio Station WEAA
Baltimore, Maryland

Dedicated to All Our Heirs;
May Their Inheritance Be an Inspiration

You Can't Take It with You,
So What Are You Going to Do About It?

♦ ♦ ♦

ACKNOWLEDGMENTS

Contributing Authors
Phillip A. Kendall
Tyler D. Kraemer

My grandfather unexpectedly died young. His perceptive estate plan included a modest family trust. Unfortunate events made the small trust a partial safety net for my grandmother and later my divorced mother as she raised, supported, and educated three children. I learned from experience. Planning works!

Writing this book began close to home. Never-ending gratitude to my wife Dorothy for her insights, support, and patience; to my children, Christina, Ericka, and Tyler, for first giving meaning to the word "heirs"; to my longtime law partner, Phillip A. Kendall, who wrote the chapter on charitable giving; Tyler D. Kraemer for all the tax calculations resulting from the 1997 tax act; and to my extraordinary legal assistant Shirley R. Hair for her intellectual and technical skills; to John S. Benson, attorney, for his overviews.

This book would not have been written without constant encouragement and review. Thank you to Ann A. Maenpaa, attorney, for her salient early contributions; to Greg Daries for his brilliant ability to change words into graphic form and give life to containers, pipelines, charts, and worksheets; to Marvin Strait, past president of the American Institute of Certified Public Accountants, and James A. Shambo C.P.A., for their tax accountant overviews; to John N. Yates, CLU, ChFC, and Daniel H. Teas II, CLU,

ix

ChFC, for perspectives from the insurance industry; to Richard A. Miller for his review from the financial planner's world; to Debbie Borst for her intellectual contributions while typing pieces of the manuscript; to Jeannie Smith for her research into the human side of inheritance; to Judges Donald E. Campbell and Rebecca S. Bromley and Probate Magistrate David Griffith for reviewing the concept of alternative estate administration.

Ellen Schneid Coleman, my editor at Prentice Hall, has provided critically important suggestions to improve the manuscript. Her professional suggestions became the glue that bonded together almost unrelated topics concerning estate planning and inheritance; Brian H. Hall provided valuable insights into the publishing industry; Dale Agthe reviewed the manuscript and made me conscious of form and style.

Friends, including Professor Robert W. Knapp, Norman F. Peterson, Randle W. Case, Jamieson D. Kennedy, M.D., and C. Milton Waldron, M.D., have suffered through endless brainstorming sessions concerning inheritance, on fishing trips and around camp fires.

All the federal and state legislators, Internal Revenue Service workers, lawyers, judges, accountants, life underwriters, financial planners, and trust officers daily stir the bubbling cauldron of changing issues we call estate planning.

Finally, the consumer deserves special recognition for not accepting the status quo and crying out for better estate planning and administration services.

Prologue

◆ ◆ ◆

HOW DO YOU WANT TO BE REMEMBERED?

You will be remembered by your heirs. Will your life be an inspiration to others, or will it represent chaos and destruction? Planning works—good or bad. Property will transfer. Taxes may become due. To whom and how much depends upon your decisions. You are the choice maker.

"He hated making any decision, however trivial"

"When I die, it will be like a shipwreck.... It will be worse than anyone imagines,"[1] Pablo Picasso predicted concerning the settlement of his estate. And he was right. When he died in 1973, his personal affairs were in chaos. He left no will or testament. He had three illegitimate children, and he was estranged from everyone in his family except his second wife, Jacqueline. No one was sure who the heirs were—or even what comprised the estate.

---

[1] Ariana Stassinopoulos Huffington, *Picasso: Creator and Destroyer* (New York: Simon & Schuster, 1988).

Why Picasso left so many loose ends in his life has been the subject of much speculation. His biographer, Arianna Stassinopoulos Huffington, wrote that his life was cluttered because "he hated making any decision, however trivial." Picasso kept everything. His Paris apartment and studio were littered with newspaper clippings, catalogues, letters, old ticket stubs, photographs, phone messages, knickknacks, and other such souvenirs of past events. The studio floor was covered with paint splotches, cigarette butts, and dust. He avoided the finality of ending relationships with the women in his life because such endings "had the ring of death." He couldn't decide to divorce his first wife even when his mistress, Françoise Gilot, gave birth to his son Claude.

Although Picasso was acclaimed as the towering genius of twentieth-century art, his disillusionment and isolation were revealed in his work. Viewing an exhibition of his paintings, the psychologist Carl Jung remarked on the similarity between them and the drawings of his schizophrenic patients. The confusion and arrogance that were part of his character as an adult appeared early on. In school, Picasso was a restless and poor student, possibly because of dyslexia. He doodled compulsively in the margins of his schoolbooks and sometimes misbehaved just so the teachers would punish him—by sending him to a detention area where he was free to draw to his heart's content.

His relationships with his wives and mistresses were characterized by ambivalence and chronicled in his paintings. Some of his frustration resulted from the lengthy and bitter negotiations when he finally decided to divorce his first wife, Olga. Before they were married, Picasso signed a community property agreement that committed them to dividing equally everything they owned, including his paintings, in the event of a separation. The ultimate property division was a compromise that both Picasso and Olga viewed as unsatisfactory.

His only legitimate child was Olga's son Paulo. Besides Claude and Paloma, he had a daughter, Maya, by another mistress. As he grew older, his relationships with his children weakened, and he had no interest in his grandchildren. After the age of 80, he locked himself within his estate with Jacqueline. At least partly because of her influence, he refused to see his children for the last ten years of his life, and they were banned from his funeral.

Although he was born in Spain, Picasso lived most of his life in France, and French law governed the disposal of his estate. Nine months after his death, a law was passed that permitted illegitimate children to inherit, and Claude, Paloma, and Maya were declared legal heirs. Paulo died in 1975, and his children, Marina and Bernard, received his share.

But it took five years of litigation to settle the estate. It was estimated that the legal fees equaled one of the shares—about one-tenth of the value of the estate. The estate was valued for tax purposes at $260 million and included almost 50,000 works. Jacqueline received the largest share—three-tenths of the estate. Marina and Bernard each received one-fifth, and Maya, Claude, and Paloma got one-tenth each. The artwork was divided into groups, and the heirs drew lots for them. Each was allowed to choose some works that had personal sentimental value.

Picasso made another prophecy before his death: "When I die, it will be like a shipwreck, and as when a huge ship sinks, many people all around will be sucked down with it."

On the day of his funeral, Paulo's son Pablito swallowed a container of bleach. He died three months later.

In 1977, Maya's mother, Marie Therese hanged herself.

In 1986, the Spanish Museum of Contemporary Art in Madrid planned an exhibition of Picasso's paintings of Jacqueline. She selected the works, and after finalizing details of the exhibition by telephone, Jacqueline put a gun to her head and shot herself.

Picasso did have a calculated estate plan—chaos and destruction—which worked to perfection. His life and death prove planning works—good or bad. The planned legacy he left through his art is priceless and timeless. His unplanned estate was a titanic family disaster. How will you be remembered by your family and the world around you? If you care—read on.

> *"It's only the inspiration of those who die that makes those who live realize what constitutes a useful life."*

Inheritance is what one person receives from another. It can be property, characteristics, culture, or traditions. Inheritance is more than the transfer of land and other forms of wealth from one generation to the next. It is also the transfer of heritage, love, and values. How are these things transferred? By communication and time spent with those about whom you care.

You can't take your money, possessions, land, love, or even your body with you when you die. Have you thought about what you are going to do with them? Remember, what is given and received, as well as how and when it is done, makes and breaks children, parents, relatives, and friends. Planning is an opportunity to show you care.

Will Rogers was right: "It's only the inspiration of those who die that makes those who live realize what constitutes a useful life."[2] The lives of your heirs can be enhanced by your thoughtful and inspired estate planning. Or they can be destroyed.

---

[2] Paula McSpadden Love, *The Will Rogers Book* (Waco, TX: Texian Press, 1972), p. 165.

Introduction
◆ ◆ ◆
PLANNING IS POWER

Your estate plan is the most powerful tool to control your heirs' financial future - and yours. You will always be remembered by the estate plan you make, or fail to make. Accept the responsibility. Your choices will enable or disable your children and grandchildren. Their opportunities and values will be directly tied to your plan.

MORE POWER WITH THE *60 MINUTE ESTATE PLANNER*
◆ ◆ ◆

The *60 Minute Estate Planner* has been acclaimed nationally as the most easily understood book ever written on this life-controlling topic. The unique pipelines and container flow charts advance flow graphics into a new dimension. Reader enthusiasm and endorsements continue unabashed. Smart, simple, fast, and easy estate plans at minimum costs have been completed by tens of thousands of satisfied users.

So why a revised edition? The simple answer is to give you even more planning power. In 1997, Congress made major changes to the estate and gift tax laws for the years 1998 through 2006. You must know and understand these changes to shield your property, or your client's property, from taxes. New flow graphics and charts quickly illustrate legal and tax principles through the year 2006.

This Revised Edition includes new pipeline and container flow graphics requested by readers. Important pay-out planning for IRAs, 401(k)s, profit sharing and other qualified plans receive expanded attention. A new concept—Personal Values Will—is introduced to encourage consideration of values when transferring property. Explanations have been updated and streamlined.

The *Planner* gives new meaning to the acronym KISS—*Keep It Smart and Simple.* The Revised Edition gives you more power to make your estate plan smart and simple, with the emphasis on smart.

EASY PLANS TO AVOID PROBATE, SAVE TAXES, AND ACHIEVE ALL YOUR GOALS

◆ ◆ ◆

If you like simplicity and illustrations, Sixty-Minute Estate Plans are for you. Flow graphic illustrations simplify explanations of confusing legalese and tax jargon. Pictures replace estate planners' wordy explanations. User-friendly charts function as personal worksheets, eliminating the need for page flipping.

If you are seeking practical "how to" knowledge, you will find it. If you are choosing to use a living trust to avoid the anguish of probate, control costs, save time, and preserve privacy, read on. Explanations of probate and other time-tested alternatives for transferring estate property follow. Advantages, disadvantages, and trade-offs of living trusts, probate, and other alternatives are explained. To save time and provide clear instructions, this book is divided into three distinct parts. Parts One and Two take you through quantitative aspects of estate planning. Part Three explains the qualitative side of inheritance.

Part One—Sixty-Minute Estate Planning: Fast, Easy, and Understandable—explains actions you should begin to think about today. You'll learn how to select a lawyer, accountant, life insurance agent, trust officer, financial planner, or stockbroker. Federal gift and estate taxes are made understandable by means of easy-to-follow graphic illustrations. Never forget, if federal estate taxes become due, rates begin at an effective 37% and go up to 55%. These taxes are based on market value of taxable estate assets and must be paid timely. If you have a large estate and desire to give property to grandchildren, be forewarned of the additional possible generation-skipping 55% flat tax. In the worst case, a federal estate tax of 55% and generation-skipping tax of 55% could be assessed on the same asset transfers, plus possible state transfer taxes.

Part Two—Sixty-Minute Estate Plans™—includes numbered plans for both married and single folks, based on estate values, to save you time. For example, Plan M5 is for a married couple, with or without minor children, with combined estate valued at

$1 million. Each plan, accompanied by a plan documentation checklist, is all that is needed for planning an estate of that value. Select the numbered plan that most closely represents your personal and financial situation and work from it.

Part Three—Inheritance Planning Always Includes Personal Values—takes you inside inheritance by going far beyond money and property. Learn how to transfer personal values. If you are interested in what other folks have done, good and bad, what works and what doesn't, you will find entertaining lessons. The right to die takes on new dimensions. Anatomical and eternal gifts live on. Lists of unusual, offbeat, and humorous bequest suggestions flow freely. Part Three explores inheritance as no other book does, providing key points to remember as an added bonus.

The Epilogue is a call for reform. You may help remove routine estate administration from our courts and save taxpayer expense, time, costs, and the anguish of probate. Neither probate nor living trusts are user friendly or consumer oriented. I propose a new choice: Alternative Estate Administration (AEA).

YOUR SIXTY-MINUTE ESTATE PLANS™

◆ ◆ ◆

If you read only Parts One and Two before meeting with a qualified estate planner, no more than 60 minutes should be required to make all key decisions and authorize document preparation. These 60 minutes of open communication may create more inheritance for your loved ones and other beneficiaries than many years of work. Goal setting, tax planning, and probate avoidance will make the difference. Sixty minutes of estate planning can erase a lifetime of indifference and procrastination.

Only a few pages of Part Two will actually apply to you. Identify and understand these pages, and you will be better informed than 95% of the people who walk into a lawyer's office for an estate planning conference. Take a few minutes and learn the easy, inexpensive way from this book instead of learning the hard, expensive way through experience, which will be too late.

CONTENTS

Part

I

◆ ◆ ◆

SIXTY-MINUTE ESTATE PLANNING
Fast, Easy, and Understandable ◆ 1

DEMYSTIFYING TAX PLANNING / 19

Part

II

◆ ◆ ◆

SIXTY-MINUTE ESTATE PLANS™ • 37

SIXTY-MINUTE ESTATE PLANNING™
Quality Selections to Satisfy Your Planning Needs / 39

Part

III
◆ ◆ ◆

INHERITANCE PLANNING
ALWAYS INCUDES PERSONAL VALUES ◆ 167

ILLUSTRATIONS

◆◆◆
FORMS AND TABLES

xxx

Part

I

◆ ◆ ◆

SIXTY-MINUTE
ESTATE PLANNING

Fast, Easy, and Understandable

Chapter 1

HOW TO DEVELOP YOUR
SIXTY-MINUTE ESTATE PLAN™

WHAT IS A SIXTY-MINUTE ESTATE PLAN™?

◆ ◆ ◆

My friend asked, "What is a Sixty-Minute Estate Plan™?" And I responded, "A Sixty-Minute Estate Plan™ is intended to be the best estate plan for you and your heirs." As I answered, my mind raced through memories from over 30 years of preparing family gift and estate plans, as well as the 35 books and hundreds of articles I reviewed to understand better the present status of inheritance in the United States. I sighed as I recalled one recent experience of a widowed new client throwing a thick package of documents on my desk, tears streaming down her face attesting to her anguish at having to go through the agony of probate and tax filings. "It's not right!" she sobbed.

She was right. The probate process is an archaic inheritance system desperately needing replacement. Estate and other transfer taxes often become the worm in the family apple, discovered after it is too late.

This widow's husband had no estate plan. Few people have good plans. Those who make the effort often walk out of the lawyer's office with a fistful of papers and a short memory intending to forget the experience quickly. This book is dedicated to bringing consumer sunshine into this primeval forest of legalese. Simplification, illustration, and clarification are key.

If you read Part One of this book before meeting with a well-trained and experienced estate planner, you will understand the basics and add-ons of a good plan. After reading Part One, no more than 60 minutes with your planner should be required to decide on the basics and add-ons to be included in your plan. These 60 minutes of focused decision making should be the most important time investment of your life. These minutes are the basis for this book.

It's fast, it's easy. Locate the Sixty-Minute Estate Plan™ illustrated example in Chapter 3 that most closely approximates your personal, family, and financial situation. Show this illustrated example to your estate planner together with your fact sheet of important information. After all your questions have been answered, authorize preparation of the necessary basic and add-on documents of a good estate plan. You're on your way. Sixty-Minute Plans™ are a compilation of what many wise teachers and clients have taught me and what I have learned. I trust you will take the practical knowledge you gain and use it to your advantage. For as the ancient sage, Confucius, advises each of us: "The essence of knowledge is, having it, to use it." I hope that you use Sixty-Minute Estate Plans™ and that, as a result, you, your children, other beneficiaries, and society learn that the essence of inheritance is to produce healthy, happy, productive heirs.

Sixty-Minute Estate Plans™: Dedicated to Simplicity and Understanding

Will Rogers, one of the legal profession's best critics, observed in 1927, "The minute you read something and can't understand it, you can almost be sure that it was drawn up by a lawyer." Little has changed in over 72 years—Will would say the same thing today about many estate-planning books on the market. *60 Minute Estate Planner* is dedicated to simplicity and understanding.

The Sixty-Minute Estate Plan™ illustrations and explanations included in the *Planner* are intended to present basic concepts so you may select your estate plan design. Complex and expensive computer programs, formulas, and printouts provide more detail. However, all the most commonly used estate-planning alternatives are presented as well for your consideration.

FIVE GUIDELINES TO SUCCESSFUL ESTATE PLANNING
◆ ◆ ◆

Once there was an intelligent couple who was looking for an effective estate planner. They had spoken with lawyers, trust officers, accountants, life insurance salespersons, financial planners, and stockbrokers. They had gone into every kind of office, large and small, luxurious and sparse, with windows and without. They were beginning to see the full spectrum of how different people planned estates. But they weren't pleased with what they saw. The couple had seen many estate planners who seemed to win while their clients lost. Some of their professional peers thought they were good estate planners. Many of their clients thought otherwise. The couple finally found a wise and effective estate planner. The couple asked, "Why does estate planning always appear to be such a complex, mysterious, expensive process?" The counselor leaned back in his chair and responded, "Because you, who need a good estate plan, don't know the right questions to ask your estate planner."

"But I read newspaper and magazine articles about living trusts and taxes all the time. I even purchased a book about estate planning, although it's just too technical and boring for me." The sage counselor smiled, "Aha!—you have just identified the first secret of estate planning."

Guideline 1: Take an Active Interest in Your Estate Plan

Begin by reading small bits and pieces of information as they appear in your usual reading materials. Gradually you will become familiar with the terms and some general concepts. It is probably a waste of time initially to read a technical book on the subject. You won't know a good book from a bad one, and there are plenty of both on the market. Also, many books are directed to just one alternative or issue, such as living trusts or federal estate taxes. Inheritance is created in many ways. Don't limit your planning options in the beginning.

The husband became puzzled. "How should I begin organizing my thoughts about a good estate plan?" he asked. The planner seized the opportunity.

Guideline 2: Understand and Distinguish Between Your Legal Estate Plan and Your Taxable Estate Plan

Your *legal estate plan* concerns property. How is it owned and titled? How will it be transferred at your death? State law controls and answers these questions. Your *taxable estate plan* concerns taxes that may be assessed on transfer of your legal estate. Lifetime transfers may be subject to federal and state gift taxes. Transfers after death may be subject to federal estate taxes and generation-skipping taxes, as well as state estate or inheritance and generation-skipping taxes. By far the largest tax bite is by the federal government, and for that reason each Sixty-Minute Plan™ considers only federal taxes. The Internal Revenue Code is the federal body of law passed by Congress that dictates all federal taxes. But, remember, taxable property may not be taxed if tax deductions and credits are used effectively. The wife asked the next logical question: "Is it possible to plan our legal estate and our taxable estate together?" The counselor clapped his hands together and said, "You have just asked the jackpot question."

Guideline 3: Dovetail Your Legal and Taxable Estate Plans

This is not only possible, it is absolutely essential. They must work together. Your advisors must be educated to work with both state laws and the federal Internal Revenue Code to prepare a good estate plan.

The husband spoke with increasing confidence; "We have investigated estate planning long enough. We must create our own plan. There is no time like the present. How should I proceed?" The counselor concluded, "Good, you are now ready to begin the estate planning process."

Guideline 4: Prepare Your Estate Plan Step by Step to Avoid Confusion

Step 1: Prepare a current financial statement identifying specifically ownership of each asset and present market value. A sample form follows on page 12.

Step 2: Select one or more planners. Use the same network of people and sources of information as you would use to obtain the names of other qualified professionals. Set up an appointment and interview the prospective planner, using questions following in this chapter beginning on page 7 as a helpful guide. There is generally no charge for a first interview, but verify this in advance.

Step 3: Select a Sixty-Minute Estate Plan™ example (see Part Two) that closely approximates your estate and goals. Use this illustration as a starting point for discussions with your counselor. Ultimately, a qualified lawyer in the state in which you live should draft the legal documents required for your estate plan.

As she reflected upon her role as marriage partner, mother to her two children, and daughter to her surviving mother, the wife wondered aloud if the counselor had any lessons to impart as they began the planning process.

"I'm glad you asked," the sage counselor reflected. "I care more about people than things. You will spend most of your planning time considering property and taxes. Excuse me if I sound old-fashioned, but there are some lessons to remember about people that I would like to share."

Guideline 5: Identify Your Estate Planning Goals in Terms of People

Remember the following:

1. The most valuable gifts to children are love, values, self-reliance, and education.
2. The work ethic of children inheriting wealth at a young age is often permanently spoiled.
3. Set examples for your family by planning ahead, maintaining open and honest communications with the next generations, and being charitable.
4. Discuss your finances fully and openly with your spouse regularly. Both husband and wife should agree on the terms and conditions of family giving and estate plans. Review executed documents regularly, and as family or finances change.

5. Make sure your wishes to benefit your family, friends, and employees are documented to guarantee they are carried out after your death.

6. Give to those you care about during your lifetime to provide reasonable security and maximum educational goals for the next generation.

7. Write your thoughts in a separate letter to special people, to be opened after you are gone.

8. Run the business and financial side of your life in an orderly manner, to avoid unnecessary and costly legal battles after your death.

9. Getting old may be a depressing and lonely experience. People often desire to financially reward those individuals who are kind and caring to them in their old age.

10. Make your estate an inspiration to those who live after you. Show by example what you believe is important. Create incentives for others.

11. When selecting an attorney, effective communication is essential. The level of estate-planning expertise required of a lawyer is dependent on the nature and extent of your estate.

QUESTIONS TO ASK BEFORE YOU HIRE A PLANNING PROFESSIONAL
❖ ❖ ❖

At a recent seminar to which I was invited to speak, a lively discussion ensued. Seminar participants indicated they had difficulty identifying good planners from bad planners. They found marketing often substituted for expertise. Poorly qualified and inefficient planners often have the most effective promotions. It was difficult to separate product sales pitches from good advice. Clients needed some method to personally evaluate planners before using their services. Out of this discussion the concept of interviewing prospective planners arose.

You ask the questions and listen to the answers first. If you are satisfied with what you hear, then authorize the planner to begin asking you questions. The following topics and matters are important in selecting a lawyer, an accountant, a life insurance agent, trust officer, financial planner, and stockbroker. Remember, cheapest is not always best. Do it right, so you don't have to do it over or suffer the consequences of poor planning. First and foremost, confirm qualities of honesty, reliability, and knowledge.

The following checklist may help you prepare your own questions and agenda.

Communications: Is the planner a good listener? Is there an objection to your interview process? Are there distractions during the meeting process? Is enough time allocated to you? Are explanations clear and concise? Do you feel comfortable disclosing intimate personal and financial matters? Is there a problem-solving atmosphere?

Preparation: Is the planner prepared? Has available factual information been reviewed before the meeting? Did you have to wait? Does the meeting progress in an orderly manner? Are diagrams and charts used to illustrate and explain legal and tax concepts?

Staff, Equipment, and Offices: Is there a competent and supportive staff? Is modern office equipment in use, including computers, software programs, copiers, and fax machines? Are you comfortable with the office environment and decor?

Education, Training, and Experience: Is the planner educated, trained, and experienced to provide the services you seek and explain the products being offered? Ask questions about formal education, special qualifications, and certifications in estate planning; continuing education to keep up with changing tax laws; legal and product issues; and years of experience.

Clarity of Explanations: Ask the planner to explain alternatives. What are the advantages and disadvantages of avoiding probate? Compare living trusts with other alternatives. What are the differences among term, whole life, universal life, survivorship life, and other types of insurance policies? What accounting services are needed? If a trust is needed, should a corporate trustee or individual trustee be named to administer the assets? Are stocks, bonds, real estate, or collectibles proper investments for you? Require explanations be repeated until you are satisfied with the answer, or go elsewhere.

Compensation: How will the planner be compensated for working with you? If on a fee basis, how will fees be charged: by the hour or by the project? What is the estimated charge for your work? When must the bill be paid? Can the bill be paid in installments? Will there be a written engagement letter or fee schedule? If payment is by product sales commission, either directly or indirectly, what will be the commissions? How, by whom, and when will they be paid?

Relationship with Planner: Who will actually do your work? Will a team of planners be used? Will this planner continue to be available and service products sold to you? If the planner is unavailable, who will take his or her place? If you die, who will assist in administering your estate?

Participation in Process: How will you participate in your estate planning process? Will you be sent drafts of documents and proposals for product purchases in advance of any required decision making? Will all your questions be answered before you are asked to make a decision?

Other Services and Products: Are other services available from the planner's office, such as financial planning, accounting and auditing, tax preparation, insurance analysis, other legal services, and investment advice? What is the total range of products being offered for sale by the planner?

HOW TO PLAN FOR CHANGE
❖ ❖ ❖

Remember the maxim "Nothing is certain but death and taxes." For estate planning purposes, add the fact the value of your estate is certain to change. Investment, consumption, inflation, and deflation will affect your security, your beneficiaries' inheritance, and payment of taxes.

What will be the rate of growth of your estate per year? Will it exceed inflation? How long is your life expectancy? A current life expectancy table for Americans is included on pages 274–275. Look up your age on any life expectancy table to determine the average life expectancy of a person your vintage.

If your estate is less than the applicable exclusion rate as shown on page 10, it is not subject to federal estate taxes. But as the table on the next page shows, if you assume a conservative 6% growth per year on $600,000, this amount will increase to $802,935 in five years and over $1,000,000 in ten years.

The Sixty-Minute Estate Plan™ models included in this book are based on the present value of your estate today. This is as it should be, because you need to make sure your estate plan will work tomorrow, and each day thereafter. There are many variables that affect your financial future and make projections very speculative. Nevertheless, you should consider and plan for an increase in value of your estate over time. You and your counselor may wish to create projections of your estate three, five, and ten years into the future.

HOW TO REDUCE OR ELIMINATE FEES, COMMISSIONS, AND OTHER ESTATE ADMINISTRATION EXPENSES
❖ ❖ ❖

Administration expenses vary from a minimal amount to 8% plus of the gross estate, depending upon the design of your plan, size and complexity of your estate, residence at death, and fee and commission agreements. Most of administration expenses arise from executor, attorney, accountant, and appraisal services. These compensation arrangements vary wildly from state to state, county to county, and firm to firm. Some are set by archaic state statutes at high fixed minimum fees. Others are determined by standards and customs in the community. Ask your planner about the fees in your state.

Books and sales personnel often quote widely varying administration expenses at death to market certain products or services. Sensational high-fee publicized cases are used for shock purposes, but cannot be ignored. There is no meaningful national standard or comparisons. Administration expenses may be subject to court review and reduction by court order.

For attorneys doing routine estate administration, an hourly charge, or fee not to exceed a fixed amount or percentage of the estate, is often a reasonable arrangement. Pay only for value received. Neither alternative is perfect. Hourly rates may reward ignorance and inefficiency, while percentage fees may be too high and overreaching.

ESTATE VALUES INCREASE OVER TIME
(Assumes a 6% Annual Growth Rate)

Estate	5 Years	10 Years	15 Years	20 Years
$ 600,000	$ 802,935	$1,074,509	$ 1,437,935	$ 1,924,281
1,000,000	1,338,225	1,790,847	2,396,558	3,207,135
2,000,000	2,676,451	3,581,695	4,793,116	6,414,270
3,000,000	4,014,676	5,372,543	7,189,674	9,621,406
5,000,000	6,691,127	8,954,238	11,982,790	16,035,677

(Assumes a 7% Annual Growth Rate)

Estate	5 Years	10 Years	15 Years	20 Years
$ 600,000	$ 841,531	$1,180,291	$ 1,655,419	$ 2,321,811
1,000,000	1,402,552	1,967,151	2,759,032	3,869,684
2,000,000	2,805,103	3,934,303	5,518,063	7,739,369
3,000,000	4,207,655	5,901,454	8,277,095	11,609,053
5,000,000	7,012,759	9,835,756	13,795,158	19,348,422

(Assumes an 8% Annual Growth Rate)

Estate	5 Years	10 Years	15 Years	20 Years
$ 600,000	$ 881,597	$ 1,295,355	$ 1,903,301	$ 2,796,574
1,000,000	1,469,328	2,158,925	3,172,169	4,660,957
2,000,000	2,938,656	4,317,850	6,344,338	9,321,914
3,000,000	4,407,984	6.476,775	9,516,507	13,982,871
5,000,000	7,346,640	10,794,625	15,860,846	23,304,786

Fiduciaries, such as executors and trustees, are entitled to compensation, which varies depending on services performed. Family executors and trustees often serve without charge. Corporate or other professional fiduciaries may charge by a published compensation schedule or going market rates. Always negotiate and insist on a written fee arrangement or letter of engagement when engaging a professional person or organization to provide legal, accounting, and administrative services.

Administration expenses are not factored into Sixty-Minute Estate Plan™ charts and worksheets for simplicity and integrity. The individual facts of each estate and the lack of predictable professional fee schedules make this necessary. Remember, one goal of your plan is to reduce or eliminate administration expenses at your death. Further discussions of administration fees and expenses appear on pages 103–104 and 257. Attorney, accounting, and appraisal costs may arise in any event. Costs can be controlled or eliminated with a good plan and communications with your estate planner.

BEGIN YOUR ESTATE PLAN BY COLLECTING FACTS

❖ ❖ ❖

A forthcoming plane trip or vacation often prompts a person to make an estate plan. A case in point is that of Will Rogers. Rogers was headed for Alaska, and his wife, Betty, was apprehensive. To reassure her, Rogers made out a new will three days before he left. Will Rogers died in a plane crash at Point Barrow, Alaska, on August 15, 1935.

There is an inhibition to even thinking about estate planning because it reminds many people of death. In general, planning sessions are somber, and there is a reluctance to talk about what might happen. Some people put off inheritance planning because they are reluctant to discuss private personal and financial matters with strangers. However, because death and taxes are unpredictable, you should begin today.

An estate plan is only as sound as the facts upon which it is based. Attorneys, insurance agents, financial planners, and accountants often use a questionnaire as a guide to obtain the necessary data and ensure that details will not be overlooked. Alternatively, the essential information may be gathered informally during an office conference. You, and your spouse, if you are married, should begin by preparing a list of all your valuable assets, including insurance, employee benefits, and property in joint names as well as your liabilities and obligations. Use any convenient form, or a blank sheet of paper. The 60 Minute Estate Planner Individual Information form on pages 12–14 will be helpful, and also includes spaces for you to identify executors, trustees and guardians.

GOOD INTENTIONS ARE NOT ENOUGH: DOCUMENTATION AND IMPLEMENTATION ARE ESSENTIAL

❖ ❖ ❖

The following brief glimpse into real life is included to introduce you to the technical world of planning opportunities and mistakes. You are not expected to understand all the legal and tax implications this early in the book. Explanations and solutions will be found in later chapters.

Personal and Confidential

INDIVIDUAL INFORMATION

Outline of basic information needed. Any informal information sheet or financial statement format may be used. Please expand and supplement relevant information.

Name: _____

Occupation and Social Security #: _____

Spouse's Name (if any) _____

Occupation and Social Security #: _____

Address and Telephone Numbers:

Children's Information:

Name	Date of Birth	Relationship	Home Town
_____	_____	_____	_____
_____	_____	_____	_____
_____	_____	_____	_____
_____	_____	_____	_____

	You	*Spouse*	*Joint*
1. Assets:			
Cash and Accounts	$_____	$_____	$_____
Notes, Accounts Receivable	$_____	$_____	$_____
Stocks, Bonds and Funds			
_____	$_____	$_____	$_____
_____	$_____	$_____	$_____
_____	$_____	$_____	$_____
Real Estate (Market Value)			
_____	$_____	$_____	$_____
_____	$_____	$_____	$_____
_____	$_____	$_____	$_____

IRA, 401(k), Qualified Pension and
Profit Sharing Plans

_____ $_____ $_____

_____ $_____ $_____

Tangible Personal Property
(furniture, automobiles, art
objects, personal effects, etc.) $_____ $_____ $_____

Business Interests

_____ $_____ $_____ $_____

_____ $_____ $_____ $_____

Other

_____ $_____ $_____ $_____

_____ $_____ $_____ $_____

                    SUBTOTALS $_____ $_____ $_____

2. Liabilities

Real Estate Mortgages $_____ $_____ $_____

Notes to Bank $_____ $_____ $_____

Accounts Payable $_____ $_____ $_____

Other $_____ $_____ $_____

Taxes $_____ $_____ $_____

                    SUBTOTALS $_____ $_____ $_____

                       TOTALS $_____ $_____ $_____

3. Expected Inheritance

From Whom? $_____ $_____ $_____

4. Life Insurance

Company	Type of Policy	Death Benefit	Insured	Owner	Beneficiary
_____	_____	_____	_____	_____	_____
_____	_____	_____	_____	_____	_____
_____	_____	_____	_____	_____	_____
_____	_____	_____	_____	_____	_____

5. Estimated Total Estate Values for Planning Purposes

You	Spouse	Joint	Combined
$_____	$_____	$_____	$_____

6. Proposed Executor/Personal Representative

	Name	Relationship	Address
Primary:	_____	_____	_____
Alternate:	_____	_____	_____

7. Proposed Trustee

	Name	Relationship	Address
Primary:	_____	_____	_____
Alternate:	_____	_____	_____

8. Proposed Guardians of Minors

	Name	Relationship	Address
Primary:	_____	_____	_____
Alternate:	_____	_____	_____

9. Other Important Information

_____

_____

_____

_____

_____

Date: _____

Don Watson's wife, fondly called Kitty, had been terminally ill with cancer for four months. Patient deaths were an accepted part of Don's medical practice. He tried to use these professional experiences to prepare his four children for the inevitable loss of their mother. Although there is never a right time to lose a loved one, Kitty's passing in 1997 was managed reasonably well by the family because they had talked about it and planned for it. The funeral was a spiritual renewal for both family and friends.

Don came into my office about a week after Kitty's burial. Although we had met socially several times, this was the first time he'd asked for legal advice. After describing Kitty's last few months, he stated "I've tried to practice what I preached to other families when a loved one is lost. Kitty and I each prepared estate plans several years ago. Our wills include so-called bypass trusts. I'm not sure what that is, but I know it was designed to save federal estate taxes. I'd like you to help with any needed administrative details. There shouldn't be much to do."

As I began reading Kitty's will, all appeared in order. The terms of the document gave all her personal effects to Don. Thereafter, a bypass trust was described, which was to receive the applicable exclusion amount of Kitty's property, to be held in trust during Don's life. It is called a bypass trust because property in this trust bypasses, and is not included in, the surviving spouse's taxable estate. Income and principal from the trust were to be used for the benefit of Don and the four children. After Don's death, the children were to receive whatever was left in the bypass trust. Don was appointed to administer the estate, and a local bank was designated trustee of the trust. The document was in a form commonly used for tax planning when a taxable estate exceeds the applicable exclusion.

"What property did Kitty have in her name at the time of her death?" I asked. Don's answer jarred me to an upright position in my chair. Just a lot in the mountains she bought with her own money—maybe worth $10,000, and some worthless mineral rights in Kansas she inherited. I was afraid to ask the next question. "Don, what would you estimate the value of your estate to be?" He responded, "Oh, about $1,600,000."

Don had made one of the most common mistakes in estate planning—one that causes additional federal and state death taxes, administrative costs, attorney's fees, time, and the anguish of probate. Don had a good estate plan on paper—but for reasons too late to change, it was not implemented.

Every good estate plan requires three steps, (1) analysis (2) documentation and (3) implementation. Analysis includes review of all legal and tax matters. Documentation is the preparation and execution of proper documents. Implementation is correctly titling assets, transferring ownership of assets if necessary to achieve tax-planning goals, naming beneficiaries for life insurance and retirement benefits, and other details. Analysis, documentation and implementation are as important to a single person whose estate is a mobile home and an automobile as it is to a wealthy married couple with children. These three steps are important to you.

THE LANGUAGE OF ESTATE PLANNING
❖ ❖ ❖

During the next 60 minutes, I gently explained to Don some basics of estate planning and administration which he needed to hear and understand. I tried to use nontechnical language whenever possible. Although Don and Kitty had previously gone through the estate planning process, most people forget the technical legal and tax jargon quickly. Therefore, I explained basic estate-planning principles and applied them to his present family situation. These same basic principles are important to you. I explained the following to Don.

Probate: Since Kitty owned real estate in her name alone, a local state court probate proceeding will be required. A second probate proceeding will be necessary in Kansas to transfer the mineral rights. Administrative costs, attorney's fees, time, and the agony of probate could have been avoided by placing the property in a living trust. Joint tenancy with right of survivorship would have been another alternative, but may have long-term tax disadvantages.

Unlimited Marital Deduction: The personal property Kitty willed to you, Don, will not be subject to federal estate taxes. Even if Kitty owned the Hope Diamond, there would be no estate taxes if she gave it to you because the Internal Revenue Code allows spouses to transfer property back and forth during life or at death without taxes. It's called the unlimited marital deduction. However, misuse of this deduction is a tax trap for the unwary. I'm afraid you fell into that trap. You could have saved large sums of estate taxes at your later death if property had been transferred into Kitty's name during her lifetime. By not titling assets in Kitty's name during her lifetime, you have lost the advantage of the unified tax credit, which may result in the payment of an additional $250,000 of federal estate taxes at your death. This breakdown in implementation may reduce your children's inheritance by a quarter of a million dollars.

Unified Tax Credit: Presently there is a federal unified tax credit, applied against estate or gift taxes, which results in every person being able to transfer the applicable exclusion to a bypass trust or directly to beneficiaries without taxes. Kitty's will included a bypass trust, which is a trust designed to receive assets thereafter available to you and your children. It is called a bypass trust because it bypasses the taxable estate of the second spouse to die. The IRS does not take a bite out of the bypass trust, and the full value eventually passes estate tax free to the beneficiaries. But to take full advantage of this estate tax-free transfer, Kitty must have the applicable exclusion value of property in her name, which would transfer to her bypass trust or to the children at her death. She only had $10,000 worth of property. Therefore, $590,000 of tax-free inheritance to the children was lost forever. Your estate may pay an additional $250,000 of federal estate tax when you die. This could have been avoided simply by transferring some additional assets to Kitty during her lifetime.

Don, you have asked what you should do to avoid more mistakes and take advantage of available planning opportunities. Let me summarize your present situation. You are close to retirement. You desire to give your estate to your children equally. You own some investment property that is increasing in value. The present federal estate tax on your estate of $1,600,000 would be $408,000 with a graduated maximum applicable rate of 45%. Every dollar you remove from your estate during your life will save 45 cents in estate taxes. I recommend the following:

Living Trust: Use a living trust to avoid probate, manage your assets in the case of your disability, and save time and anguish for your heirs. Remember, only assets transferred into the trust avoid probate.

Pour-Over Will: Include a simple pour-over will that will sweep up any assets in your name and pour them over into the trust at your death.

General Durable Power of Attorney: Sign a general durable power of attorney naming one or more of your trusted children to manage your affairs in your absence or disability.

Health Care Power of Attorney: Sign a health care power of attorney naming one or more trusted children to make health care decisions for you in the event you are unable to make them for yourself.

Family Limited Partnership or Limited Liability Company: Create a family limited partnership, with you the general partner and your four children limited partners. Transfer your appreciating investment property into the family partnership. Begin gifting interests in the family partnership to the children each year. Remember the $10,000 annual exclusion under the Internal Revenue Code, which allows you to give $10,000 to each child each year. This means that you can gift $40,000 to your four children each year without any other tax consequences whatsoever. The 1997 tax changes added possible cost of living increases to the annual exclusion. This is in addition to the applicable exclusion lifetime gifting opportunity. If you live long enough, you may be able to gift all the investment property value out of your estate, while still managing it and controlling it through the limited partnership. It will also be an opportunity to communicate with your children, and make them feel a part of this investment and their inheritance. A new fast developing alternative to family limited partnerships is the limited liability company. This should also be considered.

Good News Note: Don has completed Kitty's estate administration and implemented his new estate plan. He is spending more time than ever before with his children and their relationship has never been better.

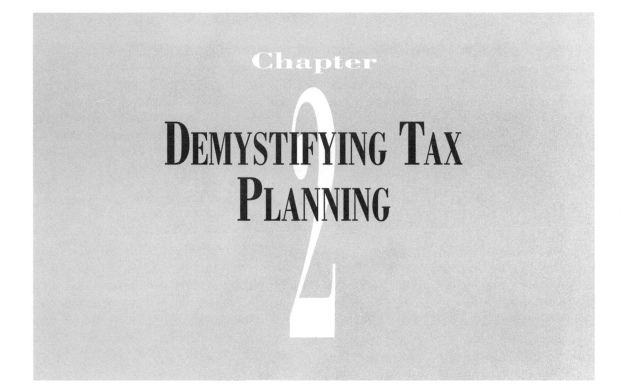

Chapter 2

DEMYSTIFYING TAX PLANNING

*"You sure do die for your country,
if you die from now on."*

Death taxes received Will Rogers's special attention. He called them inheritance taxes. Today, the federal tax is called an estate tax. But whether it is an estate tax or inheritance tax, the universal yell is always the same: "too much." Consider what Will had to say after Congress first passed the transfer tax.

"Congress knocked the rich in the creek with a [raise in the] income tax, then somebody must have told 'em: 'Yes, Congress, you got 'em while they are living. But what if they die on you to keep from paying it?' Congress says: 'Well, never thought of that so we will frame one that will get 'em alive or living, dead or deceased.' Now they got such a high inheritance tax on 'em that you won't catch these old rich boys dying promiscuously like they did. This bill makes patriots out of everybody. You sure do die for your country, if you die from now on."[1]

---

[1] Paula McSpadden Love, *The Will Rogers Book* (Waco, TX: Texian Press, 1972), p. 89.

Will Rogers always provided a humorous perspective to the most difficult problems. Consider what he had to say about inheritance taxes back in the 1930s, and then decide for yourself if anything has changed or if you can expect any help from the Congress. On tax payments, Will commented, "This is the tax paying day. There is going to be no attempt at humor for it would be mightily forced. No two can agree on what is deductible. When it's made out you don't know if you are a crook or a martyr."[2]

ESTATE PLANNING AND TAXES: AN OVERVIEW
❖ ❖ ❖

The Internal Revenue Code, rules and regulations, and court decisions comprise the most complex body of tax laws in the history of the world. Some are ambiguous, others are ridiculously complex. Many IRS agents do not completely understand the law and give incorrect answers to consumer inquiries. IRS agents deserve our sympathy, because they are often insufficiently trained to untangle the ball of worms called "The Code."

Read the following tax overview as if it were a newspaper or magazine article. Prepare a list of questions. Ask your estate planner for the answers.

There are four federal taxes that relate to estate planning. They are

- ◆ Estate taxes

- ◆ Gift taxes

- ◆ Income taxes

- ◆ Generation-skipping taxes

Each of these taxes is controlled by different sections of the Internal Revenue Code as well as rules, regulations, and court decisions. None, some, or all of these taxes may apply to your Sixty-Minute Estate Plan™. Discuss each tax with your planner. Make sure you explore each legal method to avoid, reduce, or defer these taxes. This book illustrates all commonly used estate, gift, and generation-skipping tax-planning tools.

What Assets Are Included in Your Taxable Estate?

Everything you own at death, to the extent of your interest, will be initially includable in your taxable estate. The IRS begins by looking at your total gross estate. Your taxable estate is not limited by state law concepts of property and probate. For example, if your son or daughter is the named beneficiary on a $50,000 life insurance policy owned by you, that $50,000 is included in your taxable estate.

All your property is subject to valuation as of the date of death. This often requires appraisals of real estate and business interests. The process of establishing valuation is often subjective and deserves critical consideration. Results can save or generate

---

[2] Ibid.

substantial taxes. Special rules permit an estate to be alternately valued six months after date of death.

Types of Property Commonly Included in Your Taxable Estate

- *Property Owned Individually:* This includes your stocks, bonds, business interests, real estate, collectibles, vehicles, furniture, and personal effects.

- *Your Share of Jointly Owned Property:* If you and someone not your spouse own the property jointly, whether it is real estate or a bank account, it will be fully included in your estate unless the survivor can prove what he or she contributed. The law is different when married couples jointly own property, with only 50% of the value of the property jointly owned included. For a more complete discussion of this complex area of tax, please see discussion beginning on page 114–116.

- *Property Transferred Where You Retain Control or a Beneficial Interest:* The living trust is the best example of this situation. A living trust is established to avoid probate. It does not save taxes. It is simply another pocket that you can reach into at any time and is revocable. All living trust assets are included in your taxable estate. Another example is life estates. If you leave your granddaughter your cabin by the lake, but retain the right to enjoy it for your life, the cabin will be fully includable in your estate. A final example is survivor annuities. A joint and survivor annuity, which is a common form of payout from a pension plan, provides a fixed amount of income to a person for life; on that person's death, it continues to a survivor, such as your spouse. Even though the first to die never receives the survivor annuity, its value is included in the federal taxable estate.

- *Life Insurance Transfers Within Three Years of Death:* If you transfer the ownership of an insurance policy within three years of your death, the entire proceeds of the policy, not just the cost of the policy or cash surrender value, will be included in your estate. To exclude life insurance from your estate, you generally must part with all "incidents of ownership" in the policy. This rule applies to irrevocable life insurance trusts as well as direct gifts of the policy.

THE FEDERAL ESTATE TAX

◆ ◆ ◆

Deductions and credits may eliminate all estate tax.

For estate tax calculations, your total gross estate is reduced by permitted expenses and deductions, the most significant of which is an unlimited marital deduction that lets you pass everything you own tax free to a current spouse. Once your gross estate is reduced by these amounts, a taxable estate can be calculated. The tax is then levied against that amount. A tentative tax is then calculated. A unified credit is then available and subtracted from that tentative tax. The unified credit shelters up to the applicable exclusion of property from tax. The 1997 tax law causes the applicable exclusion to increase almost yearly until the year 2007, but the changes barely keep up with inflation until 2004, as shown by the following very important schedule:

Applicable Exclusion Schedule: Important to reference the Unified Credit and Applicable Exclusion increases according to the following schedule:

Year	Unified Credit	Applicable Exclusion
1997	$192,800	$600,000
1998	$202,050	$625,000
1999	$211,300	$650,000
2000 & 2001	$220,550	$675,000
2002 & 2003	$229,800	$700,000
2004	$287,300	$850,000
2005	$326,300	$950,000
2005 and after	$345,800	$1,000,000

The effective tax rates range from 37% to 55% of taxable estates. If you are single, the unified credit alone lets you leave the applicable exclustion estate tax free. For a married couple, a combined net worth of up to two times the applicable exclusion can avoid estate taxes just by maximizing each spouse's use of the applicable exclusion which totals $1,300,000 in 1999 and $2,000,000 in 2006.

Good planning is necessary to take full advantage of these tax-free transfers. An individual spouse's taxable estate must include the applicable exclusion of property at date of death, and this property must transfer to someone other than the surviving spouse, to maximize the tax-saving opportunity. Proper planning often requires a balancing of estates between spouses to assure maximum use of the unified credit, regardless of which spouse dies first.

UNIFIED ESTATE AND GIFT TAXES
❖ ❖ ❖

There is a single tax rate schedule that applies to both gifts and estates. It is called a unified estate and gift tax.

With some exceptions, everything you own and give away, whether during life or upon death, is added together to figure out your tax liability.

The unified credit can be used to offset tax on lifetime gifts or your taxable estate. Each individual gets one unified credit, and it doesn't matter if it is used during one's lifetime or to offset estate taxes at death. The unification occurs when the amount of your taxable estate is established. All the taxable gifts you made are added to the assets you own at death to figure out your taxable estate. The tax already paid on the gifts is deducted from your final estate tax bill. The primary exception to this rule is the opportunity to make gifts of up to $10,000 plus adjustments per recipient per year completely tax free. These gifts do not figure into your taxable estate and are not reported on any tax form.

ESTATE ASSETS CONTAINER WITH TAX PIPELINES

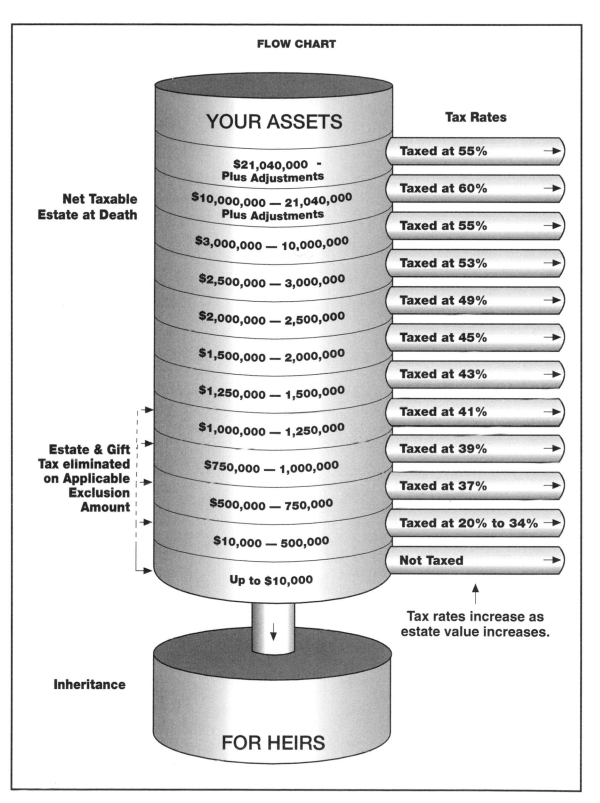

FLOW CHART

YOUR ASSETS

Tax Rates

Net Taxable Estate at Death

Asset Range	Tax Rate
$21,040,000 - Plus Adjustments	Taxed at 55%
$10,000,000 — 21,040,000 Plus Adjustments	Taxed at 60%
$3,000,000 — 10,000,000	Taxed at 55%
$2,500,000 — 3,000,000	Taxed at 53%
$2,000,000 — 2,500,000	Taxed at 49%
$1,500,000 — 2,000,000	Taxed at 45%
$1,250,000 — 1,500,000	Taxed at 43%
$1,000,000 — 1,250,000	Taxed at 41%
$750,000 — 1,000,000	Taxed at 39%
$500,000 — 750,000	Taxed at 37%
$10,000 — 500,000	Taxed at 20% to 34%
Up to $10,000	Not Taxed

Estate & Gift Tax eliminated on Applicable Exclusion Amount

Tax rates increase as estate value increases.

Inheritance

FOR HEIRS

UNIFIED FEDERAL ESTATE AND GIFT TAX RATE SCHEDULE
U.S. Citizens and Residents

Taxable Gift or Estate Transfer		Federal Unified Tax (Before Credits) $ Amount of Tax	% on Excess
0		0	18
10,000		1,800	20
20,000		3,800	22
40,000		8,200	24
60,000		13,000	26
80,000		18,200	28
100,000		23,800	30
150,000		38,800	32
200,000		54,800	32
250,000		70,800	34
300,000		87,800	34
400,000		121,800	34
500,000		155,800	37
600,000		192,800	37
700,000		229,800	37
750,000		248,300	39
800,000		267,800	39
900,000		306,800	39
1,000,000		345,800	41
1,100,000		386,800	41
1,250,000		448,300	43
1,500,000		555,800	45
1,600,000		600,800	45
2,000,000		780,800	49
2,100,000		829,800	49
2,500,000		1,025,800	53
2,600,000		1,078,800	53
3,000,000		1,290,800	55
3,100,000		1,345,800	55
3,500,000		1,565,800	55
3,600,000		1,620,800	55
4,000,000		1,840,800	55
4,100,000		1,895,800	55
4,500,000		2,115,800	55
5,000,000		2,390,800	55
5,100,000		2,445,800	55
6,000,000		2,940,800	55
6,100,000		2,995,800	55
7,000,000		3,490,800	55
7,100,000		3,545,800	55
8,000,000		4,040,800	55
8,100,000		4,095,800	55
9,000,000		4,590,800	55
9,100,000		4,645,800	55
10,000,000	plus adjustments	5,140,800	60
10,100,000		5,200,800	60
11,000,000		5,740,800	60
12,000,000		6,340,800	60
13,000,000		6,940,800	60
14,000,000		7,540,800	60
16,000,000		8,740,800	60
18,000,000		9,940,800	60
20,000,000		11,140,800	60
21,040,000		11,764,800	55
22,000,000	plus adjustments	12,292,800	55

Unified Rates: Estate and gift tax rates are combined in a single rate schedule. Lifetime transfers are subject to the gift tax and are also cumulated with transfers made at death to determine the estate tax.

Unified Credit: A unified estate and gift tax credit may be used to offset gift taxes on lifetime transfers and, to the extent not used during your lifetime, to offset taxes upon death.

Phaseout of Graduated Rates and Unified Credit: The benefits of the graduated rates and unified credit are phased out for taxable transfers between $10,000,000 plus adjustments and $21,040,000 plus adjustments by the imposition of a 5% surtax, or an effective rate of 60%.

Taxable Transfers Are Either Taxable Gifts or a Taxable Estate: "Taxable gifts" means the total amount of gifts made during the calendar year by the donor reduced by (1) any $10,000 plus adjustments annual exclusion allowable ($20,000 plus adjustments for a "split gift"), (2) unlimited gifts to a spouse subject to certain rules, (3) unlimited qualified transfers made on behalf of another for educational or medical expense payments, and (4) certain other allowable deductions. "Taxable estate" is the gross estate less the marital deduction for property passing to decedent's surviving spouse and all other allowable deductions.

Computation of Estate Tax: The estate tax is determined by computing a tentative tax under the unified tax table on the total of the decedent's taxable estate and all post-1976 gifts (other than those includable in the decedent's gross estate), then subtracting therefrom (1) the total gift tax payable on post-1976 gifts; (2) the unified credit; (3) the credit for any state inheritance or estate tax with respect to property included in the decedent's gross estate, not to exceed the maximum allowable state death tax credit; (4) the credit for gift taxes on pre-1977 gifts that are includable in the decedent's estate; (5) the credit for federal estate taxes paid by prior estates on previous transfers to the decedent; and (6) the credit for foreign death taxes.

Generation-Skipping Taxes: There may also be a tax on certain generation-skipping transfers assessed at the maximum estate and gift tax rate of 55%.

State Transfer Taxes: Most states also have separate gift and estate taxes that are not included in Sixty-Minute Estate Plan™ calculations for purposes of simplicity.

How the Unified Credit Applies to You

For a single person with an estate less than the applicable exclusion, the unified credit solves the entire federal estate and gift tax problem by eliminating transfer taxes on the applicable exclusion amount.

You can leave your property to anyone in any form that you wish, and it will pass free of any federal estate taxes. If your estate is larger than the applicable exclusion that is where your tax planning begins. For a single person with a larger estate, the unified credit can be combined with other tax-reducing strategies to reduce taxes.

If you are married, each spouse gets one full unified credit, which means each spouse has one full applicable exclusion. For couples with combined estates under one applicable exclusion, it does not matter who dies first or how much they leave to each other or their children. No special action is needed to avoid the federal estate on gift tax. Each person's unified credit alone will pass the total combined estate tax free. No taxes.

For couples with larger estates exceeding one applicable exclusion, the biggest tax planning challenge is avoiding tax in the estate of the second spouse to die. All property transferred to the surviving spouse escapes estate tax because of the unlimited marital deduction. However, two potential problems arise from this plan: (1) the deceased spouse's estate cannot take advantage of the applicable exclusion exemption equivalent because the property is being transferred to the surviving spouse, and (2) all property is stacked in the estate of the surviving spouse, to be later taxed. In the estate of the surviving spouse, there is no unlimited marital deduction unless the spouse has remarried. Planning is required to avoid or reduce the estate tax upon the death of the surviving spouse and prevent this common costly mistake.

BEWARE OF GIFT AND ESTATE TAX DIFFERENCES
◆ ◆ ◆

The highest marginal bracket of the estate tax is 122%, as measured against what a decedent's beneficiaries receive; the highest marginal rate for the gift tax is 55%, as measured against what a donor's beneficiaries receive.

The reason for the significant difference between the estate tax marginal rate and the gift tax marginal rate, even though nominally both taxes have the same marginal rate of 55%, is that the estate tax is applied not only on what is transferred, but also on the tax itself. The gift tax is only applied against what is transferred to the donor's beneficiaries. For example, assume that a parent has $100 that she wishes to dedicate to her daughter either in the form of gifts during her lifetime or transfers by her will. If that parent uses the $100 during her lifetime, she will be able to transfer $65 to her daughter and pay a gift tax of $35 (i.e. 55% x 65 = 35). In calculating the gift tax there is no additional tax applied on the payment of the gift tax. If, on the other hand, that parent dies with that same $100 and she dedicates that same amount to her daughter, that daughter will only receive $45 because the estate tax is assessed not only against what is transferred to the daughter, but also against what is paid to the federal government. The estate tax is calculated by taxing the tax (i.e., $100 x 55% = $55). Since the estate tax is $55, and what the daughter receives is only $45, the estate tax is in reality a "122%" tax on what is transferred to the daughter (as opposed to the "55%" tax if a gift tax had been paid.)

HOW YOU MAY CALCULATE YOUR OWN ESTATE TAXES
◆ ◆ ◆

Once you have determined the tax due on your net assets from the schedule, subtract from it the available unified tax credit for estate and gift taxes (assuming you have not made any taxable gifts). The unified credit allows estates of up to the applicable exclusiton to pass to heirs untaxed and twice the applicable exclusion for a married couple if each owns an applicable exclusion amount that passes to heirs other than the surviving spouse. Then select the numbered Sixty-Minute Estate Plan™ that most closely approximates your estate. Do your own comparison tax calculations in the blank spaces on the chart and worksheet or use the worksheet provided for that purpose.

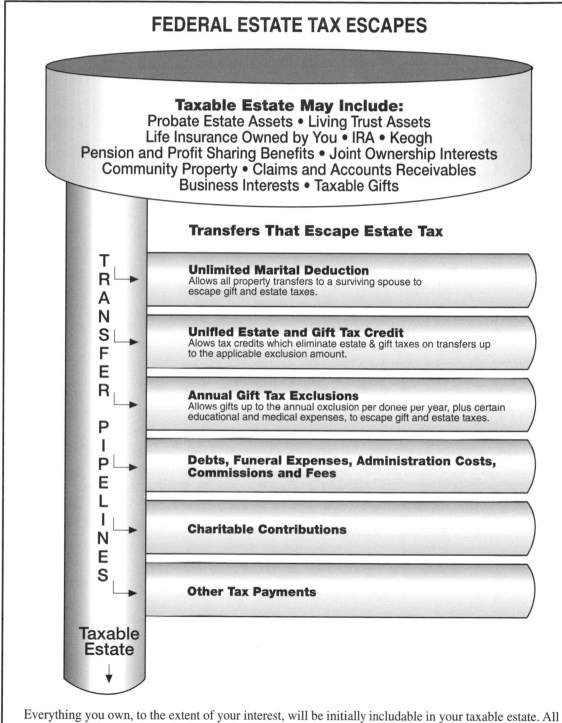

FEDERAL ESTATE TAX ESCAPES

Taxable Estate May Include:
Probate Estate Assets • Living Trust Assets
Life Insurance Owned by You • IRA • Keogh
Pension and Profit Sharing Benefits • Joint Ownership Interests
Community Property • Claims and Accounts Receivables
Business Interests • Taxable Gifts

Transfers That Escape Estate Tax

Unlimited Marital Deduction
Allows all property transfers to a surviving spouse to
escape gift and estate taxes.

Unified Estate and Gift Tax Credit
Alows tax credits which eliminate estate & gift taxes on transfers up
to the applicable exclusion amount.

Annual Gift Tax Exclusions
Allows gifts up to the annual exclusion per donee per year, plus certain
educational and medical expenses, to escape gift and estate taxes.

Debts, Funeral Expenses, Administration Costs, Commissions and Fees

Charitable Contributions

Other Tax Payments

TRANSFER PIPELINES

Taxable Estate

Everything you own, to the extent of your interest, will be initially includable in your taxable estate. All your property is subject to valuation as of the date of your death, or an alternate valuation date six months later. Your taxable estate may be reduced by the transfer of property to your surviving spouse, the unified estate and tax credit (which is equivalent to the applicable exclusion amount of a taxable estate), debts, funeral expenses, administration costs, commissions and fees, charitable contributions and tax payments.

Planning Opportunities
for Married Couples
❖ ❖ ❖

A good strategy for married couples with combined estates of between the applicable exclusion and two times the applicable exclusion is to equalize the estates to the extent necessary to assure that the estate of the surviving spouse does not exceed the applicable exclusion on date of death.

If each spouse owns half the value of the total assets, each spouse can be assured of maximizing the unified credit, regardless of who dies first. The chart illustrations included in Chapter 3 indicate equal estates. The charts may also be used as worksheets to illustrate your present asset ownership. It is not necessary that estates be equal, only that sufficient assets are owned by each spouse, to assure that no estate taxes become due at either death.

Leaving all the assets to the surviving spouse, when that spouse will likely have an estate over the applicable exclusion, is a sure way to feel patriotic by making large tax payments to the IRS. Protect your children's inheritance with good tax planning now.

The unlimited marital deduction allows you to transfer everything to your spouse during your life, or at death, without taxes. The marital deduction is unlimited. Tax considerations are important, and as previously discussed in this chapter, unlimited transfers to the surviving spouse are not always the best solution. But the transfers are estate and gift tax free!

You can take advantage of the marital deduction only if you leave property to someone the IRS considers your spouse. State laws regarding the validity of a marriage or common law marriage may control. Former spouses and future spouses do not count. To qualify for the unlimited marital deduction, the property must be included in your estate, the interest that passes must generally include all the rights of the owner, and the rights usually cannot terminate. There are a few exceptions, such as the standard marital deduction trust and the QTIP trust, which are explained later in this chapter.

Trusts Commonly Used with the Marital Deduction

Bypass Trust

This trust is designed not to qualify for the unlimited estate tax marital deduction.

It takes advantage of your lifetime applicable exclusion. This trust is called the bypass trust because it bypasses the surviving spouse's taxable estate and is not subject to estate taxes. The trust is also technically referred to as an applicable exclusion trust or credit shelter trust, and commonly referred to as a family trust. Often an applicable exclusion value of assets is placed in the trust with your surviving spouse entitled to receive the income for life plus limited principal. It may also sprinkle benefits to your children and other beneficiaries. Ultimately it establishes the conditions and beneficiaries for final distribution. The bypass trust is the most universally used method of saving estate taxes in family situations, and is illustrated in charts in Chapter 3.

Marital Deduction Trust

This trust is designed to qualify for the unlimited estate tax marital deduction.

Under this trust, the surviving spouse is provided with income for life and the power to appoint who will get the trust principal. There is lots of flexibility regarding the powers to the trustee to withdraw principal or even of the surviving spouse to withdraw principal, or even to collapse the entire trust and receive the trust corpus. The main feature of the marital trust is that the management of the funds is taken out of the surviving spouse's hands. The ultimate management and control rests with the trustee. The surviving spouse has the power to decide who ultimately receives the property. State law may allow a surviving spouse to elect against a will or trust establishing a marital deduction trust with his or her statutory share of your estate property.

The Qualified Terminal Interest Property Trust (QTIP)

This trust—the qualified terminal interest (QTIP) trust—is designed to qualify for the unlimited estate tax marital deduction.

This is the second form of a marital deduction trust. In this trust your spouse's rights in the property you leave come to an end when he or she dies. The IRS has created this special case, and if you follow the rules, this type of property transfer will qualify for the marital deduction, even though the surviving spouse does not have the full right of possession, enjoyment, and disposition. Under the QTIP trust, your surviving spouse must be given all the trust income for life payable at least quarterly, but you can determine how the trust principal will be split up when your spouse dies. For practical purposes, your surviving spouse is given what is called a life estate in the trust assets. QTIP trust property must be included in your surviving spouse's estate, even if he or she is not given the right to dispose of the trust property.

With a QTIP trust, the powers of the trustee can be as broad or narrow as you desire. There is no requirement that the survivor be given the right to invade the trust or withdraw principal, although these rights are permitted. The surviving spouse cannot be given the power to direct trust principal to any other beneficiary during his or her lifetime, but can be given the option to decide who gets the trust property at death.

A QTIP trust removes the trust assets from the control of the surviving spouse, while still qualifying for the unlimited marital deduction. Since a QTIP trust limits control and disposition rights of the surviving spouse, it is a good idea for married couples to discuss this plan in the decision-making process. Otherwise, there is the risk a surviving spouse who has a right to some or all of the property being transferred into the QTIP trust under state inheritance laws would elect against the trust and assert statutory rights to the property outright. Before establishing a QTIP trust, discuss these issues with your estate planner.

Annual Gift Exclusion

❖ ❖ ❖

Probably the most frequently used tool for reducing estates during life is the annual gift exclusion. You can give up to the annual exclusion to any person, relative or not, each year from your own assets without paying a gift tax. In fact, you need not even file a gift tax return to report the gifts. If you are married and your spouse concurs, the two of you can give twice the annual exclusion of your assets to any one person without paying a tax or filing a gift tax return. If you and your spouse choose, you may give up to two times the annual exclusion to each of your three children, for example, and your taxable estate would shrink by that amount. If you made maximum annual gifts to these same three children for five years, you could reduce your estates' value with no taxes, no gift tax returns, and no reduction of your applicable exclusion. The annual gift exclusion is 10,000 per donor plus cost of living adjustments.

You should realize that these gifts are from after-tax property. You cannot deduct annual gifts from your income tax bill. Recipients of annual gifts pay no taxes on the money received. No time limits prior to death apply to the annual gifts. You could, for example, make gifts to select people from your death bed and the value of these gifts would be excluded from your taxable estate. But you must give these annual gifts during your lifetime. Your executor cannot make the gifts for you after your death.

Stepped-up Basis to Save Taxes

❖ ❖ ❖

Stepped-up basis is an income tax trade-off between gift and estate transfers that can save your heirs big taxes.

Basis is a term used for federal income tax purposes. Basis, or "cost basis," as it is sometimes referred to, is the amount that is used to compute taxable gain for federal income tax purposes on the sale of property. Estate assets take as their cost basis a new fair market value as of the date of death, or six months after date of death, whenever a valuation date is elected. If the property has increased in value, the resultant increase in basis is called a step up in basis. Estate planning should always include taking maximum advantage of this income-tax-reducing opportunity.

A lifetime gift of property does not receive a stepped-up basis. This means that all gifts carry the gift maker's cost basis over to the gift receiver. When the property is later sold, there may be a big capital gain tax to pay. Consider the following example; then ask your estate planner to answer any remaining questions.

You may decide to give your son or daughter 100 shares of Family Corporation. You paid $10 per share when you bought them years ago. At the time of your gift, the appraised market value was $50 per share. Your gift amounted to a value of $5,000, which was less than the gift tax exclusion on annual gifts. Therefore, there will be no gift tax, you need not file a gift tax return, and there will be no reduction of your lifetime applicable exclusion. However, your son or daughter will maintain your cost basis of $10 per share. If he or she should sell the stock later, the difference between the net proceeds and the cost basis of $10 per share will be subject to a capital gains tax. If the

100 shares are sold for $50 per share, a capital gain of $4,000 ($5,000 net proceeds less cost basis of $1,000) occurs.

If the shares of Family Corporation had remained in your estate, they would have received a stepped-up value equal to your price at the close of the market on the day you died. Your son or daughter would inherit the 100 shares of Family Corporation with the value stepped up to $50 per share. If the shares were then sold at $50 per share, there would be no capital gain because the sales price equals the stepped-up cost basis. This is a good example of why knowing the value of your estate assets is critical. Taking property through your estate may save your heirs from paying capital gains taxes and costs you nothing as long as your taxable estate is less than the applicable exclusion.

If you own community property with your spouse, acquired in one of the community property states, there is further good news. Although only one-half of the community property is included in the gross estate, both halves of a community property asset receive a new basis. Community property states include Louisiana, Texas, New Mexico, Arizona, California, Nevada, Washington, and Idaho. This adjustment to the surviving spouse's basis is a major incentive for classifying property as community property. Compare this with the treatment of property held as joint tenants with rights of survivorship where there is a step up or down of only the decedent's one-half share. Tax rules are often not logical or uniformly enforced.

INCOME TAXES ON ESTATES AND TRUSTS

❖ ❖ ❖

Income taxes on estate and trust income should be avoided. Since the 1993 tax changes, the rates almost free fall to the maximum income tax rate. Although the following rate table is adjusted annually for cost of living increases, consider it a red flag to watch out for this tax. You may avoid this tax by timely distributing the income from estates and trusts to the beneficiaries within 65 days after the close of the tax year. The beneficiaries pay the income tax at the beneficiaries' rate.

INCOME TAX RATES FOR ESTATES AND TRUSTS

If taxable income is		the tax is:			of the amount over
Over	*but not over*				
$ 0	$1,500			15 %	0
$1,500	$3,500	$ 225.00	+	28 %	1,500
$3,500	$5,500	$ 785.00	+	31 %	3,500
$5,500	$7,500	$1,405.00	+	36 %	5,500
$7,500	--	$2,215.00	+	39.6%	7,500

RETIREMENT AND IRA ACCOUNTS

◆ ◆ ◆

Pension, profit sharing, IRA, 401(k), Keogh, and other deferred tax qualified plans may be subject to both income and estate taxes. In worst case scenarios, over 77% of the account may be paid to the government as a result of federal estate and income taxes when the account is transferred to the next generation. The rules governing distribution are complex and changing. Seek professional tax advice before selecting a payout or transfer plan.

Income taxes are due when a tax-deferred qualified plan benefit is distributed. The manner in which these amounts are taxed as income depends on the timing and form in which they are received, primarily as an annuity or lump sum. These same account benefits are included in the gross taxable estate when someone dies. However, the benefit will not be subject to income tax or estate tax if the benefit rolls over to the surviving spouse who may then make new payment and beneficiary choices. The law requires employees' spouses to be the beneficiaries of employees' qualified plan benefits, unless the spouse consents otherwise. This rule does not apply to IRA accounts. To achieve maximum deferrals of distributions and income tax, a "designated beneficiary" must be named as of the required beginning date or date of death, whichever occurs first. A designated beneficiary must be either an individual or a trust that is irrevocable at the death of the account owner, such as a bypass trust. To develop your retirement and IRA account strategy, refer to the more detailed planning guidance beginning on page 124.

THE ROTH NONDEDUCTIBLE IRA WILL BECOME THE PREFERRED IRA OF THE 21ST CENTURY

◆ ◆ ◆

The Roth IRA is the hot new retirement plan introduced in the 1997 tax act. Misinformation and misunderstandings abound. A Roth is available to any individual, subject to certain income and other limitations. Eligibility fazes out at $95,000 for single taxpayers and $150,000 for married taxpayers filing jointly. Up to $2,000 can be contributed depending on other plan participation. Roths allow tax free withdrawals of contributions and earnings after five years and age 59½ for first time home purchases, qualified education expenses, disability or death.

Investigate opportunities to convert traditional IRAs to Roth IRAs if your adjusted gross income for the calendar year is less than $100,000. The income from the conversion does not count in determining the limit.

After conversion to a Roth IRA, no further income taxes are payable. A Roth does not escape estate taxes. This innovative financial and estate planning tool will create new planning options for children and grandchildren. It will become the preferred IRA in the 21st Century. Watch for changes. Try to capitalize on this income tax free planning opportunity as soon as possible.

CHARITABLE DEDUCTIONS

◆ ◆ ◆

If life has been generous to you, or you have no obvious beneficiary, consider giving some or all of your estate to charity. There is an estate tax deduction for gifts to charity. It is another very effective planning tool to reduce your taxable estate. Help yourself while helping others.

A comparison with the personal income tax deduction for charitable contributions is helpful. Income tax deductions have conditions and limitations, although few people ever maximize the deduction. The good news for estate tax purposes is that you can give it all away and get a full deduction.

Charitable giving is a useful tax planning tool, and important to our society. A full chapter of this book has been devoted to that planning option. Charitable alternatives include outright gifts, charitable bequests in trust, charitable remainder trusts, and charitable remainder trusts with insurance replacement trusts, all with illustrated examples and charts.

Small gifts can be made simply and quickly. With large estates, or where large donations are contemplated, gifts should be carefully integrated with your overall estate plan to be sure all bases are covered. The input of experts should be sought to help you select the type of property that should be the subject of such gifts or bequests and determine the tax consequences. Sixty-Minute charitable plans in Chapter 5 are intended to help you move forward quickly and easily.

GENERATION-SKIPPING TRANSFER TAX

◆ ◆ ◆

The generation-skipping transfer (GST) tax is added to any estate or gift tax if it applies. If you are planning to leave assets to your grandchildren, you should be aware of the generation-skipping transfer tax. If you omit your children as beneficiaries and leave the inheritance directly to your grandchildren and younger generations, this tax applies.

In the past, generation-skipping trusts were common, especially among the wealthy. The grandfather would set up a trust that distributed only income from the trust to his children. The trust principal would be distributed later to his grandchildren and future generations. This allowed the trust to grow tax free and appreciate in value. It avoided the heavy taxation that would have occurred if each generation had been taxed on the full inheritance. This method built generation after generation of wealth in such families as the Rockefellers and Kennedys.

Congress saw an opportunity to pick up more taxes by taxing each generational transfer. Now, if you leave substantial assets to your grandchildren and future generations, bypassing your children's generation, these assets may be subject to generation-skipping transfer tax.

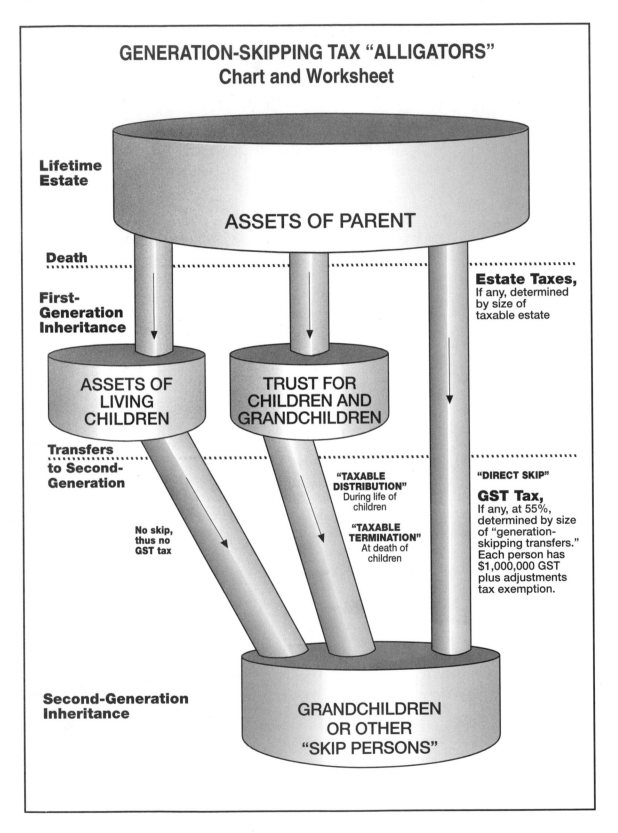

GENERATION-SKIPPING TAX "ALLIGATORS"
Chart and Worksheet

Lifetime Estate

ASSETS OF PARENT

Death

First-Generation Inheritance

Estate Taxes, If any, determined by size of taxable estate

ASSETS OF LIVING CHILDREN

TRUST FOR CHILDREN AND GRANDCHILDREN

Transfers to Second-Generation

No skip, thus no GST tax

"TAXABLE DISTRIBUTION" During life of children

"TAXABLE TERMINATION" At death of children

"DIRECT SKIP"

GST Tax, If any, at 55%, determined by size of "generation-skipping transfers." Each person has $1,000,000 GST plus adjustments tax exemption.

Second-Generation Inheritance

GRANDCHILDREN OR OTHER "SKIP PERSONS"

The GST is bad news. It is a very expensive flat rate tax of 55%. And remember, this tax is in addition to estate taxes, which can also be as high as 55%. As an example, in 1998, if a $10 million estate were left to grandchildren in 1998 with no estate tax planning, $5.5 million would be paid in estate taxes and another $2,475,000 would be paid in GST taxes. Only $2,025,000 would be left for the beneficiaries.

A "skip person" is a person assigned to a generation which is two or more generations below the person making the gift (for example, a grandchild or a great grandchild), or any trust where all the beneficiaries are skip persons. A "direct skip" occurs when a transfer subject to federal gift or estate tax is made to a skipped person. For example, where a transfer is made during life or at death to the transferor's grandchild or great grandchild, a direct skip occurs. A "taxable termination" occurs upon the termination of all the beneficial interests held by nonskip persons in a trust, if thereafter any of the beneficiaries are skip persons. For example, where a trust is established for the lifetime benefit of your children, and is eventually to be distributed to your grandchildren, a taxable termination will occur at your children's death. A "taxable distribution" occurs when any distribution of income or principal is made from a generation-skipping trust to a skip person (other than a taxable termination or a direct skip). For example, where a discretionary sprinkle trust is established for your spouse and descendants, any distribution made during your spouse's lifetime to your grandchild or great grandchild is a taxable distribution. Special rules apply to special situations and generations are defined in the Code.

Congress softened the punch by giving you a $1,000,000 GST plus cost of living adjustments tax exemption which may be used during your lifetime or at death. If married, your spouse has an identical exemption. Also, certain educational and medical expenses are excluded. Finally, gifts that qualify for the annual gift tax exclusion escape GST taxability. Complex tax elections may be required to maximize tax exemptions in large estates.

In the case of a taxable termination or taxable distribution, the GST tax is computed on a tax-inclusive basis. This means that the GST tax base, or "taxable amount," is the value of the property actually received by the heir and is not grossed up by the GST taxes owed by the generous original owner.

State Taxes

◆ ◆ ◆

Most states impose some form of estate or inheritance, gift, generation-skipping, and income taxes. A state death tax credit is available in computing federal estate taxes, but it is limited. State taxes vary widely from state to state. Therefore, they have not been considered in any of the charts or examples in this book. Typically, state taxes are very limited in proportion to federal taxes. However, they may impact on the overall tax results in states with significant death taxes. Discuss this matter with your planner.

TAXES: TOO MANY AND TOO MUCH

◆ ◆ ◆

When we have to pay taxes the cry is always the same—too many and too much. My clients become exasperated when they realize planning and the resulting legal documents will produce more inheritance for their heirs than several years of business activities, investing, farming, or other hard work. Taxes are not fair! That's why you must care!

The taxes discussed in this chapter are major, but they are only a small portion of all the tax issues that must be analyzed in a complex estate plan or administration. Throughout this book other tax issues are identified and discussed along with tax-planning options with recommendations.

Congress, the Internal Revenue Service, state and local revenue departments, and our courts are constantly changing the laws and their interpretations. Watch for changes that affect you. Confer with your professional planner regularly.

Part

II

• • •

Sixty-Minute Estate Plans™

Chapter 3

SIXTY-MINUTE ESTATE PLANNING
Quality Selections to Satisfy Your Planning Needs

Sixty-Minute Estate Plans™ offer you an illustrated menu of different selections. Compare using them to entering an unfamiliar restaurant for a family dinner. When you look at the restaurant's menu, you won't find a detailed list of ingredients, the temperature at which the food was prepared, cooking equipment used, or the names of the chef and staff. Your interest is only that competent people prepare a quality meal that satisfies your needs.

Sixty-Minute Estate Plans™ is like a family restaurant, offering a full menu of quality selections intended to meet all your needs. You must read the menu and make your decisions. The menu is divided into main dishes (basics of a good plan) and supplemental dishes (add-ons of a good plan). After reading through the first portion of this chapter, you should be familiar with the menu. You'll then be able to list all your questions and know the answers to them before placing your order.

USING A LIVING TRUST TO AVOID PROBATE

◆ ◆ ◆

Wills Versus Living Trusts

Newspapers and magazine articles headline the national debate. Best-selling books argue the issue. Crowds gather when the topic is argued. Property passing pursuant to your

39

will is subject to a court procedure called "probate." If you create a living trust, property transferred into your living trust prior to death avoids probate. The advantages, disadvantages, and trade-offs of the living trust should be discussed thoroughly with your estate planner before making your decision. Chapter 4, How to Select the Pipelines of Distribution That's Right for You: Living Trusts, Probate, and Direct Transfers, discusses in detail the probate process, the living trust alternatives, and other ways to avoid probate.

Living trusts are being highly promoted as the best presently available alternative to avoiding the anguish of probate. Sixty-Minute Estate Plans™ recommends the use of the living trust as the foundation of your estate plan. However, Sixty-Minute Estate Plans™ also includes a plan for you if you choose a will or direct transfers instead of the living trust. Listen to your estate planner's analysis and recommendations before deciding between a will and probate or a living trust. Neither is user friendly, which is the reason I shout out a message of reform in the epilogue of this book.

BASIC AND ADD-ON DOCUMENTS OF A GOOD PLAN
◆ ◆ ◆

Following is a list of the documents (with simplified definitions) you will need to complete your plan. In the plans that follow, they are broken down into basic and add-on documents and are recommended depending on your specific factual situation and goals. For a more complete alphabetical list of simplified legal and tax definitions used in this book, please refer to the Digest of Legal and Tax Terminology. Advice of your chosen estate planner should always be utilized in selecting your final Sixty-Minute Estate Plan™ documents.

Living Trust—A trust created during your lifetime. It is revocable, which means it can be amended or terminated anytime while you are competent and is legally referred to as a revocable inter vivos trust. The trust becomes irrevocable upon your death. A living trust is used primarily to avoid probate and manage property. It does not save taxes.

Pour-Over Will—A will that transfers property owned by you at your death to a trust. There must be a previously existing trust to receive these assets. The will "pours over" assets to the trust by use of the probate transfer process. A pour-over will should be used with a living trust to sweep up any assets that may not have been transferred to the trust during your lifetime.

Last Will and Testament—A will that satisfies all legal requirements for enforceability to transfer property owned by you at your death by use of the court-empowered probate transfer process. It is an alternative to the living trust and pour-over will.

Joint Ownership Documents with Right of Survivorship—A legal method of owning property in joint names, with two or more people, each survivor having an automatic ownership right to the property after the death of one owner. Often called joint tenancy, this method of owning property avoids probate, but may produce unintended legal results and tax disadvantages, and loss of property control, especially in larger estates.

Beneficiary Designations—Forms used to transfer life insurance, pension, profit-sharing, Keogh, IRA, and annuity survivor and death benefits and other pay-on-death proceeds to your designated beneficiaries at your death. The communication must be in writing, usually on forms provided by the benefit administrator.

Durable Power of Attorney—A power of attorney that continues to remain in effect if you become disabled or that comes into existence after you become disabled.

Medical Durable Power of Attorney (Proxy) for Health Care—A power of attorney that authorizes someone to make medical decisions on your behalf if you are unable to do so.

Living Will—Not a will, but a document that specifies whether life-sustaining measures should be undertaken to preserve life when a person is not expected to recover. Living wills are limited. A medical durable power of attorney for health care covers a broader range of health care decisions.

Appointment of Guardian of Minor or Incapacitated Heirs— A guardian of the person is a named individual designated to have the physical care and custody of minor or incapacitated heirs. Often the same individual manages the financial affairs for these same heirs. Sometimes a separate individual or corporate trust department is designated to manage the financial affairs for these heirs, and may be called guardian of the estate, conservator, trustee, or other fiduciary, depending on the legal status and conditions under which the individual or corporation manages and distributes assets.

Anatomical Gift—A gift of one or more of your organs during your life or upon your death. Use forms approved in your state.

Letters of Instruction—Informal letters or documents that you can prepare without professional help to express affection, give advice, describe your philosophy, assist your survivors to inventory and collect your assets and comply with funeral and burial instructions, and so on. They are not legally binding.

Spousal Transfer Documents—Documents that transfer ownership of assets from one spouse to another. The purpose of the transfer is to assure that each spouse will have sufficient assets in his or her estate to take advantage of the applicable exclusion.

Testamentary Trust—A trust that becomes effective upon your death. The trust provisions are typically contained in your will to take care of special situations such as minor or incapacitated heirs.

Bypass Trust—A trust designed not to qualify for the unlimited estate tax marital deduction. It takes advantage of your lifetime applicable exclusion (derived from the federal gift and estate tax unified credit). This trust is called the bypass trust because it bypasses the surviving spouse's taxable estate and is not subject to estate taxes. The trust is also technically referred to as an applicable exclustion trust or credit shelter trust, and is commonly referred to as a family trust. Often the applicable exclusion worth of assets is placed in the trust with your surviving spouse entitled to receive the income for life plus limited principal. It may also sprinkle benefits to your children and other beneficiaries. Ultimately, it establishes the conditions and beneficiaries for final distribution. The bypass trust is the most universally used method of saving estate taxes in family situations.

Irrevocable Life Insurance Trust—A trust used to hold life insurance policies. Annual gifts pay insurance premiums. It cannot be materially changed or terminated. If properly designed, the life insurance proceeds payable upon death will not be part of your probate estate or be subject to estate taxes. This is a good method to deliver benefits to the next generation or provide liquidity for an estate. Paperwork and annual trustee costs are factors to consider.

QTIP Qualified Terminal Interest Property (QTIP) Trust—A trust that requires a surviving spouse to receive all income from the trust at least annually but that ultimately transfers property to persons designated by the deceased. The trust qualifies for the unlimited marital deduction. The trust assets are included in the taxable estate of the second spouse to die.

Family Partnerships, Corporations, and Limited Liability Companies—Business organizations owned by family members. Control of management and operation is usually retained by a parent, but the economic benefits are often transferred to children through a series of gifts to reduce the value of the parent's taxable estate. These organizations can be used to operate family businesses or hold assets, such as real estate. Partnerships may be either general or limited. Limited partnerships may name the parents as general partners with full control and risk, and the children as limited partners with no control and limited risk. Corporations may elect under the Internal Revenue Code to be taxed as a C corporation with full tax exposure or as an S corporation, under which there is no tax at the corporate level. Limited liability companies are a new form of business entity which provide the liability protection of a corporation and the tax benefits of a partnership. Limited liability companies are destined to become very important business and estate-planning entities. All family businesses should have written agreements concerning ownership, sale, and management continuation under specific situations, including death.

Community Property and Separate Property Agreement— Community property is created through acquisition of property during marriage while living in the states of Louisiana, Texas, New Mexico, Arizona, California, Nevada, Washington, Idaho, and Wisconsin. If a couple resides in a community property state, all property acquired by either spouse during the marriage is community property. Each spouse is deemed to own a presently vested, undivided one-half interest in community property, until the community relationship is terminated. Property that a spouse acquired before the marriage or acquired by gift or inheritance during the marriage remains his or her separate property, as long as it is not commingled with community property. Special rules apply in each state. Once property is classified as community property, it retains that identity, even if the couple moves to a common law state. The classification of property as community or separate may be changed by agreement between the spouses. A community and separate property agreement is recommended to avoid conflict and confusion if a married couple own community property. Legal and tax considerations for community and separate property differ depending on facts and state and tax laws.

Nuptial Agreement—An agreement made between two persons who are married, or who are about to marry, that specifies the rights of each spouse in property in the event of marriage dissolution or death. These agreements are often used in second marriage situations and can be helpful to ensure that children of prior marriages will enjoy a share of the estate of their parent upon death.

Charitable Gift—A gift to a legal charity. The gift is typically made to an organization that meets specific requirements so that the gift will be deductible for income and estate tax purposes. There are many charitable gift alternatives that create varying tax advantages.

Qualified domestic trusts (QDOTs) is a variation of the QTIP trust that must be used (along with the QTIP trust) when one spouse is a noncitizen of the United States and the goal is to defer payment of estate taxes until the death of the second spouse.

Uncommon Trusts—These trusts are not commonly used because they require special situations, are subject to complex tax rules, and trade-offs make utilization difficult. However, they can be useful under the right circumstances.

A *minor's trust* is an irrevocable trust to receive lifetime gifts to permanently move property outside of your estate. The tax law allows accumulation or distribution of principal and income for a child before reaching age 21. Final total distribution usually occurs when the child reaches age 21. Warning: If the beneficiaries are children under the age of 14, the income is attributable to the parents at their income tax rates under the *kiddie tax.* By utilizing the $10,000 plus adjustments-per-person-per-year gift exclusion or the applicable exclusion, these types of trusts may be funded aggressively.

A *dynasty trust* allows you to provide benefits to successive generations without initial payment of gift, estate, or generation-skipping taxes (GSTs). The trust may last as long as state perpetuities laws allow. Funding is designed to take advantage of the applicable exclusion and the $1,000,000 plus adjustments GST exemption. Eventually, as the trust property vests in final beneficiaries, transfer taxes may be payable at rates as high as 55% federal, plus possible state tax. Principal and income may be distributed to or accumulated for successive generations of beneficiaries. This is a complex but powerful shield designed to preserve special family assets or distribute benefits over several generations.

A *grantor retained income trust (GRIT)* is a lifetime irrevocable trust created by naming your beneficiaries as the remaindermen to receive the trust principal. The trust lasts for a period of years, for example, ten. You receive the income or benefit during the term of years. If you die before the specified term expires, the trust value may be included in your estate. If you outlive the period, the income or benefit stops, and the gift is complete and excluded from your estate. GRITs are often used for the transfer of high-value residences, vacation properties, or valuable art.

Grantor retained annuity trusts (GRATs) and grantor retained unitrusts (GRUTs) are also types of irrevocable lifetime trusts that include features that permit the grantor to enjoy some use of the transferred property, avoid probate, and save estate taxes while subject to complex tax laws and regulations.

Qualified Subchapter S Trust (QSST) to hold stock in an S corporation without causing termination of the S election. The trust must have only one beneficiary and satisfy other qualifying conditions as described in the Internal Revenue Code.

Other Trusts—Other estate, gift, and tax planning tools beyond the scope of this book for very large or unusual estates. Ask your estate planner.

SIXTY-MINUTE ESTATE PLANS™: IMPORTANT ASSUMPTIONS AND PARAMETERS
◆ ◆ ◆

As on a restaurant menu, all details about the selections are not included, but they are important. You should be told of important information, such as ingredients, not on the menu that may concern you. In Sixty-Minute Estate Plans™, the important ingredients are the parameters and assumptions underlying the plans. Ask your estate planning counselor specifically about the parameters and assumptions listed here. Make sure that you and your counselor both understand how these assumptions affect the facts of your specific factual situation.

1. The net federal taxable estate is assumed to be equal to the lifetime estate as shown.

2. The applicable exclustion is assumed to be fully available.

3. In married couples' estates subject to estate tax, sufficient assets in the estate of the first spouse to die are assumed to take full advantage of the applicable exclusion. Also, it is assumed both spouses die the same year. If spouses die in different years, changing estate values and the applicable exclusion may produce different results at the second death.

4. State taxes, if any, have not been included.

5. Attorney fees and administration expenses have not been included.

Your Menu of Complete Sixty-Minute Estate Plans™

A menu of Sixty-Minute Estate Plans™ follows. Each plan includes a chart, which may also be used as a worksheet, illustrating flow of assets and estate taxes. Charts are in the form of containers holding or receiving assets and pipelines transferring assets. The design emphasizes user friendliness. Following each chart worksheet are basic documents that should be included in this estate plan and add-on documents that should be considered, depending on your individual fact situation and goals.

The menu includes selections for married couples with estates from $0 to $3,000,000 and for singles with estates from $0 to $3,000,000.

Match your circumstances to the Sixty-Minute Estate Plan™ that most closely approximates your estate. Space has been provided in the containers, and along the pipelines, in which to write in your own facts and figures. Use the chart as a worksheet by writing in the value of your lifetime estate, your spouse's lifetime estate if married, projected property transfers, and value of assets in the receiving containers. Study your chart until you understand it.

Following each chart is a list of the documentation recommended to implement the plan you have selected, with brief summary. A more detailed explanation of basics and add-ons of documents appear earlier in this chapter.

When you are ready, call for an appointment with a qualified estate planner, and you are on track to a fast and easy completion of one of the most important projects of your lifetime—your estate plan.

PLAN S1—SINGLE PERSON
WITH ESTATE NOT EXCEEDING APPLICABLE EXCLUSION
Without Minor or Incapacitated Heirs

If your estate situation fits closely to this example, the following plan documentation is recommended. For a more detailed explanation of basics and add-ons, refer to pages 40–44.

Basics of a Good Plan

Living trust with appropriate support and funding documents to avoid the anguish and cost of probate, save time, and preserve privacy; *pour-over will* to transfer into your living trust assets that remain outside the trust at time of death (alternative to last will and testament below—check only one alternative); or

Last will and testament that transfers property owned by you at your death by use of the probate transfer process (alternative to living trust and pour-over will earlier—check only one alternative).

Joint ownership documents with right of survivorship to cause an automatic transfer of your property interest to the surviving joint owner or owners at your death. Often referred to as joint tenancy. Avoids probate and is not affected by will. Watch out for tax traps and loss of control.

Beneficiary designations for life insurance, pension, profit-sharing, Keogh, IRA, and annuity survivor and death benefits and other pay-on-death proceeds. You must complete the proper forms and submit them to the company or administrator in charge of benefits.

Durable power of attorney to name an individual to act for you if you become incapacitated.

Medical durable power of attorney for health care naming someone to make health care decisions if you are unable to do so yourself.

Living will to die with dignity and not be kept alive by a machine under certain conditions.

Add-ons to Consider

Anatomical gift document to give vital organs.

Letters of instruction to help organize your estate, provide vital information and final instructions to your heirs, and express your thoughts. Include funeral and burial letter, inheritance letter, and family and friends letter.

Testamentary trust after death to manage, control, and defer distribution of assets.

Charitable gifts which may take many forms.

Other gift, estate planning, and tax-saving tools.

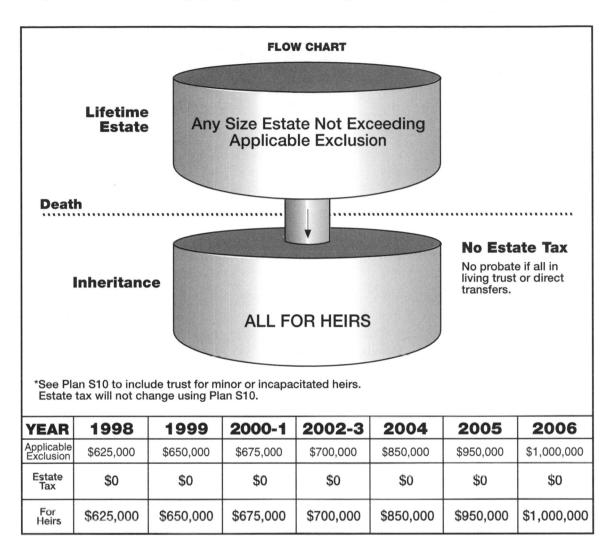

FLOW CHART

Lifetime Estate

Any Size Estate Not Exceeding Applicable Exclusion

Death

Inheritance

ALL FOR HEIRS

No Estate Tax

No probate if all in living trust or direct transfers.

*See Plan S10 to include trust for minor or incapacitated heirs. Estate tax will not change using Plan S10.

YEAR	1998	1999	2000-1	2002-3	2004	2005	2006
Applicable Exclusion	$625,000	$650,000	$675,000	$700,000	$850,000	$950,000	$1,000,000
Estate Tax	$0	$0	$0	$0	$0	$0	$0
For Heirs	$625,000	$650,000	$675,000	$700,000	$850,000	$950,000	$1,000,000

PLAN S2—SINGLE PERSON
WITH $700,000 ESTATE
Without Minor or Incapacitated Heirs

If your estate situation fits closely to this example, the following plan documentation is recommended. For a more detailed explanation of basics and add-ons, refer to pages 40–44. For Flow Chart and Table illustrations, see samples beginning on page 64.

Basics of a Good Plan

Living trust with appropriate support and funding documents to avoid the anguish and cost of probate, save time, and preserve privacy; *pour-over will* to transfer into your living trust assets that remain outside the trust at time of death (alternative to last will and testament below—check only one alternative); or

Last will and testament that transfers property owned by you at your death by use of the probate transfer process (alternative to living trust and pour-over will earlier—check only one alternative).

Joint ownership documents with right of survivorship to cause an automatic transfer of your property interest to the surviving joint owner or owners at your death. Often referred to as joint tenancy. Avoids probate and is not affected by will. Watch out for tax traps and loss of control.

Beneficiary designations for life insurance, pension, profit-sharing, Keogh, IRA, and annuity survivor and death benefits and other pay-on-death proceeds. You must complete the proper forms and submit them to the company or administrator in charge of benefits.

Durable power of attorney to name an individual to act for you if you become incapacitated.

Medical durable power of attorney for health care naming someone to make health care decisions if you are unable to do so yourself.

Living will to die with dignity and not be kept alive by a machine under certain conditions.

Add-ons to Consider

Anatomical gift document to give vital organs.

Letters of instruction to help organize your estate, provide vital information and final instructions to your heirs, and express your thoughts. Include funeral and burial letter, inheritance letter, and family and friends letter.

Testamentary trust after death to manage, control and defer distribution of assets.

Irrevocable life insurance trust to save estate taxes by excluding death benefits from estate.

Charitable gifts which may take many forms.

Other gift, estate planning, and tax-saving tools.

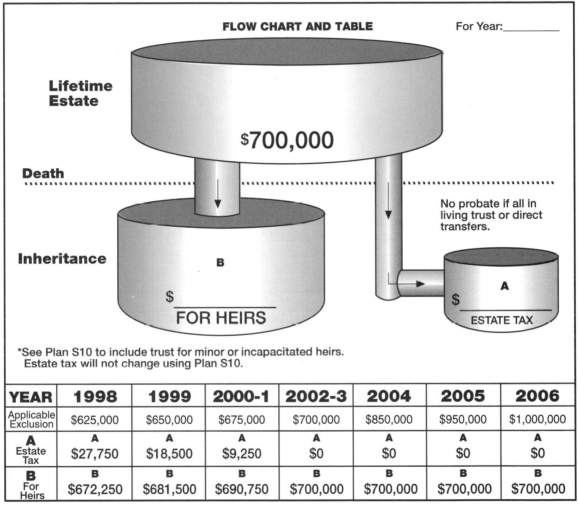

FLOW CHART AND TABLE   For Year:_____

Lifetime Estate

$700,000

Death

Inheritance

B

$_____
FOR HEIRS

No probate if all in living trust or direct transfers.

A

$_____
ESTATE TAX

*See Plan S10 to include trust for minor or incapacitated heirs. Estate tax will not change using Plan S10.

YEAR	1998	1999	2000-1	2002-3	2004	2005	2006
Applicable Exclusion	$625,000	$650,000	$675,000	$700,000	$850,000	$950,000	$1,000,000
A Estate Tax	A $27,750	A $18,500	A $9,250	A $0	A $0	A $0	A $0
B For Heirs	B $672,250	B $681,500	B $690,750	B $700,000	B $700,000	B $700,000	B $700,000

Select year. Insert into Flow Chart blanks A and B the corresponding amounts from table.

PLAN S3—SINGLE PERSON
WITH $850,000 ESTATE
Without Minor or Incapacitated Heirs

If your estate situation fits closely to this example, the following plan documentation is recommended. For a more detailed explanation of basics and add-ons, refer to pages 40–44. For Flow Chart and Table illustrations, see samples beginning on page 64.

Basics of a Good Plan

Living trust with appropriate support and funding documents to avoid the anguish and cost of probate, save time, and preserve privacy; *pour-over will* to transfer into your living trust assets that remain outside the trust at time of death (alternative to last will and testament below—check only one alternative); or

Last will and testament that transfers property owned by you at your death by use of the probate transfer process (alternative to living trust and pour-over will earlier—check only one alternative).

Joint ownership documents with right of survivorship to cause an automatic transfer of your property interest to the surviving joint owner or owners at your death. Often referred to as joint tenancy. Avoids probate and is not affected by will. Watch out for tax traps and loss of control.

Beneficiary designations for life insurance, pension, profit-sharing, Keogh, IRA, and annuity survivor and death benefits and other pay-on-death proceeds. You must complete the proper forms and submit them to the company or administrator in charge of benefits.

Durable power of attorney to name an individual to act for you if you become incapacitated.

Medical durable power of attorney for health care naming someone to make health care decisions if you are unable to do so yourself.

Living will to die with dignity and not be kept alive by a machine under certain conditions.

Add-ons to Consider

Anatomical gift document to give vital organs.

Letters of instruction to help organize your estate, provide vital information and final instructions to your heirs, and express your thoughts. Include funeral and burial letter, inheritance letter, and family and friends letter.

Testamentary trust after death to manage, control, and defer distribution of assets.

Irrevocable life insurance trust to save taxes by excluding death benefits from estate.

Charitable gifts which may take many forms.

Other gift, estate planning, and tax-saving tools.

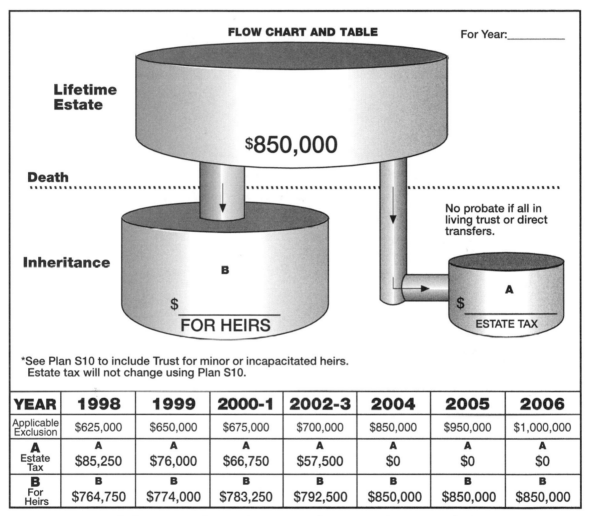

YEAR	1998	1999	2000-1	2002-3	2004	2005	2006
Applicable Exclusion	$625,000	$650,000	$675,000	$700,000	$850,000	$950,000	$1,000,000
A Estate Tax	A $85,250	A $76,000	A $66,750	A $57,500	A $0	A $0	A $0
B For Heirs	B $764,750	B $774,000	B $783,250	B $792,500	B $850,000	B $850,000	B $850,000

Select year. Insert into Flow Chart blanks A and B the corresponding amounts from table.

PLAN S4—SINGLE PERSON
WITH $1,000,000 ESTATE
Without Minor or Incapacitated Heirs

If your estate situation fits closely to this example, the following plan documentation is recommended. For a more detailed explanation of basics and add-ons, refer to pages 40–44. For Flow Chart and Table illustrations, see samples beginning on page 64.

Basics of a Good Plan

Living trust with appropriate support and funding documents to avoid the anguish and cost of probate, save time, and preserve privacy; *pour-over will* to transfer into your living trust assets that remain outside the trust at time of death (alternative to last will and testament below—check only one alternative); or

Last will and testament that transfers property owned by you at your death by use of the probate transfer process (alternative to living trust and pour-over will earlier—check only one alternative).

Joint ownership documents with right of survivorship to cause an automatic transfer of your property interest to the surviving joint owner or owners at your death. Often referred to as joint tenancy. Avoids probate and is not affected by will. Watch out for tax traps and loss of control.

Beneficiary designations for life insurance, pension, profit-sharing, Keogh, IRA, and annuity survivor and death benefits and other pay-on-death proceeds. You must complete the proper forms and submit them to the company or administrator in charge of benefits.

Durable power of attorney to name an individual to act for you if you become incapacitated.

Medical durable power of attorney for health care naming someone to make health care decisions if you are unable to do so yourself.

Living will to die with dignity and not be kept alive by a machine under certain conditions.

Add-ons to Consider

Anatomical gift document to give vital organs.

Letters of instruction to help organize your estate, provide vital information and final instructions to your heirs, and express your thoughts. Include funeral and burial letter, inheritance letter, and family and friends letter.

Testamentary trust after death to manage, control, and defer distribution of assets.

Irrevocable life insurance trust to save estate taxes for excluding death benefits from estate.

Family partnerships, corporations, and limited liability companies to allow gifting interests in business and investments while establishing management and control options.

Charitable gifts which may take many forms.

Other gift, estate planning, and tax-saving tools.

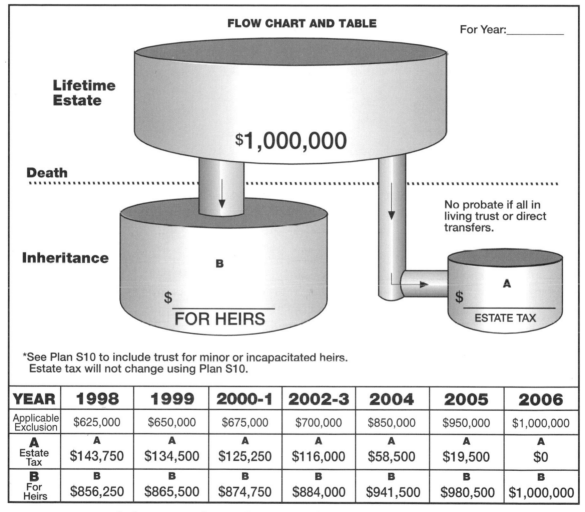

FLOW CHART AND TABLE   For Year:_____

Lifetime Estate

$1,000,000

Death

No probate if all in living trust or direct transfers.

Inheritance

B

$_____
FOR HEIRS

$_____ A
ESTATE TAX

*See Plan S10 to include trust for minor or incapacitated heirs. Estate tax will not change using Plan S10.

YEAR	1998	1999	2000-1	2002-3	2004	2005	2006
Applicable Exclusion	$625,000	$650,000	$675,000	$700,000	$850,000	$950,000	$1,000,000
A Estate Tax	A $143,750	A $134,500	A $125,250	A $116,000	A $58,500	A $19,500	A $0
B For Heirs	B $856,250	B $865,500	B $874,750	B $884,000	B $941,500	B $980,500	B $1,000,000

Select year. Insert into Flow Chart blanks A and B the corresponding amounts from table.

PLAN S5—SINGLE PERSON
WITH $1,250,000 ESTATE
Without Minor or Incapacitated Heirs

If your estate situation fits closely to this example, the following plan documentation is recommended. For a more detailed explanation of basics and add-ons, refer to pages 40–44. For Flow Chart and Table illustrations, see samples beginning on page 64.

Basics of a Good Plan

Living trust with appropriate support and funding documents to avoid the anguish and cost of probate, save time, and preserve privacy; *pour-over will* to transfer into your living trust assets that remain outside the trust at time of death (alternative to last will and testament below—check only one alternative); or

Last will and testament that transfers property owned by you at your death by use of the probate transfer process (alternative to living trust and pour-over will earlier—check only one alternative).

Joint ownership documents with right of survivorship to cause an automatic transfer of your property interest to the surviving joint owner or owners at your death. Often referred to as joint tenancy. Avoids probate and is not affected by will. Watch out for tax traps and loss of control.

Beneficiary designations for life insurance, pension, profit-sharing, Keogh, IRA, and annuity survivor and death benefits and other pay-on-death proceeds. You must complete the proper forms and submit them to the company or administrator in charge of benefits.

Durable power of attorney to name an individual to act for you if you become incapacitated.

Medical durable power of attorney for health care naming someone to make health care decisions if you are unable to do so yourself.

Living will to die with dignity and not be kept alive by a machine under certain conditions.

Add-on to Consider

Anatomical gift document to give vital organs.

Letters of instruction to help organize your estate, provide vital information and final instructions to your heirs, and express your thoughts. Include funeral and burial letter, inheritance letter, and family and friends letter.

Testamentary trust after death to manage, control, and defer distribution of assets.

Irrevocable life insurance trust to save estate taxes by excluding death benefits from estate.

Family partnerships, corporations, and limited liability companies to allow gifting interests in business and investments while establishing management and control options.

Charitable gifts which may take many forms.

Other gift, estate planning, and tax saving tools.

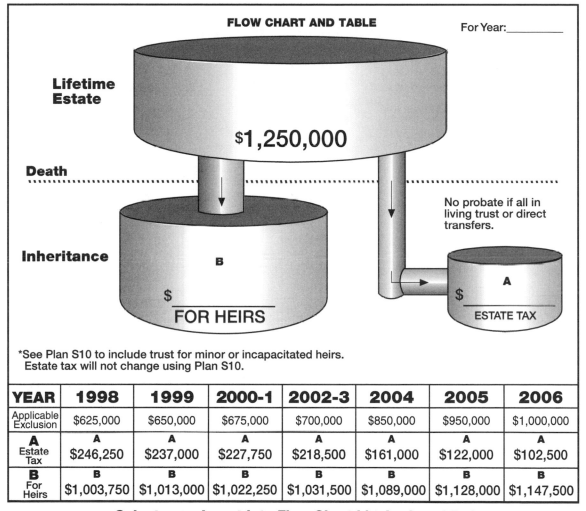

FLOW CHART AND TABLE

For Year:_____

Lifetime Estate

$1,250,000

Death

Inheritance

No probate if all in living trust or direct transfers.

B

$ _____ **FOR HEIRS**

A

$ _____ ESTATE TAX

*See Plan S10 to include trust for minor or incapacitated heirs. Estate tax will not change using Plan S10.

YEAR	1998	1999	2000-1	2002-3	2004	2005	2006
Applicable Exclusion	$625,000	$650,000	$675,000	$700,000	$850,000	$950,000	$1,000,000
A Estate Tax	A $246,250	A $237,000	A $227,750	A $218,500	A $161,000	A $122,000	A $102,500
B For Heirs	B $1,003,750	B $1,013,000	B $1,022,250	B $1,031,500	B $1,089,000	B $1,128,000	B $1,147,500

Select year. Insert into Flow Chart blanks A and B the corresponding amounts from table.

PLAN S6—SINGLE PERSON
WITH $1,500,000 ESTATE
Without Minor or Incapacitated Heirs

If your estate situation fits closely to this example, the following plan documentation is recommended. For a more detailed explanation of basics and add-ons, refer to pages 40–44. For Flow Chart and Table illustrations, see samples beginning on page 64.

Basics of a Good Plan

Living trust with appropriate support and funding documents to avoid the anguish and cost of probate, save time, and preserve privacy; *pour-over will* to transfer into your living trust assets that remain outside the trust at time of death (alternative to last will and testament below—check only one alternative); or

Last will and testament that transfers property owned by you at your death by use of the probate transfer process (alternative to living trust and pour-over will earlier—check only one alternative).

Joint ownership documents with right of survivorship to cause an automatic transfer of your property interest to the surviving joint owner or owners at your death. Often referred to as joint tenancy. Avoids probate and is not affected by will. Watch out for tax traps and loss of control.

Beneficiary designations for life insurance, pension, profit-sharing, Keogh, IRA, and annuity survivor and death benefits and other pay-on-death proceeds. You must complete the proper forms and submit them to the company or administrator in charge of benefits.

Durable power of attorney to name an individual to act for you if you become incapacitated.

Medical durable power of attorney for health care naming someone to make health care decisions if you are unable to do so yourself.

Living will to die with dignity and not be kept alive by a machine under certain conditions.

Add-ons to Consider

Anatomical gift document to give vital organs.

Letters of instruction to help organize your estate, provide vital information and final instructions to your heirs, and express your thoughts. Include funeral and burial letter, inheritance letter, and family and friends letter.

Testamentary trust after death to manage, control, and defer distribution of assets.

Irrevocable life insurance trust to save estate taxes by excluding death benefits from estate.

Family partnerships, corporations, and limited liability companies to allow gifting interests in business and investments while establishing management and control options.

Charitable gifts which may take many forms.

Other gift, estate planning, and tax-saving tools.

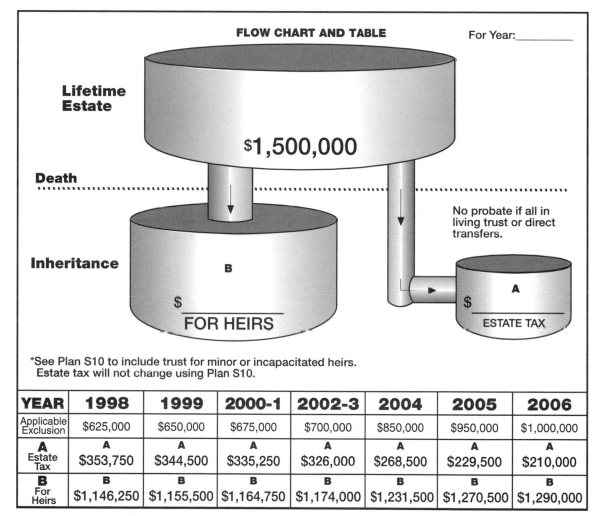

FLOW CHART AND TABLE   For Year:_____

Lifetime Estate

$1,500,000

Death

Inheritance

B

$ ____
FOR HEIRS

No probate if all in living trust or direct transfers.

A

$ ____
ESTATE TAX

*See Plan S10 to include trust for minor or incapacitated heirs. Estate tax will not change using Plan S10.

YEAR	1998	1999	2000-1	2002-3	2004	2005	2006
Applicable Exclusion	$625,000	$650,000	$675,000	$700,000	$850,000	$950,000	$1,000,000
A Estate Tax	**A** $353,750	**A** $344,500	**A** $335,250	**A** $326,000	**A** $268,500	**A** $229,500	**A** $210,000
B For Heirs	**B** $1,146,250	**B** $1,155,500	**B** $1,164,750	**B** $1,174,000	**B** $1,231,500	**B** $1,270,500	**B** $1,290,000

Select year. Insert into Flow Chart blanks A and B the corresponding amounts from table.

PLAN S7—SINGLE PERSON
WITH $2,000,000 ESTATE
Without Minor or Incapacitated Heirs

If your estate situation fits closely to this example, the following plan documentation is recommended. For a more detailed explanation of basics and add-ons, refer to pages 40–44. For Flow Chart and Table illustrations, see samples beginning on page 64.

Basics of a Good Plan

Living trust with appropriate support and funding documents to avoid the anguish and cost of probate, save time, and preserve privacy; *pour-over will* to transfer into your living trust assets that remain outside the trust at time of death (alternative to last will and testament below—check only one alternative); or

Last will and testament that transfers property owned by you at your death by use of the probate transfer process (alternative to living trust and pour-over will earlier—check only one alternative).

Joint ownership documents with right of survivorship to cause an automatic transfer of your property interest to the surviving joint owner or owners at your death. Often referred to as joint tenancy. Avoids probate and is not affected by will. Watch out for tax traps and loss of control.

Beneficiary designations for life insurance, pension, profit-sharing, Keogh, IRA, and annuity survivor and death benefits and other pay-on-death proceeds. You must complete the proper forms and submit them to the company or administrator in charge of benefits.

Durable power of attorney to name an individual to act for you if you become incapacitated.

Medical durable power of attorney for health care naming someone to make health care decisions if you are unable to do so yourself.

Living will to die with dignity and not be kept alive by a machine under certain conditions.

Add-ons to Consider

Anatomical gift document to give vital organs.

Letters of instruction to help organize your estate, provide vital information and final instructions to your heirs, and express your thoughts. Include funeral and burial letter, inheritance letter, and family and friends letter.

Testamentary trust after death to manage, control, and defer distribution of assets.

Irrevocable life insurance trust to save estate taxes by excluding death benefits from estate.

Family partnerships, corporations, and limited liability companies to allow gifting interests in business and investments while establishing management and control options.

Charitable gifts which may take many forms.

Uncommon trusts, including minor's trust if minor heirs, dynasty trust, grantor retained income trust (GRIT), grantor retained annuity trust (GRAT), grantor retained unitrust (GRUT), and qualified subchapter S trust (QSST) in uncommon situations if trade-offs are acceptable and complex tax laws allow achievement of goals.

Other gift, estate planning, and tax-saving tools.

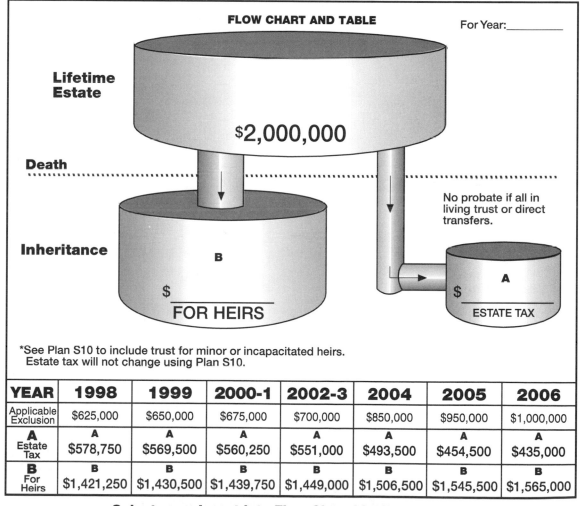

FLOW CHART AND TABLE   For Year:_____

Lifetime Estate

$2,000,000

Death

Inheritance   B

No probate if all in living trust or direct transfers.

$_____
FOR HEIRS

$_____ A
ESTATE TAX

*See Plan S10 to include trust for minor or incapacitated heirs. Estate tax will not change using Plan S10.

YEAR	1998	1999	2000-1	2002-3	2004	2005	2006
Applicable Exclusion	$625,000	$650,000	$675,000	$700,000	$850,000	$950,000	$1,000,000
A Estate Tax	A $578,750	A $569,500	A $560,250	A $551,000	A $493,500	A $454,500	A $435,000
B For Heirs	B $1,421,250	B $1,430,500	B $1,439,750	B $1,449,000	B $1,506,500	B $1,545,500	B $1,565,000

Select year. Insert into Flow Chart blanks A and B the corresponding amounts from table.

PLAN S8—SINGLE PERSON
WITH $2,500,000 ESTATE
Without Minor or Incapacitated Heirs

If your estate situation fits closely to this example, the following plan documentation is recommended. For a more detailed explanation of basics and add-ons, refer to pages 40–44. For Flow Chart and Table illustrations, see samples beginning on page 64.

Basics of a Good Plan

Same as Plan S7 for $2,000,000 estate.

Add-ons to Consider

Same as Plan S7 for $2,000,000 estate.

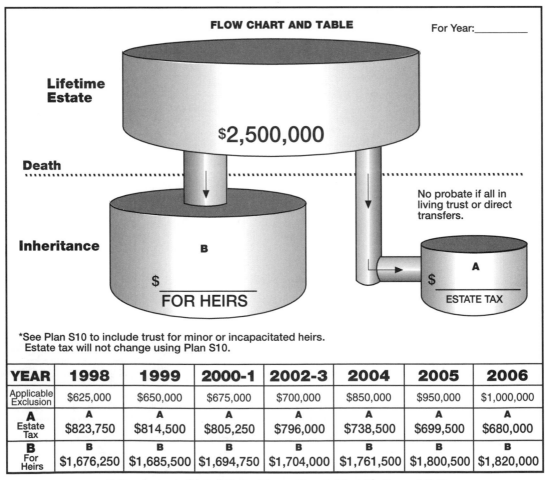

FLOW CHART AND TABLE For Year:_____

Lifetime Estate

$2,500,000

Death

No probate if all in living trust or direct transfers.

Inheritance

B

$ _____
FOR HEIRS

A

$ _____
ESTATE TAX

*See Plan S10 to include trust for minor or incapacitated heirs. Estate tax will not change using Plan S10.

YEAR	1998	1999	2000-1	2002-3	2004	2005	2006
Applicable Exclusion	$625,000	$650,000	$675,000	$700,000	$850,000	$950,000	$1,000,000
A Estate Tax	**A** $823,750	**A** $814,500	**A** $805,250	**A** $796,000	**A** $738,500	**A** $699,500	**A** $680,000
B For Heirs	**B** $1,676,250	**B** $1,685,500	**B** $1,694,750	**B** $1,704,000	**B** $1,761,500	**B** $1,800,500	**B** $1,820,000

Select year. Insert into Flow Chart blanks A and B the corresponding amounts from table.

PLAN S9—SINGLE PERSON
WITH $3,000,00 ESTATE
Without Minor or Incapacitated Heirs

If your estate situation fits closely to this example, the following plan documentation is recommended. For a more detailed explanation of basics and add-ons, refer to pages 40–44. For Flow Chart and Table illustrations, see samples beginning on page 64.

Basics of a Good Plan

Same as Plan S7 for $2,000,000 estate.

Add-ons to Consider

Same as Plan S7 for $2,000,000 estate.

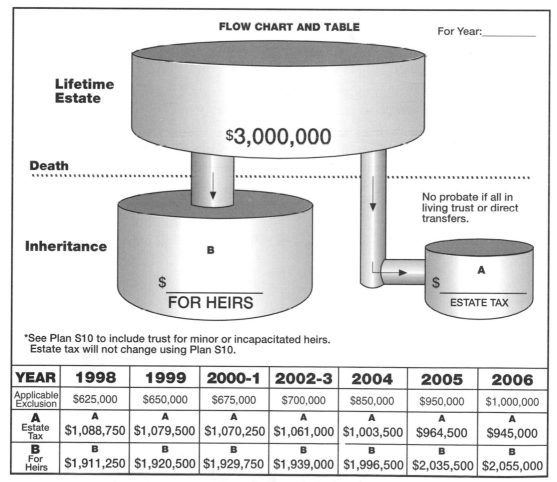

FLOW CHART AND TABLE   For Year:_____

Lifetime Estate

$3,000,000

Death

Inheritance

B

$_____
FOR HEIRS

No probate if all in living trust or direct transfers.

A

$_____
ESTATE TAX

*See Plan S10 to include trust for minor or incapacitated heirs. Estate tax will not change using Plan S10.

YEAR	1998	1999	2000-1	2002-3	2004	2005	2006
Applicable Exclusion	$625,000	$650,000	$675,000	$700,000	$850,000	$950,000	$1,000,000
A Estate Tax	A $1,088,750	A $1,079,500	A $1,070,250	A $1,061,000	A $1,003,500	A $964,500	A $945,000
B For Heirs	B $1,911,250	B $1,920,500	B $1,929,750	B $1,939,000	B $1,996,500	B $2,035,500	B $2,055,000

Select year. Insert into Flow Chart blanks A and B the corresponding amounts from table.

PLAN S10—SINGLE PERSON
WITH ANY SIZE ESTATE
With Minor or Incapacitated Heirs

If your estate situation fits closely to this example, the following plan documentation is recommended. For a more detailed explanation of basics and add-ons, refer to pages 40–44.

Basics of a Good Plan

Living trust with appropriate support and funding documents to avoid the anguish and cost of probate, save time, and preserve privacy; *pour-over will* to transfer into your living trust assets that remain outside the trust at time of death (alternative to last will and testament below—check only one alternative); or

Last will and testament that transfers property owned by you at your death by use of the probate transfer process (alternative to living trust and pour-over will earlier—check only one alternative).

Appointment of guardian of the person and guardian of the estate for minor or incapacitated heirs. Guardian of the person will be responsible for physical management, and guardian of the estate will be responsible for financial management. Actual titles may vary.

Testamentary trust for minor or incapacitated heirs to manage assets after death, control and defer distribution of assets, and avoid court-supervised conservatorships.

Joint ownership documents with right of survivorship to cause an automatic transfer of your property interest to the surviving joint owner or owners at your death. Often referred to as joint tenancy. Avoids probate and is not affected by will. Watch out for tax traps and loss of control.

Beneficiary designations for life insurance, pension, profit-sharing, Keogh, IRA, and annuity survivor and death benefits and other pay-on-death proceeds. You must complete the proper forms and submit them to the company or administrator in charge of benefits.

Durable power of attorney to name an individual to act for you if you become incapacitated.

Medical durable power of attorney for health care naming someone to make health care decisions if you are unable to do so yourself.

Living will to die with dignity and not be kept alive by a machine under certain conditions.

Add-ons to Consider

Anatomical gift document to give vital organs.

Letters of instruction to help organize your estate, provide vital information and final instructions to your heirs, and express your thoughts. Include funeral and burial letter, inheritance letter, and family and friends letter.

Testamentary trust after death to manage, control, and defer distribution of assets.

Irrevocable life insurance trust to save estate taxes by excluding death benefits from estate.

Family partnerships, corporations, and limited liability companies to allow gifting interests in business and investments while establishing management and control options.

Charitable gifts which may take many forms.

Uncommon trusts, including minor's trust if minor heirs, dynasty trust, grantor retained income trust (GRIT), grantor retained annuity trust (GRAT), grantor retained unitrust (GRUT), and qualified subchapter S trust (QSST) in uncommon situations if trade-offs are acceptable and complex tax laws allow achievement of goals.

Other gift, estate planning, and tax-saving tools.

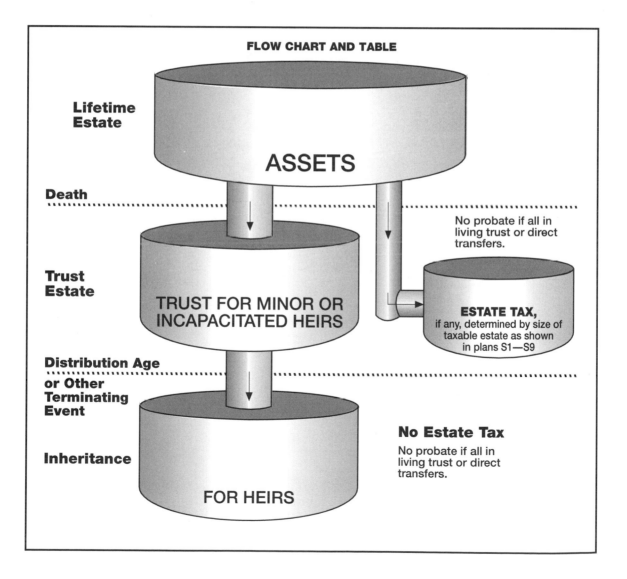

SAMPLE PERSONALIZED WORKSHEET USING CALCULATIONS FOR SINGLE PERSON WITH $775,000 ESTATE
Without Minor or Incapacitated Heirs

This sample worksheet illustrates how any chart in this book may be adapted to the reader's personal estate plan facts. In this example, a single person has a taxable estate of $775,000 in the year 2001. By applying the Unified Federal Estate and Gift Tax Rate Schedule for U.S. Citizens and Residents appearing on page 24 and deducting the full unified tax credit of $220,550 available in 2001, her estate would be subject to estate taxes of $37,500, leaving $737,500 for heirs. By writing in your own flow chart amounts in the spaces available, you may easily chart the flow of your own estate.

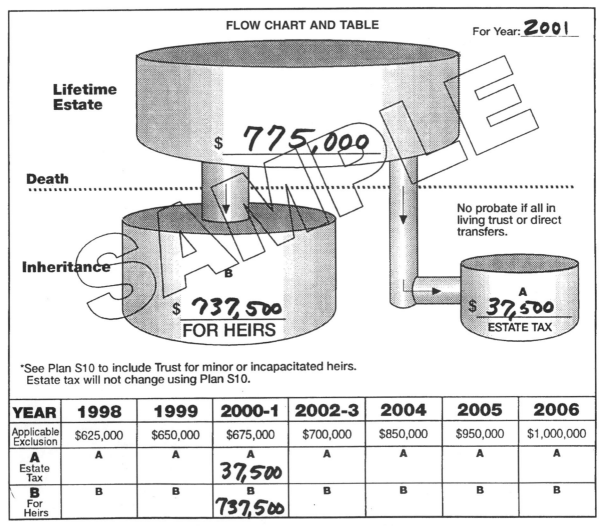

FLOW CHART AND TABLE   For Year: **2001**

Lifetime Estate

$ **775,000**

Death

No probate if all in living trust or direct transfers.

Inheritance   B

$ **737,500**
FOR HEIRS

$ **37,500**
ESTATE TAX

*See Plan S10 to include Trust for minor or incapacitated heirs. Estate tax will **not** change using Plan S10.

YEAR	1998	1999	2000-1	2002-3	2004	2005	2006
Applicable Exclusion	$625,000	$650,000	$675,000	$700,000	$850,000	$950,000	$1,000,000
A Estate Tax	A	A	A **37,500**	A	A	A	A
B For Heirs	B	B	B **737,500**	B	B	B	B

Select year. Insert calculations made using Unified Federal Estate and Gift Schedule and Applicable (credit) Exclusion.

SAMPLE PERSONALIZED FLOW CHART USING TABLE FOR SINGLE PERSON WITH $850,000 ESTATE
Without Minor or Incapacitated Heirs

This sample flow chart and table illustrates how to select a calendar year (2001) and fill in blanks A (Estate Tax) and B (For Heirs) for the selected year.

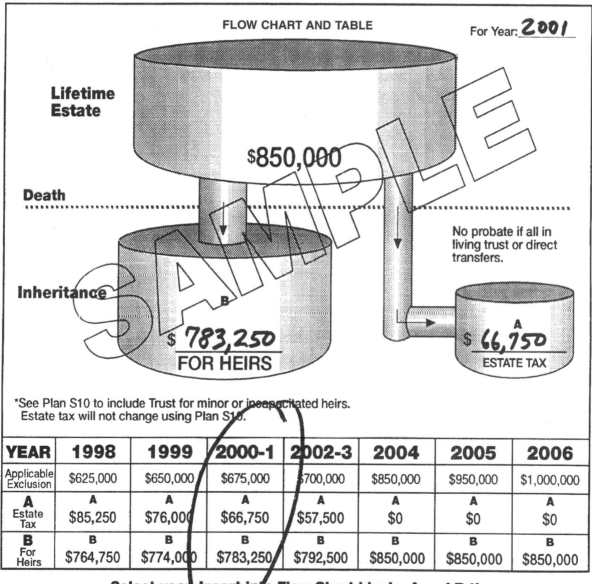

FLOW CHART AND TABLE   For Year: **2001**

Lifetime Estate

$850,000

Death

No probate if all in living trust or direct transfers.

Inheritance

$ 783,250
FOR HEIRS

$ 66,750
ESTATE TAX

*See Plan S10 to include Trust for minor or incapacitated heirs. Estate tax will not change using Plan S10.

YEAR	1998	1999	2000-1	2002-3	2004	2005	2006
Applicable Exclusion	$625,000	$650,000	$675,000	$700,000	$850,000	$950,000	$1,000,000
A Estate Tax	**A** $85,250	**A** $76,000	**A** $66,750	**A** $57,500	**A** $0	**A** $0	**A** $0
B For Heirs	**B** $764,750	**B** $774,000	**B** $783,250	**B** $792,500	**B** $850,000	**B** $850,000	**B** $850,000

Select year. Insert into Flow Chart blanks A and B the corresponding amounts from table.

WORKSHEET FOR SINGLE PERSON
WITH $_____ ESTATE

This blank worksheet can be used to develop alternative estate plans, identify various heirs, consider charitable gifts, and calculate potential estate taxes.

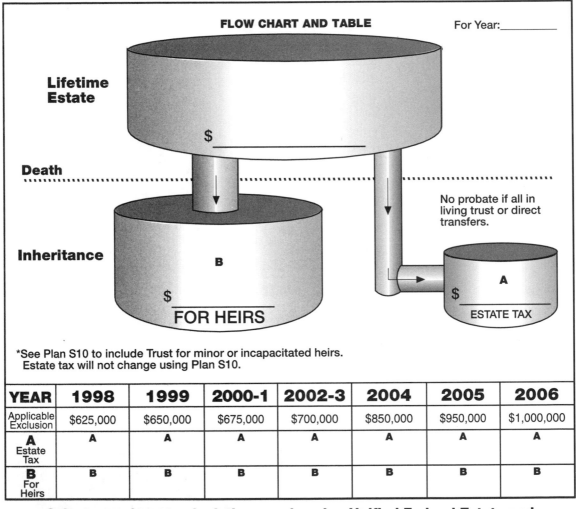

FLOW CHART AND TABLE   For Year:_____

Lifetime Estate

$ _____

Death

No probate if all in living trust or direct transfers.

Inheritance

B

$ _____
FOR HEIRS

A

$ _____
ESTATE TAX

*See Plan S10 to include Trust for minor or incapacitated heirs. Estate tax will not change using Plan S10.

YEAR	1998	1999	2000-1	2002-3	2004	2005	2006
Applicable Exclusion	$625,000	$650,000	$675,000	$700,000	$850,000	$950,000	$1,000,000
A Estate Tax	A	A	A	A	A	A	A
B For Heirs	B	B	B	B	B	B	B

Select year. Insert calculations made using Unified Federal Estate and Gift Schedule and Applicable (credit) Exclusion.

PLAN M1—MARRIED COUPLE WITH COMBINED ESTATE NOT EXCEEDING APPLICABLE EXCLUSION
Without Minor or Incapacitated Heirs

If your estate situation fits closely to this example, the following plan documentation is recommended. For a more detailed explanation of basics and add-ons, refer to pages 40–44.

Basics of a Good Plan

Living trust with appropriate support and funding documents to avoid the anguish and cost of probate, save time, and preserve privacy; *pour-over will* to transfer into your living trust assets that remain outside the trust at time of death (alternative to last will and testament below—check only one alternative); or

Last will and testament that transfers property owned by you at your death by use of the probate transfer process (alternative to living trust and pour-over will earlier—check only one alternative).

Joint ownership documents with right of survivorship to cause an automatic transfer of your property interest to the surviving joint owner or owners at your death. Often referred to as joint tenancy. Avoids probate and is not affected by will. Watch out for tax traps and loss of control.

Beneficiary designations for life insurance, pension, profit-sharing, Keogh, IRA, and annuity survivor and death benefits and other pay-on-death proceeds. You must complete the proper forms and submit them to the company or administrator in charge of benefits.

Durable power of attorney to name an individual to act for you if you become incapacitated.

Medical durable power of attorney for health care naming someone to make health care decisions if you are unable to do so yourself.

Living will to die with dignity and not be kept alive by a machine under certain conditions.

Add-ons to Consider

Anatomical gift document to give vital organs.

Letters of instruction to help organize your estate, provide vital information and final instructions to your heirs, and express your thoughts. Include funeral and burial letter, inheritance letter, and family and friends letter.

Testamentary trust after death to manage, control, and defer distribution of assets.

Charitable gifts which may take many forms.

Other gift and estate planning tools.

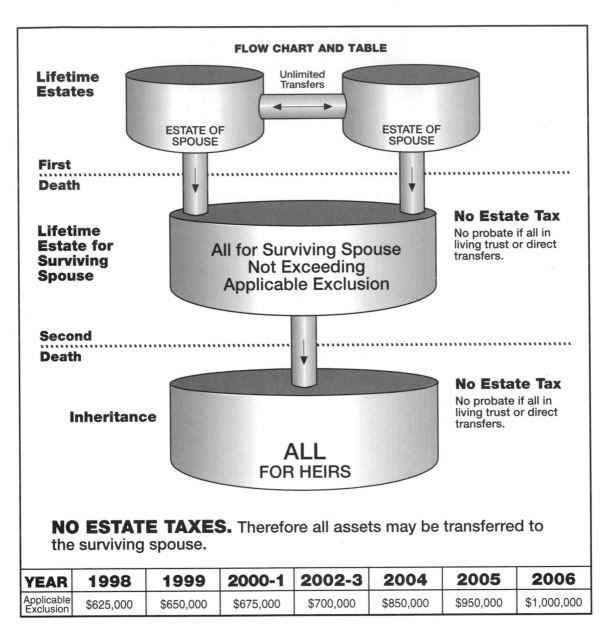

FLOW CHART AND TABLE

Lifetime Estates

Unlimited Transfers

ESTATE OF SPOUSE

ESTATE OF SPOUSE

First Death

Lifetime Estate for Surviving Spouse

All for Surviving Spouse Not Exceeding Applicable Exclusion

No Estate Tax
No probate if all in living trust or direct transfers.

Second Death

Inheritance

No Estate Tax
No probate if all in living trust or direct transfers.

ALL FOR HEIRS

NO ESTATE TAXES. Therefore all assets may be transferred to the surviving spouse.

YEAR	1998	1999	2000-1	2002-3	2004	2005	2006
Applicable Exclusion	$625,000	$650,000	$675,000	$700,000	$850,000	$950,000	$1,000,000

PLAN M2—MARRIED COUPLE WITH COMBINED ESTATE NOT EXCEEDING APPLICABLE EXCLUSION
With Minor or Incapacitated Heirs

If your estate situation fits closely to this example, the following plan documentation is recommended. For a more detailed explanation of basics and add-ons, refer to pages 40–44.

Basics of a Good Plan

Living trust with appropriate support and funding documents to avoid the anguish and cost of probate, save time, and preserve privacy; *pour-over will* to transfer into your living trust assets that remain outside the trust at time of death (alternative to last will and testament below—check only one alternative); or

Last will and testament that transfers property owned by you at your death by use of the probate transfer process (alternative to living trust and pour-over will earlier—check only one alternative).

Appointment of guardian of minor or incapacitated heirs guardian of the person will be responsible for personal physical care and control, and guardian of the estate will be responsible for financial management. Actual titles may vary.

Testamentary trust for minor or incapacitated heirs to manage assets after second death, control and defer distribution of assets, and avoid court-supervised conservatorships.

Joint ownership documents with right of survivorship to cause an automatic transfer of your property interest to the surviving joint owner or owners at your death. Often referred to as joint tenancy. Avoids probate and is not affected by will. Watch out for tax traps and loss of control.

Beneficiary designations for life insurance, pension, profit-sharing, Keogh, IRA, and annuity survivor and death benefits and other pay-on-death proceeds. You must complete the proper forms and submit them to the company or administrator in charge of benefits.

Durable power of attorney to name an individual to act for you if you become incapacitated.

Medical durable power of attorney for health care naming someone to make health care decisions if you are unable to do so yourself.

Living will to die with dignity and not be kept alive by a machine under certain conditions.

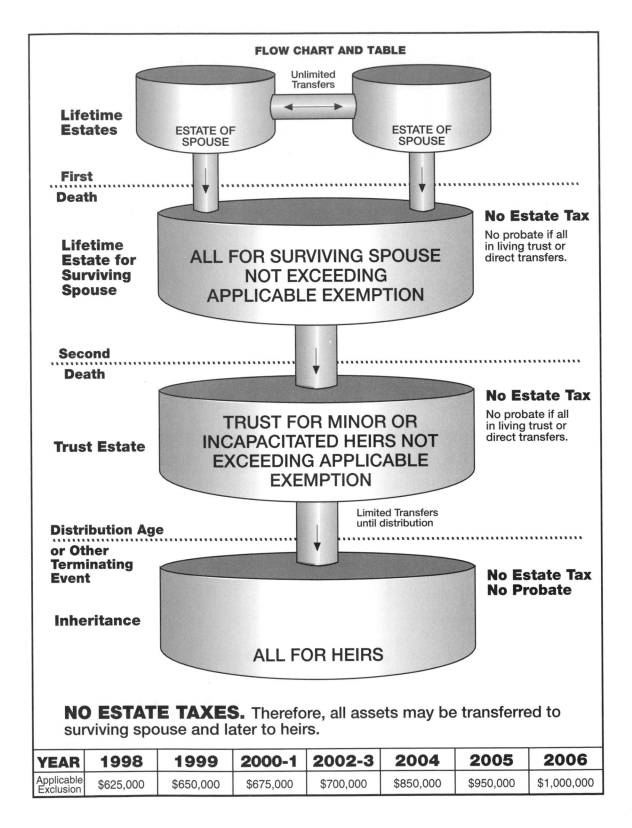

FLOW CHART AND TABLE

Unlimited Transfers

Lifetime Estates

ESTATE OF SPOUSE   ESTATE OF SPOUSE

First Death

No Estate Tax

No probate if all in living trust or direct transfers.

Lifetime Estate for Surviving Spouse

ALL FOR SURVIVING SPOUSE NOT EXCEEDING APPLICABLE EXEMPTION

Second Death

No Estate Tax

No probate if all in living trust or direct transfers.

Trust Estate

TRUST FOR MINOR OR INCAPACITATED HEIRS NOT EXCEEDING APPLICABLE EXEMPTION

Limited Transfers until distribution

Distribution Age or Other Terminating Event

No Estate Tax No Probate

Inheritance

ALL FOR HEIRS

NO ESTATE TAXES. Therefore, all assets may be transferred to surviving spouse and later to heirs.

YEAR	1998	1999	2000-1	2002-3	2004	2005	2006
Applicable Exclusion	$625,000	$650,000	$675,000	$700,000	$850,000	$950,000	$1,000,000

Add-ons to Consider

Anatomical gift document to give vital organs.

Letters of instruction to help organize your estate, provide vital information and final instructions to your heirs, and express your thoughts. Include funeral and burial letter, inheritance letter, and family and friends letter.

Testamentary trust after death to manage, control, and defer distribution of assets.

Charitable gifts which may take many forms.

Other gift and estate planning tools.

PLAN M3 —MARRIED COUPLE
WITH $700,000 COMBINED ESTATE USING BYPASS TRUST
With or Without Minor or Incapacitated Heirs

If your estate situation fits closely to this example, the following plan documentation is recommended. For a more detailed explanation of basics and add-ons, refer to pages 40–44. For Flow Chart and Table illustrations, see samples beginning on page 95.

Basics of a Good Plan

Living trust with appropriate support and funding documents to avoid the anguish and cost of probate, save time, and preserve privacy; *pour-over will* to transfer into your living trust assets that remain outside the trust at time of death (alternative to last will and testament below—check only one alternative); or

Last will and testament that transfers property owned by you at your death by use of the probate transfer process (alternative to living trust and pour-over will earlier—check only one alternative).

Bypass trust to keep limited assets out of taxable estate of surviving spouse to save estate taxes and provide lifetime security to surviving spouse.

Appointment of guardian of minor or incapacitated heirs guardian of the person will be responsible for personal physical care and control, and guardian of the estate will be responsible for financial management. Actual titles may vary.

Testamentary trust for minor or incapacitated heirs to manage assets after death, control and defer distribution of assets, and avoid court-supervised conservatorships.

Joint ownership documents including joint tenancy with right of survivorship to cause an automatic transfer of your property interest to the surviving joint owner or owners at your death. Avoids probate and is not affected by will. Watch out for tax traps and loss of control.

Beneficiary designations for life insurance, pension, profit-sharing, Keogh, IRA, and annuity survivor and death benefits and other pay-on-death proceeds. You must complete the proper forms and submit them to the company or administrator in charge of benefits.

Durable power of attorney to name an individual to act for you if you become incapacitated.

Medical durable power of attorney for health care naming someone to make health care decisions if you are unable to do so yourself.

Living will to die with dignity and not be kept alive by a machine under certain conditions.

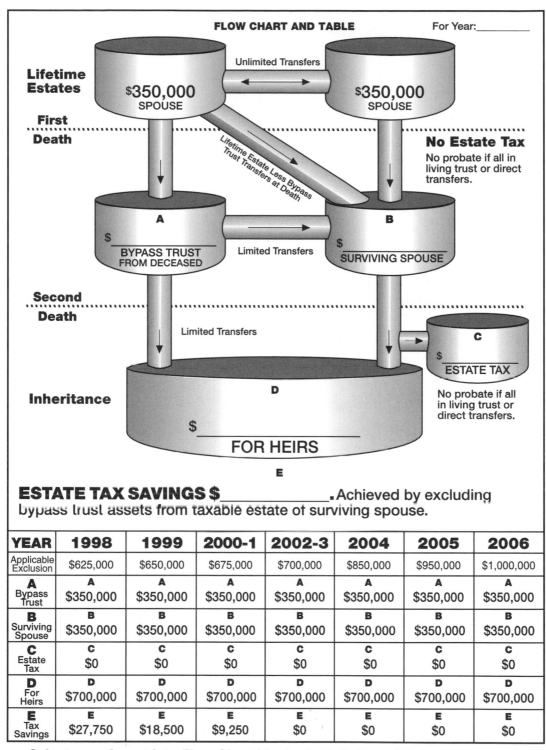

FLOW CHART AND TABLE   For Year:_____

Lifetime Estates — $350,000 SPOUSE — Unlimited Transfers — $350,000 SPOUSE

First Death .... **No Estate Tax** No probate if all in living trust or direct transfers.

Lifetime Estate Less Bypass Trust Transfers at Death

A $____ BYPASS TRUST FROM DECEASED — Limited Transfers — **B** $____ SURVIVING SPOUSE

Second Death ....

Limited Transfers

C $____ ESTATE TAX — No probate if all in living trust or direct transfers.

Inheritance — **D** $____ FOR HEIRS

E

ESTATE TAX SAVINGS $_____. Achieved by excluding bypass trust assets from taxable estate of surviving spouse.

YEAR	1998	1999	2000-1	2002-3	2004	2005	2006
Applicable Exclusion	$625,000	$650,000	$675,000	$700,000	$850,000	$950,000	$1,000,000
A Bypass Trust	A $350,000	A $350,000	A $350,000	A $350,000	A $350,000	A $350,000	A $350,000
B Surviving Spouse	B $350,000	B $350,000	B $350,000	B $350,000	B $350,000	B $350,000	B $350,000
C Estate Tax	C $0	C $0	C $0	C $0	C $0	C $0	C $0
D For Heirs	D $700,000	D $700,000	D $700,000	D $700,000	D $700,000	D $700,000	D $700,000
E Tax Savings	E $27,750	E $18,500	E $9,250	E $0	E $0	E $0	E $0

Select year. Insert into Flow Chart blanks A, B, C, D, and E the corresponding amounts from table.

Add-ons to Consider

Anatomical gift document to give vital organs.

Letters of instruction to help organize your estate, provide vital information and final instructions to your heirs, and express your thoughts. Include funeral and burial letter, inheritance letter, and family and friends letter.

Testamentary trust after death to manage, control, and defer distribution of assets.

Spousal transfer documents to assure that each spouse will have sufficient assets in his or her estate to take maximum advantage of the applicable exclusion and thereby reduce or eliminate federal estate taxes.

Community property and separate property agreement for a married couple who has lived in a community property state and accumulated community property while living there. Agreement is a joint declaration identifying community and separate property for legal and tax purposes.

Nuptial agreements before or after marriage agreeing to the separate property and rights of each spouse in the event of marriage dissolution or death. Often used in second marriage situations.

Qualified Domestic Trust (QDOT) if spouse is a noncitizen of the United States and goal is to defer estate taxes until second death.

Charitable gifts which may take many forms.

Other gift, estate planning, and tax-saving tools.

PLAN M4—MARRIED COUPLE WITH $850,000 COMBINED ESTATE USING BYPASS TRUST
With or Without Minor or Incapacitated Heirs

If your estate situation fits closely to this example, the following plan documentation is recommended. For a more detailed explanation of basics and add-ons, refer to pages 40–44. For Flow Chart and Table illustrations, see samples beginning on page 95.

Basics of a Good Plan

Living trust with appropriate support and funding documents to avoid the anguish and cost of probate, save time, and preserve privacy; *pour-over will* to transfer into your living trust assets that remain outside the trust at time of death (alternative to last will and testament below—check only one alternative); or

Last will and testament that transfers property owned by you at your death by use of the probate transfer process (alternative to living trust and pour-over will earlier—check only one alternative).

Bypass trust to keep limited assets out of taxable estate of surviving spouse to save estate taxes and provide lifetime security to surviving spouse.

Appointment of guardian of minor or incapacitated heirs guardian of the person will be responsible for personal physical care and control, and guardian of the estate will be responsible for financial management. Actual titles may vary.

Testamentary trust for minor or incapacitated heirs to manage assets after death, control and defer distribution of assets, and avoid court-supervised conservatorships.

Joint ownership documents with right of survivorship to cause an automatic transfer of your property interest to the surviving joint owner or owners at your death. Often referred to as joint tenancy. Avoids probate and is not affected by will. Watch out for tax traps and loss of control.

Beneficiary designations for life insurance, pension, profit-sharing, Keogh, IRA, and annuity survivor and death benefits and other pay-on-death proceeds. You must complete the proper forms and submit them to the company or administrator in charge of benefits.

Durable power of attorney to name an individual to act for you if you become incapacitated.

Medical durable power of attorney for health care naming someone to make health care decisions if you are unable to do so yourself.

Living will to die with dignity and not be kept alive by a machine under certain conditions.

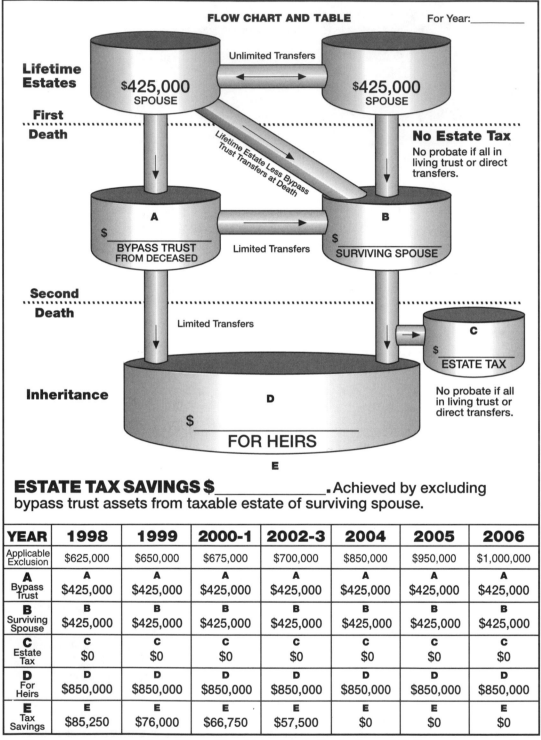

FLOW CHART AND TABLE   For Year:_____

Unlimited Transfers

**Lifetime
Estates** $425,000 $425,000
                   SPOUSE   SPOUSE

**First
Death**   Lifetime Estate Less Bypass   **No Estate Tax**
                Trust Transfers at Death   No probate if all in
                                                     living trust or direct
                                                     transfers.

A   B

$_____ $_____
BYPASS TRUST   Limited Transfers   SURVIVING SPOUSE
FROM DECEASED

**Second
Death**

Limited Transfers   C

$_____
ESTATE TAX

Inheritance   D

$_____   No probate if all
FOR HEIRS   in living trust or
                  direct transfers.

E

ESTATE TAX SAVINGS $_____.Achieved by excluding
bypass trust assets from taxable estate of surviving spouse.

YEAR	1998	1999	2000-1	2002-3	2004	2005	2006
Applicable Exclusion	$625,000	$650,000	$675,000	$700,000	$850,000	$950,000	$1,000,000
A Bypass Trust	A $425,000	A $425,000	A $425,000	A $425,000	A $425,000	A $425,000	A $425,000
B Surviving Spouse	B $425,000	B $425,000	B $425,000	B $425,000	B $425,000	B $425,000	B $425,000
C Estate Tax	C $0	C $0	C $0	C $0	C $0	C $0	C $0
D For Heirs	D $850,000	D $850,000	D $850,000	D $850,000	D $850,000	D $850,000	D $850,000
E Tax Savings	E $85,250	E $76,000	E $66,750	E $57,500	E $0	E $0	E $0

**Select year. Insert into Flow Chart blanks A, B, C, D, and E the corresponding
amounts from table.**

Add-ons to Consider

Anatomical gift document to give vital organs.

Letters of instruction to help organize your estate, provide vital information and final instructions to your heirs, and express your thoughts. Include funeral and burial letter, inheritance letter, and family and friends letter.

Testamentary trust after death to manage, control, and defer distribution of assets.

Irrevocable life insurance trust to save estate taxes by excluding death benefits from estate.

Spousal transfer documents to assure that each spouse will have sufficient assets in his or her estate to take maximum advantage of the applicable exclusion and thereby reduce or eliminate federal estate taxes.

Community property and separate property agreement for a married couple who has lived in a community property state and accumulated community property while living there. Agreement is a joint declaration identifying community and separate property for legal and tax purposes.

Nuptial agreements before or after marriage agreeing to the separate property and rights of each spouse in the event of marriage dissolution or death. Often used in second marriage situations.

Qualified Domestic Trust (QDOT) if spouse is a noncitizen of the United States and goal is to defer estate taxes until second death.

Charitable gifts which may take many forms.

Other gift, estate planning, and tax-saving tools.

PLAN M5—MARRIED COUPLE
WITH $1,000,000 COMBINED ESTATE USING BYPASS TRUST
With or Without Minor or Incapacitated Heirs

If your estate situation fits closely to this example, the following plan documentation is recommended. For a more detailed explanation of basics and add-ons, refer to pages 40–44. For Flow Chart and Table illustrations, see samples beginning on page 95.

Basics of a Good Plan

Living trust with appropriate support and funding documents to avoid the anguish and cost of probate, save time, and preserve privacy; *pour-over will* to transfer into your living trust assets that remain outside the trust at time of death (alternative to last will and testament below—check only one alternative); or

Last will and testament that transfers property owned by you at your death by use of the probate transfer process (alternative to living trust and pour-over will earlier—check only one alternative).

Bypass trust to keep limited assets out of taxable estate of surviving spouse to save estate taxes and provide lifetime security to surviving spouse.

Appointment of guardian of minor or incapacitated heirs guardian of the person will be responsible for personal physical care and control, and guardian of the estate will be responsible for financial management. Actual titles may vary.

Testamentary trust for minor or incapacitated heirs to manage assets after death, control and defer distribution of assets, and avoid court-supervised conservatorships.

Joint ownership documents with right of survivorship to cause an automatic transfer of your property interest to the surviving joint owner or owners at your death. Often referred to as joint tenancy. Avoids probate and is not affected by will. Watch out for tax traps and loss of control.

Beneficiary designations for life insurance, pension, profit-sharing, Keogh, IRA, and annuity survivor and death benefits and other pay-on-death proceeds. You must complete the proper forms and submit them to the company or administrator in charge of benefits.

Durable power of attorney to name an individual to act for you if you become incapacitated.

Medical durable power of attorney for health care naming someone to make health care decisions if you are unable to do so yourself.

Living will to die with dignity and not be kept alive by a machine under certain conditions.

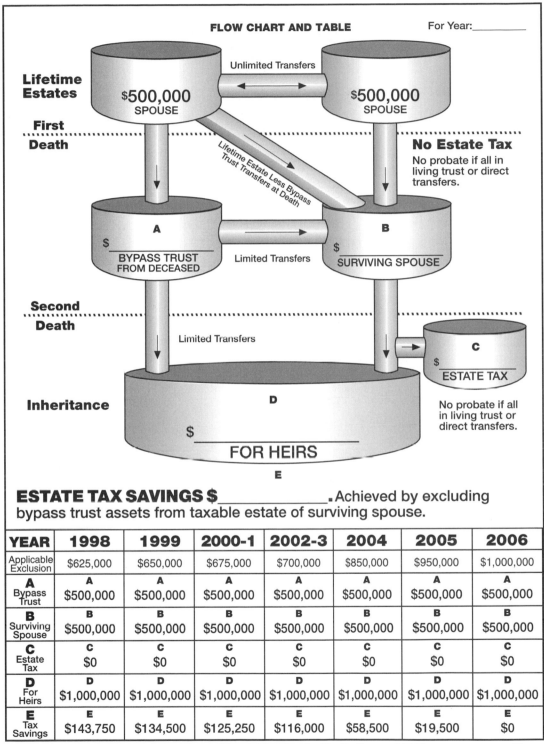

FLOW CHART AND TABLE   For Year:_____

Lifetime Estates

Unlimited Transfers

$500,000 SPOUSE ⟷ $500,000 SPOUSE

First Death

Lifetime Estate Less Bypass Trust Transfers at Death

No Estate Tax
No probate if all in living trust or direct transfers.

A $ _____ BYPASS TRUST FROM DECEASED

Limited Transfers

B $ _____ SURVIVING SPOUSE

Second Death

Limited Transfers

C $ _____ ESTATE TAX

Inheritance

D $ _____ FOR HEIRS

No probate if all in living trust or direct transfers.

E

ESTATE TAX SAVINGS $_____. Achieved by excluding bypass trust assets from taxable estate of surviving spouse.

YEAR	1998	1999	2000-1	2002-3	2004	2005	2006
Applicable Exclusion	$625,000	$650,000	$675,000	$700,000	$850,000	$950,000	$1,000,000
A Bypass Trust	A $500,000	A $500,000	A $500,000	A $500,000	A $500,000	A $500,000	A $500,000
B Surviving Spouse	B $500,000	B $500,000	B $500,000	B $500,000	B $500,000	B $500,000	B $500,000
C Estate Tax	C $0	C $0	C $0	C $0	C $0	C $0	C $0
D For Heirs	D $1,000,000	D $1,000,000	D $1,000,000	D $1,000,000	D $1,000,000	D $1,000,000	D $1,000,000
E Tax Savings	E $143,750	E $134,500	E $125,250	E $116,000	E $58,500	E $19,500	E $0

Select year. Insert into Flow Chart blanks A, B, C, D, and E the corresponding amounts from table.

Add-ons to Consider

Anatomical gift document to give vital organs.

Letters of instruction to help organize your estate, provide vital information and final instructions to your heirs, and express your thoughts. Include funeral and burial letter, inheritance letter, and family and friends letter.

Testamentary trust after death to manage, control, and defer distribution of assets.

Irrevocable life insurance trust to save estate taxes by excluding death benefits from estate.

Spousal transfer documents to assure that each spouse will have sufficient assets in his or her estate to take maximum advantage of the applicable exclusion and thereby reduce or eliminate federal estate taxes.

Community property and separate property agreement for a married couple who has lived in a community property state and accumulated community property while living there. Agreement is a joint declaration identifying community and separate property for legal and tax purposes.

Nuptial agreements before or after marriage agreeing to the separate property and rights of each spouse in the event of marriage dissolution or death. Often used in second marriage situations.

Qualified Domestic Trust (QDOT) if spouse is a noncitizen of the United States and goal is to defer estate taxes until second death.

Charitable gifts which may take many forms.

Other gift, estate planning, and tax-saving tools.

PLAN M6—MARRIED COUPLE WITH $1,250,000 COMBINED ESTATE USING BYPASS TRUST
With or Without Minor or Incapacitated Heirs

If your estate situation fits closely to this example, the following plan documentation is recommended. For a more detailed explanation of basics and add-ons, refer to pages 40–44. For Flow Chart and Table illustrations, see samples beginning on page 95.

Basics of a Good Plan

Living trust with appropriate support and funding documents to avoid the anguish and cost of probate, save time, and preserve privacy; *pour-over will* to transfer into your living trust assets that remain outside the trust at time of death (alternative to last will and testament below—check only one alternative); or

Last will and testament that transfers property owned by you at your death by use of the probate transfer process (alternative to living trust and pour-over will earlier—check only one alternative).

Bypass trust to keep limited assets out of taxable estate of surviving spouse to save estate taxes and provide lifetime security to surviving spouse.

Appointment of guardian of minor or incapacitated heirs guardian of the person will be responsible for personal physical care and control and guardian of the estate will be responsible for financial management. Actual titles may vary.

Testamentary trust for minor or incapacitated heirs to manage assets after death, control and defer distribution of assets, and avoid court-supervised conservatorships.

Joint ownership documents with right of survivorship to cause an automatic transfer of your property interest to the surviving joint owner or owners at your death. Often referred to as joint tenancy. Avoids probate and is not affected by will. Watch out for tax traps and loss of control.

Beneficiary designations for life insurance, pension, profit-sharing, Keogh, IRA, and annuity survivor and death benefits and other pay-on-death proceeds. You must complete the proper forms and submit them to the company or administrator in charge of benefits.

Durable power of attorney to name an individual to act for you if you become incapacitated.

Medical durable power of attorney for health care naming someone to make health care decisions if you are unable to do so yourself.

Living will to die with dignity and not be kept alive by a machine under certain conditions.

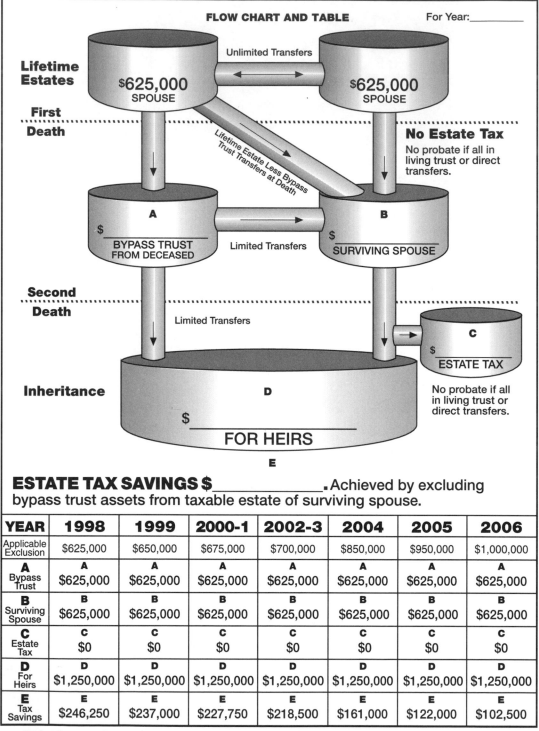

FLOW CHART AND TABLE   For Year:_____

Unlimited Transfers

Lifetime Estates

$625,000 SPOUSE $625,000 SPOUSE

First Death

Lifetime Estate Less Bypass Trust Transfers at Death

No Estate Tax
No probate if all in living trust or direct transfers.

A
$ _____
BYPASS TRUST FROM DECEASED

Limited Transfers

B
$ _____
SURVIVING SPOUSE

Second Death

Limited Transfers

C
$ _____
ESTATE TAX

No probate if all in living trust or direct transfers.

Inheritance

D
$ _____
FOR HEIRS

E

ESTATE TAX SAVINGS $_____. Achieved by excluding
bypass trust assets from taxable estate of surviving spouse.

YEAR	1998	1999	2000-1	2002-3	2004	2005	2006
Applicable Exclusion	$625,000	$650,000	$675,000	$700,000	$850,000	$950,000	$1,000,000
A Bypass Trust	A $625,000	A $625,000	A $625,000	A $625,000	A $625,000	A $625,000	A $625,000
B Surviving Spouse	B $625,000	B $625,000	B $625,000	B $625,000	B $625,000	B $625,000	B $625,000
C Estate Tax	C $0	C $0	C $0	C $0	C $0	C $0	C $0
D For Heirs	D $1,250,000	D $1,250,000	D $1,250,000	D $1,250,000	D $1,250,000	D $1,250,000	D $1,250,000
E Tax Savings	E $246,250	E $237,000	E $227,750	E $218,500	E $161,000	E $122,000	E $102,500

Select year. Insert into Flow Chart blanks A, B, C, D, and E the corresponding amounts from table.

Add-ons to Consider

Anatomical gift document to give vital organs.

Letters of instruction to help organize your estate, provide vital information and final instructions to your heirs, and express your thoughts. Include funeral and burial letter, inheritance letter, and family and friends letter.

Testamentary trust after death to manage, control, and defer distribution of assets.

Irrevocable life insurance trust to save estate taxes by excluding death benefits from estate.

Spousal transfer documents to assure that estates are sufficiently balanced to take advantage of the applicable exclusion at the second spouse's death.

Qualified terminable interest property (QTIP) trust for married couples to defer estate taxes and impose controls while providing income to surviving spouse.

Family partnerships, corporations, and limited liability companies to allow gifting interests in business and investments while establishing management and control options.

Community property and separate property agreement for a married couple who has lived in a community property state and accumulated community property while living there. Agreement is a joint declaration identifying community and separate property for legal and tax purposes.

Nuptial agreements before or after marriage agreeing to the separate property and rights of each spouse in the event of marriage dissolution or death. Often used in second marriage situations.

Qualified Domestic Trust (QDOT) if spouse is a noncitizen of the United States and goal is to defer estate taxes until second death.

Charitable gifts which may take many forms.

Other gift, estate planning, and tax-saving tools.

PLAN M7—MARRIED COUPLE
WITH $1,500,000 COMBINED ESTATE USING BYPASS TRUST
With or Without Minor or Incapacitated Heirs

If your estate situation fits closely to this example, the following plan documentation is recommended. For a more detailed explanation of basics and add-ons, refer to pages 40–44. For Flow Chart and Table illustrations, see samples beginning on page 95.

Basics of a Good Plan

Living trust with appropriate support and funding documents to avoid the anguish and cost of probate, save time, and preserve privacy; *pour-over will* to transfer into your living trust assets that remain outside the trust at time of death (alternative to last will and testament below—check only one alternative); or

Last will and testament that transfers property owned by you at your death by use of the probate transfer process (alternative to living trust and pour-over will earlier—check only one alternative).

Bypass trust to keep limited assets out of taxable estate of surviving spouse to save estate taxes and provide lifetime security to surviving spouse.

Appointment of guardian of minor or incapacitated heirs guardian of the person will be responsible for personal physical care and control, and guardian of the estate will be responsible for financial management. Actual titles may vary.

Testamentary trust for minor or incapacitated heirs to manage assets after death, control and defer distribution of assets, and avoid court-supervised conservatorships.

Joint ownership documents with right of survivorship to cause an automatic transfer of your property interest to the surviving joint owner or owners at your death. Often referred to as joint tenancy. Avoids probate and is not affected by will. Watch out for tax traps and loss of control.

Beneficiary designations for life insurance, pension, profit-sharing, Keogh, IRA, and annuity survivor and death benefits and other pay-on-death proceeds. You must complete the proper forms and submit them to the company or administrator in charge of benefits.

Durable power of attorney to name an individual to act for you if you become incapacitated.

Medical durable power of attorney for health care naming someone to make health care decisions if you are unable to do so yourself.

Living will to die with dignity and not be kept alive by a machine under certain conditions.

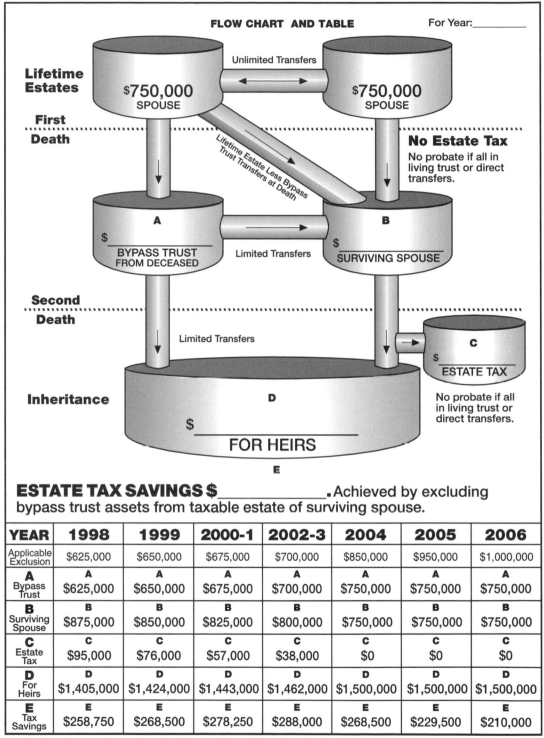

FLOW CHART AND TABLE   For Year:_____

Lifetime Estates

Unlimited Transfers

$750,000 SPOUSE $750,000 SPOUSE

First Death

No Estate Tax
No probate if all in living trust or direct transfers.

Lifetime Estate Less Bypass Trust Transfers at Death

A
$_____
BYPASS TRUST FROM DECEASED

Limited Transfers

B
$_____
SURVIVING SPOUSE

Second Death

Limited Transfers

C
$_____
ESTATE TAX

No probate if all in living trust or direct transfers.

Inheritance

D
$_____
FOR HEIRS

E

ESTATE TAX SAVINGS $_____. Achieved by excluding
bypass trust assets from taxable estate of surviving spouse.

YEAR	1998	1999	2000-1	2002-3	2004	2005	2006
Applicable Exclusion	$625,000	$650,000	$675,000	$700,000	$850,000	$950,000	$1,000,000
A Bypass Trust	**A** $625,000	**A** $650,000	**A** $675,000	**A** $700,000	**A** $750,000	**A** $750,000	**A** $750,000
B Surviving Spouse	**B** $875,000	**B** $850,000	**B** $825,000	**B** $800,000	**B** $750,000	**B** $750,000	**B** $750,000
C Estate Tax	**C** $95,000	**C** $76,000	**C** $57,000	**C** $38,000	**C** $0	**C** $0	**C** $0
D For Heirs	**D** $1,405,000	**D** $1,424,000	**D** $1,443,000	**D** $1,462,000	**D** $1,500,000	**D** $1,500,000	**D** $1,500,000
E Tax Savings	**E** $258,750	**E** $268,500	**E** $278,250	**E** $288,000	**E** $268,500	**E** $229,500	**E** $210,000

Select year. Insert into Flow Chart blanks A, B, C, D, and E the corresponding amounts from table.

Add-ons to Consider

Anatomical gift document to give vital organs.

Letters of instruction to help organize your estate, provide vital information and final instructions to your heirs, and express your thoughts. Include funeral and burial letter, inheritance letter, and family and friends letter.

Testamentary trust after death to manage, control, and defer distribution of assets.

Irrevocable life insurance trust to save estate taxes by excluding death benefits from estate.

Spousal transfer documents to assure that each spouse will have sufficient assets in his or her estate to take maximum advantage of the applicable exclusion and thereby reduce or eliminate federal estate taxes.

Qualified terminable interest property (QTIP) trust for married couples to defer estate taxes and impose controls while providing income to surviving spouse.

Family partnerships, corporations, and limited liability companies to allow gifting interests in business and investments while establishing management and control options.

Community property and separate property agreement for a married couple who has lived in a community property state and accumulated community property while living there. Agreement is a joint declaration identifying community and separate property for legal and tax purposes.

Nuptial agreements before or after marriage agreeing to the separate property and rights of each spouse in the event of marriage dissolution or death. Often used in second marriage situations.

Qualified Domestic Trust (QDOT) if spouse is a noncitizen of the United States and goal is to defer estate taxes until second death.

Charitable gifts which may take many forms.

Other gift, estate planning, and tax-saving tools.

PLAN M8—MARRIED COUPLE WITH $2,000,000 COMBINED ESTATE USING BYPASS TRUST
With or Without Minor or Incapacitated Heirs

If your estate situation fits closely to this example, the following plan documentation is recommended. For a more detailed explanation of basics and add-ons, refer to pages 40–44. For Flow Chart and Table illustrations, see samples beginning on page 95.

Basics of a Good Plan

Living trust with appropriate support and funding documents to avoid the anguish and cost of probate, save time, and preserve privacy; *pour-over will* to transfer into your living trust assets that remain outside the trust at time of death (alternative to last will and testament below—check only one alternative); or

Last will and testament that transfers property owned by you at your death by use of the probate transfer process (alternative to living trust and pour-over will earlier—check only one alternative).

Bypass trust to keep limited assets out of taxable estate of surviving spouse to save estate taxes and provide lifetime security to surviving spouse.

Appointment of guardian of minor or incapacitated heirs guardian of the person will be responsible for personal physical care and control, and guardian of the estate will be responsible for financial management. Actual titles may vary.

Testamentary trust for minor or incapacitated heirs to manage assets after death, control and defer distribution of assets, and avoid court-supervised conservatorships.

Joint ownership documents with right of survivorship to cause an automatic transfer of your property interest to the surviving joint owner or owners at your death. Often referred to as joint tenancy. Avoids probate and is not affected by will. Watch out for tax traps and loss of control.

Beneficiary designations for life insurance, pension, profit-sharing, Keogh, IRA, and annuity survivor and death benefits and other pay-on-death proceeds. You must complete the proper forms and submit them to the company or administrator in charge of benefits.

Durable power of attorney to name an individual to act for you if you become incapacitated.

Medical durable power of attorney for health care naming someone to make health care decisions if you are unable to do so yourself.

Living will to die with dignity and not be kept alive by a machine under certain conditions.

FLOW CHART AND TABLE

For Year:_____

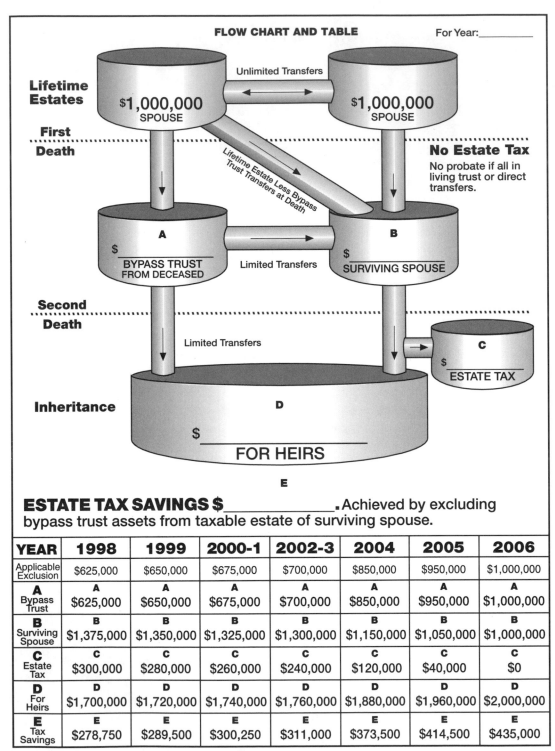

Lifetime Estates

$1,000,000 SPOUSE

Unlimited Transfers

$1,000,000 SPOUSE

First Death

No Estate Tax

No probate if all in living trust or direct transfers.

Lifetime Estate Less Bypass Trust Transfers at Death

A

$_____

BYPASS TRUST FROM DECEASED

Limited Transfers

B

$_____

SURVIVING SPOUSE

Second Death

Limited Transfers

C

$_____

ESTATE TAX

Inheritance

D

$_____

FOR HEIRS

E

ESTATE TAX SAVINGS $_____. Achieved by excluding bypass trust assets from taxable estate of surviving spouse.

YEAR	1998	1999	2000-1	2002-3	2004	2005	2006
Applicable Exclusion	$625,000	$650,000	$675,000	$700,000	$850,000	$950,000	$1,000,000
A Bypass Trust	A $625,000	A $650,000	A $675,000	A $700,000	A $850,000	A $950,000	A $1,000,000
B Surviving Spouse	B $1,375,000	B $1,350,000	B $1,325,000	B $1,300,000	B $1,150,000	B $1,050,000	B $1,000,000
C Estate Tax	C $300,000	C $280,000	C $260,000	C $240,000	C $120,000	C $40,000	C $0
D For Heirs	D $1,700,000	D $1,720,000	D $1,740,000	D $1,760,000	D $1,880,000	D $1,960,000	D $2,000,000
E Tax Savings	E $278,750	E $289,500	E $300,250	E $311,000	E $373,500	E $414,500	E $435,000

Select year. Insert into Flow Chart blanks A, B, C, D, and E the corresponding amounts from table.

Add-ons to Consider

Anatomical gift document to give vital organs.

Letters of instruction to help organize your estate, provide vital information and final instructions to your heirs, and express your thoughts. Include funeral and burial letter, inheritance letter, and family and friends letter.

Testamentary trust after death to manage, control, and defer distribution of assets.

Irrevocable life insurance trust to save estate taxes by excluding death benefits from estate.

Spousal transfer documents to assure that estates are sufficiently balanced to take advantage of the applicable exclusion at the second spouse's death.

Qualified terminable interest property (QTIP) trust for married couples to defer estate taxes and impose controls while providing income to surviving spouse.

Family partnerships, corporations, and limited liability companies to allow gifting interests in business and investments while establishing management and control options.

Community property and separate property agreement for a married couple who has lived in a community property state and accumulated community property while living there. Agreement is a joint declaration identifying community and separate property for legal and tax purposes.

Nuptial agreements before or after marriage agreeing to the separate property and rights of each spouse in the event of marriage dissolution or death. Often used in second marriage situations.

Qualified Domestic Trust (QDOT) if spouse is a noncitizen of the United States and goal is to defer estate taxes until second death.

Charitable gifts which may take many forms.

Uncommon trusts, including minor's trust, dynasty trust, grantor retained income trust (GRIT), grantor retained annuity trust (GRAT), grantor retained unitrust (GRUT), and qualified subchapter S trust (QSST) for special situations if trade-offs acceptable and complex tax laws allow achievement of goals.

Other gift, estate planning, and tax-saving tools for large or unusual estates.

PLAN M9—MARRIED COUPLE
WITH $2,500,000 COMBINED ESTATE USING BYPASS TRUST
With or Without Minor or Incapacitated Heirs

If your estate situation fits closely to this example, the following plan documentation is recommended.

Basics of a Good Plan and Add-ons to Consider

Same as Plan M8—Married Couple with $2,000,000 Using Bypass Trust.

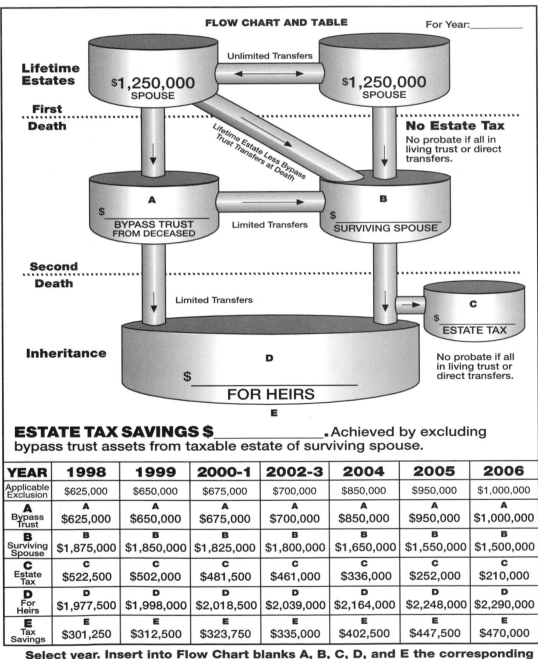

FLOW CHART AND TABLE For Year:_____

Lifetime Estates

$1,250,000 SPOUSE — Unlimited Transfers — $1,250,000 SPOUSE

First Death

No Estate Tax
No probate if all in living trust or direct transfers.

Lifetime Estate Less Bypass Trust Transfers at Death

A $_____ **BYPASS TRUST FROM DECEASED** — Limited Transfers — B $_____ **SURVIVING SPOUSE**

Second Death

Limited Transfers

C $_____ **ESTATE TAX**

Inheritance

D $_____ **FOR HEIRS**

E

No probate if all in living trust or direct transfers.

ESTATE TAX SAVINGS $_____. Achieved by excluding
bypass trust assets from taxable estate of surviving spouse.

YEAR	1998	1999	2000-1	2002-3	2004	2005	2006
Applicable Exclusion	$625,000	$650,000	$675,000	$700,000	$850,000	$950,000	$1,000,000
A Bypass Trust	A $625,000	A $650,000	A $675,000	A $700,000	A $850,000	A $950,000	A $1,000,000
B Surviving Spouse	B $1,875,000	B $1,850,000	B $1,825,000	B $1,800,000	B $1,650,000	B $1,550,000	B $1,500,000
C Estate Tax	C $522,500	C $502,000	C $481,500	C $461,000	C $336,000	C $252,000	C $210,000
D For Heirs	D $1,977,500	D $1,998,000	D $2,018,500	D $2,039,000	D $2,164,000	D $2,248,000	D $2,290,000
E Tax Savings	E $301,250	E $312,500	E $323,750	E $335,000	E $402,500	E $447,500	E $470,000

Select year. Insert into Flow Chart blanks A, B, C, D, and E the corresponding amounts from table.

PLAN M10—MARRIED COUPLE
WITH $3,000,000 COMBINED ESTATE USING BYPASS TRUST
With or Without Minor or Incapacitated Heirs

If your estate situation fits closely to this example, the following plan documentation is recommended.

Basics of a Good Plan and Add-ons to Consider

Same as Plan M8—Married Couple with $2,000,000 Using Bypass Trust.

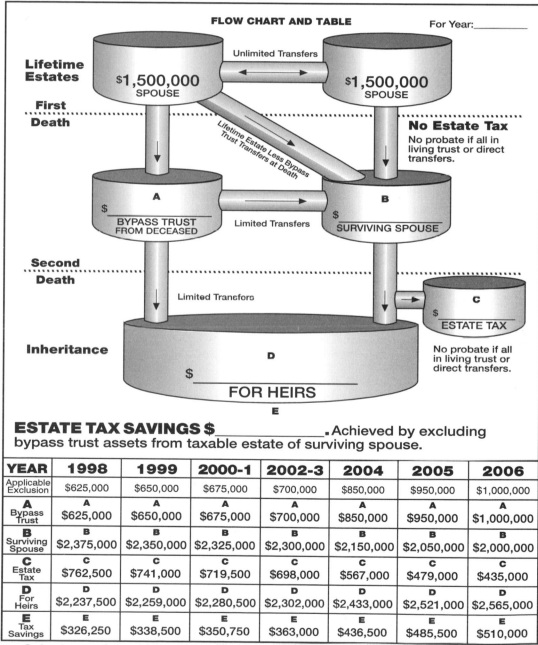

FLOW CHART AND TABLE   For Year:_____

Lifetime Estates
$1,500,000 SPOUSE — Unlimited Transfers — $1,500,000 SPOUSE

First Death

Lifetime Estate Less Bypass Trust Transfers at Death

No Estate Tax
No probate if all in living trust or direct transfers.

A — $_____ BYPASS TRUST FROM DECEASED — Limited Transfers — B — $_____ SURVIVING SPOUSE

Second Death

Limited Transfers

Limited Transfers

Inheritance — D — $_____ FOR HEIRS

C — $_____ ESTATE TAX

No probate if all in living trust or direct transfers.

E

ESTATE TAX SAVINGS $_____ . Achieved by excluding bypass trust assets from taxable estate of surviving spouse.

YEAR	1998	1999	2000-1	2002-3	2004	2005	2006
Applicable Exclusion	$625,000	$650,000	$675,000	$700,000	$850,000	$950,000	$1,000,000
A Bypass Trust	A $625,000	A $650,000	A $675,000	A $700,000	A $850,000	A $950,000	A $1,000,000
B Surviving Spouse	B $2,375,000	B $2,350,000	B $2,325,000	B $2,300,000	B $2,150,000	B $2,050,000	B $2,000,000
C Estate Tax	C $762,500	C $741,000	C $719,500	C $698,000	C $567,000	C $479,000	C $435,000
D For Heirs	D $2,237,500	D $2,259,000	D $2,280,500	D $2,302,000	D $2,433,000	D $2,521,000	D $2,565,000
E Tax Savings	E $326,250	E $338,500	E $350,750	E $363,000	E $436,500	E $485,500	E $510,000

Select year. Insert into Flow Chart blanks A, B, C, D, and E the corresponding amounts from table.

PLAN M11—MARRIED COUPLE WITH $2,000,000 COMBINED ESTATE USING BYPASS TRUST AND QTIP TRUST With or Without Minor or Incapacitated Heirs

If your estate situation fits closely to this example, the following plan documentation is recommended. For a more detailed explanation of basics and add-ons, refer to pages 40–44. For Flow Chart and Table illustrations, see samples beginning on page 98.

Basics of a Good Plan

Living trust with appropriate support and funding documents to avoid the anguish and cost of probate, save time, and preserve privacy; *pour-over will* to transfer into your living trust assets that remain outside the trust at time of death (alternative to last will and testament below—check only one alternative); or

Last will and testament that transfers property owned by you at your death by use of the probate transfer process (alternative to living trust and pour-over will earlier—check only one alternative).

Appointment of guardian of minor or incapacitated heirs guardian of the person will be responsible for personal physical care and control, and guardian of the estate will be responsible for financial management. Titles may vary.

Testamentary trust for minor or incapacitated heirs to manage assets after death, control and defer distribution of assets, and avoid court-supervised conservatorships.

Bypass trust to keep limited assets out of taxable estate of surviving spouse to save estate taxes and provide lifetime security to surviving spouse.

Qualified terminable interest property (QTIP) trust for married couples to defer estate taxes and impose controls while providing income to surviving spouse.

Joint ownership documents including joint tenancy with right of survivorship to cause an automatic transfer of your property interest to the surviving joint owner or owners at your death. Avoids probate and is not affected by will. Watch out for tax traps and loss of control.

Beneficiary designations for life insurance, pension, profit-sharing, Keogh, IRA, and annuity survivor and death benefits and other pay-on-death proceeds. You must complete the proper forms and submit them to the company or administrator in charge of benefits.

Durable power of attorney to name an individual to act for you if you become incapacitated.

Medical durable power of attorney for health care naming someone to make health care decisions if you are unable to do so yourself.

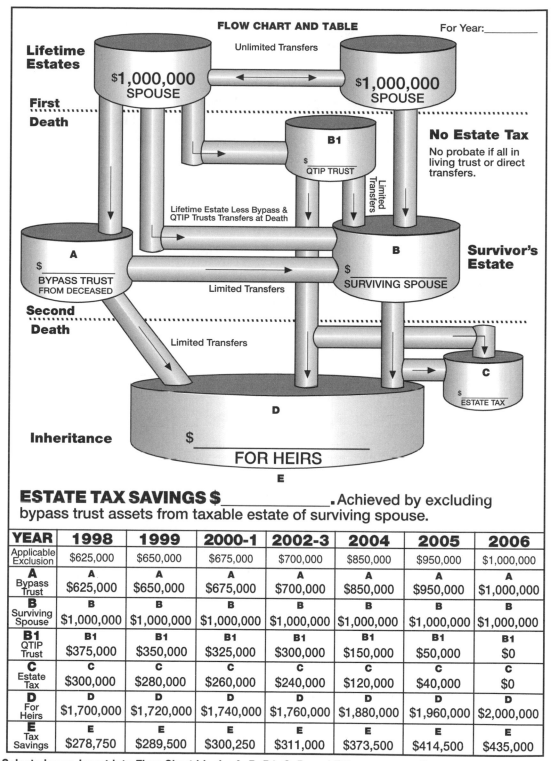

FLOW CHART AND TABLE   For Year:_____

Lifetime Estates

Unlimited Transfers

$1,000,000 SPOUSE $1,000,000 SPOUSE

First Death

No Estate Tax

No probate if all in living trust or direct transfers.

B1

$_____ QTIP TRUST

Limited Transfers

Lifetime Estate Less Bypass & QTIP Trusts Transfers at Death

A

$_____ BYPASS TRUST FROM DECEASED

B

$_____ SURVIVING SPOUSE

Survivor's Estate

Limited Transfers

Second Death

Limited Transfers

C

$_____ ESTATE TAX

D

Inheritance $_____ **FOR HEIRS**

E

ESTATE TAX SAVINGS $_____ .Achieved by excluding
bypass trust assets from taxable estate of surviving spouse.

YEAR	1998	1999	2000-1	2002-3	2004	2005	2006
Applicable Exclusion	$625,000	$650,000	$675,000	$700,000	$850,000	$950,000	$1,000,000
A Bypass Trust	A $625,000	A $650,000	A $675,000	A $700,000	A $850,000	A $950,000	A $1,000,000
B Surviving Spouse	B $1,000,000	B $1,000,000	B $1,000,000	B $1,000,000	B $1,000,000	B $1,000,000	B $1,000,000
B1 QTIP Trust	B1 $375,000	B1 $350,000	B1 $325,000	B1 $300,000	B1 $150,000	B1 $50,000	B1 $0
C Estate Tax	C $300,000	C $280,000	C $260,000	C $240,000	C $120,000	C $40,000	C $0
D For Heirs	D $1,700,000	D $1,720,000	D $1,740,000	D $1,760,000	D $1,880,000	D $1,960,000	D $2,000,000
E Tax Savings	E $278,750	E $289,500	E $300,250	E $311,000	E $373,500	E $414,500	E $435,000

Selected year. Insert into Flow Chart blanks A, B, B1, C, D, and E the corresponding amounts from table.

Living will to die with dignity and not be kept alive by a machine under certain conditions.

Add-ons to Consider

Anatomical gift document to give vital organs.

Letters of instruction to help organize your estate, provide vital information and final instructions to your heirs, and express your thoughts. Include funeral and burial letter, inheritance letter, and family and friends letter.

Testamentary trust after death to manage, control, and defer distribution of assets.

Irrevocable life insurance trust to save estate taxes by excluding death benefits from estate.

Spousal transfer documents to assure that estates are sufficiently balanced to take advantage of the applicable exclusion at the second spouse's death.

Family partnerships, corporations, and limited liability companies to allow gifting interests in business and investments while establishing management and control options.

Community property and separate property agreement for a married couple who has lived in a community property state and accumulated community property while living there. Agreement is a joint declaration identifying community and separate property for legal and tax purposes.

Nuptial agreements before or after marriage agreeing to the separate property and rights of each spouse in the event of marriage dissolution or death. Often used in second marriage situations.

Qualified Domestic Trust (QDOT) if spouse is a noncitizen of the United States and goal is to defer estate taxes until second death.

Uncommon trusts, including minor's trust, dynasty trust, grantor retained income trust (GRIT), grantor retained annuity trust (GRAT), grantor retained unitrust (GRUT), and qualified subchapter S trust (QSST) for special situations if trade-offs acceptable and complex tax laws allow achievement of goals.

Charitable gifts which may take many forms.

Other gift, estate planning, and tax-saving tools for large or unusual estates.

SAMPLE PERSONALIZED FLOW CHART USING TABLE FOR MARRIED COUPLE WITH $850,000 COMBINED ESTATE USING BYPASS TRUST
With or Without Minor or Incapacitated Heirs

This sample flow chart and table illustrates how to select a calendar year (2001) and fill in blanks A (Bypass Trust), B (Surviving Spouse), C (Estate Tax), D (For Heirs), and E (Tax Savings).

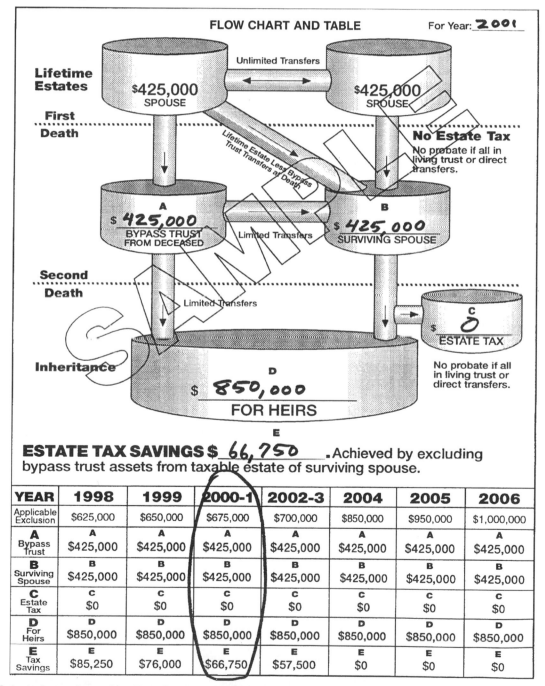

FLOW CHART AND TABLE   For Year: **2001**

Lifetime Estates

$425,000 SPOUSE — Unlimited Transfers — $425,000 SPOUSE

First Death

Lifetime Estate Less Bypass Trust Transfers at Death

No Estate Tax
No probate if all in living trust or direct transfers.

A
$ **425,000**
BYPASS TRUST FROM DECEASED — Limited Transfers — B
$ **425,000**
SURVIVING SPOUSE

Second Death

Limited Transfers

C
$ **0**
ESTATE TAX

No probate if all in living trust or direct transfers.

Inheritance

D
$ **850,000**
FOR HEIRS

E
ESTATE TAX SAVINGS $ 66,750 .Achieved by excluding bypass trust assets from taxable estate of surviving spouse.

YEAR	1998	1999	2000-1	2002-3	2004	2005	2006
Applicable Exclusion	$625,000	$650,000	$675,000	$700,000	$850,000	$950,000	$1,000,000
A Bypass Trust	A $425,000	A $425,000	A $425,000	A $425,000	A $425,000	A $425,000	A $425,000
B Surviving Spouse	B $425,000	B $425,000	B $425,000	B $425,000	B $425,000	B $425,000	B $425,000
C Estate Tax	C $0	C $0	C $0	C $0	C $0	C $0	C $0
D For Heirs	D $850,000	D $850,000	D $850,000	D $850,000	D $850,000	D $850,000	D $850,000
E Tax Savings	E $85,250	E $76,000	E $66,750	E $57,500	E $0	E $0	E $0

Selected year. Insert into Flow Chart blanks A, B, B1, C, D, and E the corresponding amounts from table.

SAMPLE PERSONALIZED WORKSHEET USING CALCULATIONS
FOR MARRIED COUPLE USING BYPASS TRUST

This sample worksheet illustrates how any chart in this book may be adapted to the reader's personal estate plan facts. In this example, a married couple have a taxable estate of $1,320,000 in the year 2001. By applying the Unified Federal Estate and Gift Tax Rate Schedule of U.S. Citizens and Residents appearing on page 24 and deducting the unified credit of $220,550, which allows $675,000 of assets to transfer to the bypass trust, upon the second death the estate would be subject to estate taxes of $0, leaving $1,320,000 for heirs. Estate tax savings of $257,850 are realized by keeping bypass trust assets out of the taxable estate of the surviving spouse. By writing in your own flow chart amounts in the spaces available, you may easily chart the flow of your own estate.

SAMPLE PERSONALIZED WORKSHEET USING CALCULATIONS FOR MARRIED COUPLE WITH $1,320,000 COMBINED ESTATE USING BYPASS TRUST
With or Without Minor or Incapacitated Heirs

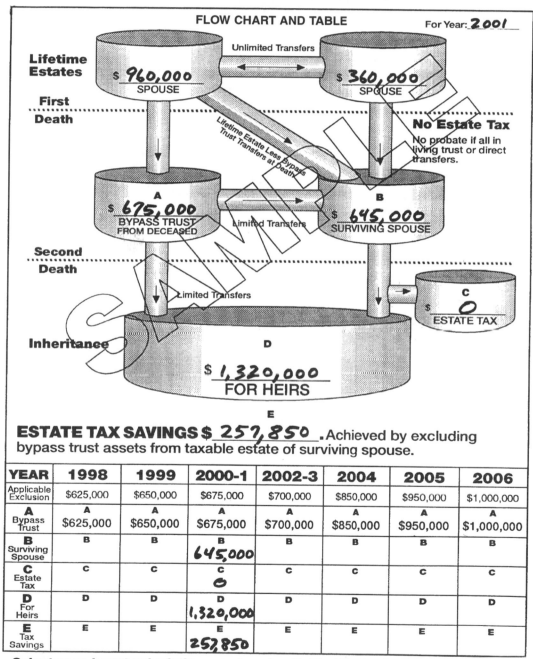

FLOW CHART AND TABLE   For Year: *2001*

Lifetime Estates $ *960,000* SPOUSE   Unlimited Transfers $ *360,000* SPOUSE

First Death   **No Estate Tax**   No probate if all in living trust or direct transfers.

Lifetime Estate Less Bypass Trust Transfers at Death

A $ *675,000* BYPASS TRUST FROM DECEASED   Limited Transfers   B $ *645,000* SURVIVING SPOUSE

Second Death

Limited Transfers   C $ *0* ESTATE TAX

Inheritance   D $ *1,320,000* FOR HEIRS

E

ESTATE TAX SAVINGS $ *257,850* . Achieved by excluding bypass trust assets from taxable estate of surviving spouse.

YEAR	1998	1999	2000-1	2002-3	2004	2005	2006
Applicable Exclusion	$625,000	$650,000	$675,000	$700,000	$850,000	$950,000	$1,000,000
A Bypass Trust	A $625,000	A $650,000	A $675,000	A $700,000	A $850,000	A $950,000	A $1,000,000
B Surviving Spouse	B	B	B *645,000*	B	B	B	B
C Estate Tax	C	C	C *0*	C	C	C	C
D For Heirs	D	D	D *1,320,000*	D	D	D	D
E Tax Savings	E	E	E *257,850*	E	E	E	E

Select year. Insert calculations made using Unified Federal Estate and Gift Tax Schedule and Applicable (credit) Exclusion.

SAMPLE PERSONALIZED FLOW CHART USING TABLE FOR MARRIED COUPLE WITH $2,000,000 COMBINED ESTATE USING BYPASS TRUST AND QTIP TRUST
With or Without Minor or Incapacitated Heirs

This sample flow chart and table illustrates how to select calendar year (2001) and fill in A (Bypass Trust), B (Surviving Spouse), B1 (QTIP Trust), C (Estate Tax), D (For Heirs), and E (Tax Savings).

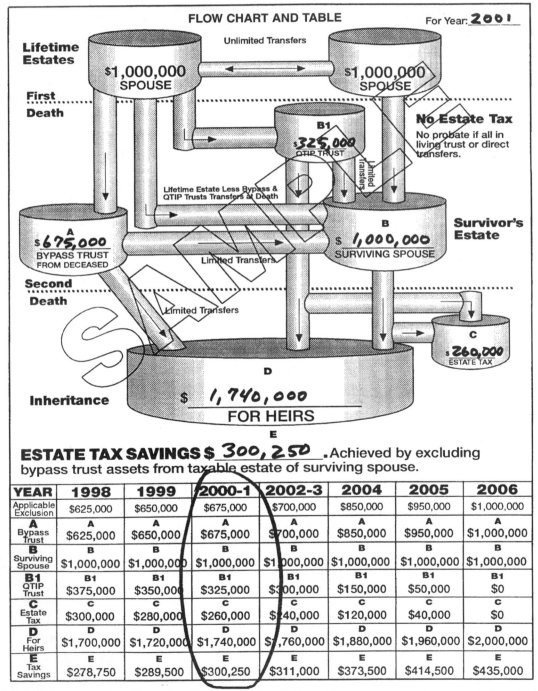

FLOW CHART AND TABLE   For Year: **2001**

Lifetime Estates   Unlimited Transfers

$1,000,000 SPOUSE $1,000,000 SPOUSE

First Death

No Estate Tax
No probate if all in living trust or direct transfers.

B1
$325,000
QTIP TRUST

Lifetime Estate Less Bypass & QTIP Trusts Transfers at Death

Limited Transfers

A
$675,000
BYPASS TRUST FROM DECEASED

B
$1,000,000
SURVIVING SPOUSE

Survivor's Estate

Limited Transfers

Second Death

Limited Transfers

C
$260,000
ESTATE TAX

D
$1,740,000
FOR HEIRS

Inheritance

E

ESTATE TAX SAVINGS $ 300,250 .Achieved by excluding
bypass trust assets from taxable estate of surviving spouse.

YEAR	1998	1999	2000-1	2002-3	2004	2005	2006
Applicable Exclusion	$625,000	$650,000	$675,000	$700,000	$850,000	$950,000	$1,000,000
A Bypass Trust	A $625,000	A $650,000	A $675,000	A $700,000	A $850,000	A $950,000	A $1,000,000
B Surviving Spouse	B $1,000,000	B $1,000,000	B $1,000,000	B $1,000,000	B $1,000,000	B $1,000,000	B $1,000,000
B1 QTIP Trust	B1 $375,000	B1 $350,000	B1 $325,000	B1 $300,000	B1 $150,000	B1 $50,000	B1 $0
C Estate Tax	C $300,000	C $280,000	C $260,000	C $240,000	C $120,000	C $40,000	C $0
D For Heirs	D $1,700,000	D $1,720,000	D $1,740,000	D $1,760,000	D $1,880,000	D $1,960,000	D $2,000,000
E Tax Savings	E $278,750	E $289,500	E $300,250	E $311,000	E $373,500	E $414,500	E $435,000

Selected year. Insert into Flow Chart blanks A, B, B1, C, D, and E the corresponding amounts from table.

SAMPLE PERSONALIZED WORKSHEET USING TABLE FOR MARRIED COUPLE WITH $2,280,000 COMBINED ESTATE USING BYPASS TRUST AND QTIP TRUST
With or Without Minor or Incapacitated Heirs

This sample worksheet illustrates how any chart in this book may be adapted to the reader's personal estate plan facts. In this example, a married couple have a taxable estate of $2,280,000 in the year 2001. By applying the Unified Federal Estate and Gift Tax Rate Schedule of U.S. Citizens and Residents appearing on page 24 and deducting the unified credit of $220,550, which allows $675,000 of assets to transfer to the bypass trust, upon the second death the estate would be subject to estate taxes of $382,500, leaving $1,897,500 for heirs. Estate tax savings of $314,950 are realized by keeping bypass trust assets out of the taxable estate of the surviving spouse. The QTIP trust is an additional trust for managing and controlling distribution of assets after the first death. By writing in your own flow chart amounts in the spaces available, you may easily chart the flow of your own estate.

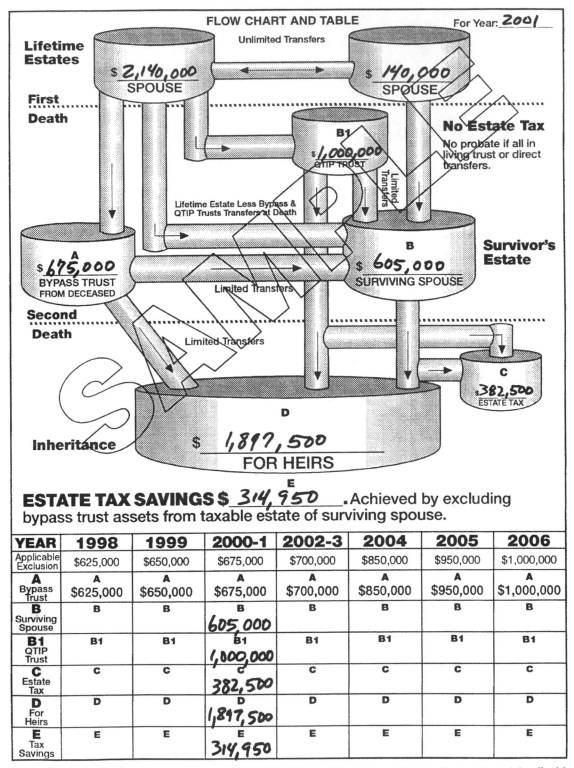

FLOW CHART AND TABLE   For Year: *2001*

Lifetime Estates   Unlimited Transfers

$ *2,140,000* SPOUSE $ *140,000* SPOUSE

First Death

No Estate Tax
No probate if all in living trust or direct transfers.

B1
$ *1,000,000* QTIP TRUST

Lifetime Estate Less Bypass & QTIP Trusts Transfers at Death

Limited Transfers

A
$ *675,000* BYPASS TRUST FROM DECEASED

B
$ *605,000* SURVIVING SPOUSE

Survivor's Estate

Limited Transfers

Second Death

Limited Transfers

C
$ *382,500* ESTATE TAX

Inheritance

D
$ *1,897,500*
FOR HEIRS

ESTATE TAX SAVINGS $ *314,950* **.**Achieved by excluding bypass trust assets from taxable estate of surviving spouse.

YEAR	1998	1999	2000-1	2002-3	2004	2005	2006
Applicable Exclusion	$625,000	$650,000	$675,000	$700,000	$850,000	$950,000	$1,000,000
A Bypass Trust	A $625,000	A $650,000	A $675,000	A $700,000	A $850,000	A $950,000	A $1,000,000
B Surviving Spouse	B	B	B *605,000*	B	B	B	B
B1 QTIP Trust	B1	B1	B1 *1,000,000*	B1	B1	B1	B1
C Estate Tax	C	C	C *382,500*	C	C	C	C
D For Heirs	D	D	D *1,897,500*	D	D	D	D
E Tax Savings	E	E	E *314,950*	E	E	E	E

Selected year. Insert calculations made using Unified Federal Estate and Gift Tax Schedule and Applicable (credit) Exclusion.

WORKSHEET FOR MARRIED COUPLE WITH $ _____
COMBINED ESTATE USING BYPASS TRUST
With or Without Minor or Incapacitated Heirs

This blank worksheet can be used to (1) insert estimated estate valuations, (2) calculate potential estate taxes, (3) develop alternative estate plans, (4) identify various heirs, and (5) consider charitable gifts.

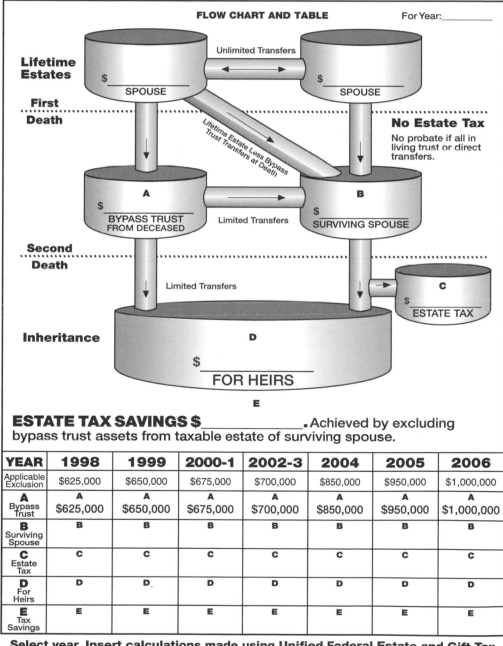

FLOW CHART AND TABLE   For Year: _____

ESTATE TAX SAVINGS $_____. Achieved by excluding bypass trust assets from taxable estate of surviving spouse.

YEAR	1998	1999	2000-1	2002-3	2004	2005	2006
Applicable Exclusion	$625,000	$650,000	$675,000	$700,000	$850,000	$950,000	$1,000,000
A Bypass Trust	A $625,000	A $650,000	A $675,000	A $700,000	A $850,000	A $950,000	A $1,000,000
B Surviving Spouse	B	B	B	B	B	B	B
C Estate Tax	C	C	C	C	C	C	C
D For Heirs	D	D.	D	D	D	D	D
E Tax Savings	E	E	E	E	E	E	E

Select year. Insert calculations made using Unified Federal Estate and Gift Tax Schedule and Applicable (credit) Exclusion.

WORKSHEET FOR MARRIED COUPLE WITH $ _____ COMBINED ESTATE USING BYPASS TRUST AND QTIP TRUST
With or Without Minor or Incapacitated Heirs

This blank worksheet can be used to (1) estimate estate valuations, (2) calculate potential estate taxes, (3) develop alternative estate plans, (4) identify various heirs, and (5) consider charitable gifts. Consider funding alternatives for QTIP trust.

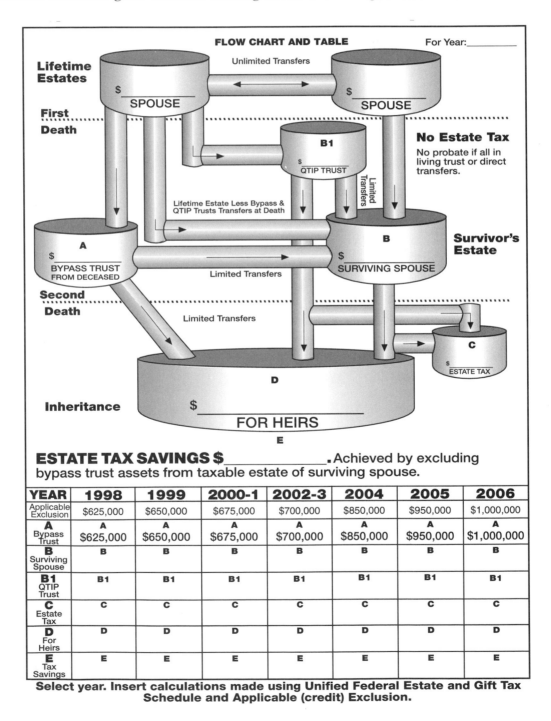

ESTATE TAX SAVINGS $_____. Achieved by excluding bypass trust assets from taxable estate of surviving spouse.

YEAR	1998	1999	2000-1	2002-3	2004	2005	2006
Applicable Exclusion	$625,000	$650,000	$675,000	$700,000	$850,000	$950,000	$1,000,000
A Bypass Trust	A $625,000	A $650,000	A $675,000	A $700,000	A $850,000	A $950,000	A $1,000,000
B Surviving Spouse	B	B	B	B	B	B	B
B1 QTIP Trust	B1	B1	B1	B1	B1	B1	B1
C Estate Tax	C	C	C	C	C	C	C
D For Heirs	D	D	D	D	D	D	D
E Tax Savings	E	E	E	E	E	E	E

Select year. Insert calculations made using Unified Federal Estate and Gift Tax Schedule and Applicable (credit) Exclusion.

LIVING TRUST, PROBATE, JOINT OWNERSHIP, RETIREMENT AND IRA ACCOUNT PIPELINES

Each of your assets, including insurance death benefits and retirement accounts, must be transferred upon your death. Probate, living trusts, and direct transfers are some of the many available pipelines of distribution. Direct transfers include beneficiary designations, joint ownership with right of survivorship, and pay-on-death accounts. You and your estate planner should plan how each of your assets will be transferred. As in a jigsaw puzzle, each piece is important.

THE PROBLEM WITH PROBATE

◆ ◆ ◆

The problem most often cited with probate is cost. The executor (personal representative) has a right to be compensated, and state statutes often set forth what is reasonable. Statutory executor fees vary radically from state to state. Texas law provides the executor's fee is not to exceed 5% of gross fair market value of the estate. New York has a descending percentage as the estate increases, with a reasonableness limit of 2% of the gross estate value over $5,000,000. The good news is that many executors charge far less and family executors often waive rights to all compensation.

The executor regularly hires an attorney, and sometimes an accountant, to provide legal, accounting, and tax services for the estate. An attorney is required for probate through the courts. The fees of these professionals may equal or exceed the fees of the executor. Often the professional does most of the estate administration work if the executor is untrained in estate administration matters.

Many executors, attorneys, and accountants charge an hourly rate. Others may charge a percentage of the gross estate, or some combination of hourly rate and percentage. Costs for estate administration are constantly quoted in publications across the country. Surveys and selected case histories conclude executor, attorney, and accountant fees for estates range between 1 and 10%. The most publicly quoted percentage is 8% of the value of the gross estate.

In fact, probate costs, fees, and commissions are often overstated because of downward pressure from competition and negotiation of fixed and percentage compensation schedules. Family executors and trustees usually provide services without compensation. Attorneys' fees vary so widely from state to state and office to office that most generalized fee estimates are quite meaningless. Adoption of forms of the Uniform Probate Code and other simplified procedures in various states have simplified the probate process in most cases. However, one conclusion is clear—total probate costs are unnecessarily high because the process is archaic and fraught with too many forms, rules, and waiting periods.

❖ ❖ ❖

PROBATE AND NONPROBATE TRANSFERS:
Pipelines That Legally Transfer Your Assets

These pipelines illustrate the legal methods by which your property will flow after your death. Each pipeline requires your attention to assure the flow to your selected beneficiaries in the correct amounts at predetermined times. You turn the valves by how you title assets. Probate will be directed by your will or, if you have no will, by state law. Taxes are not considered.

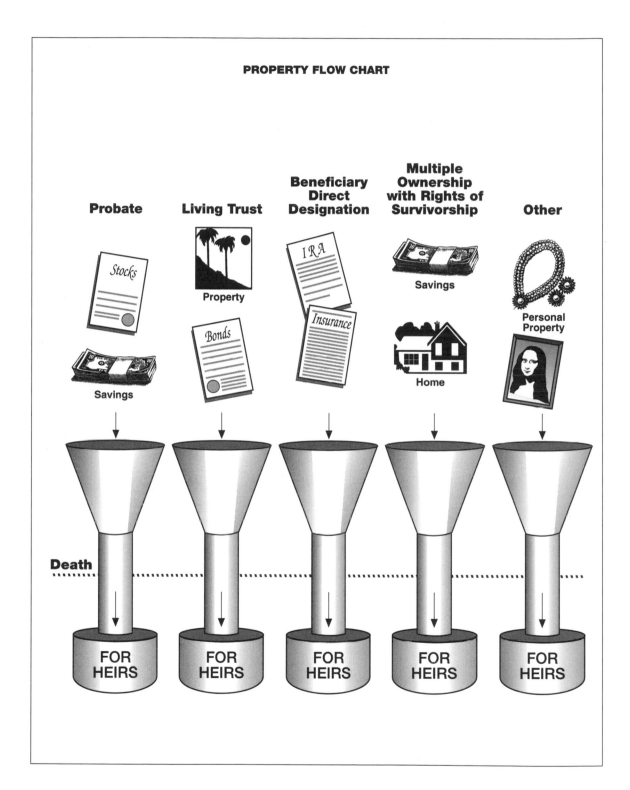

INHERITANCE LEAKS:
Pipelines That Reduce Flow of Assets to Heirs

You do not have to be a plumber to realize that there are many valves that open and close causing leaks and reduce the flow of assets to your beneficiaries. Your estate plan will control these valves. You may wish to roughly estimate the dollar value of each pipeline leak. These leaks can be controlled or eliminated by a good plan.

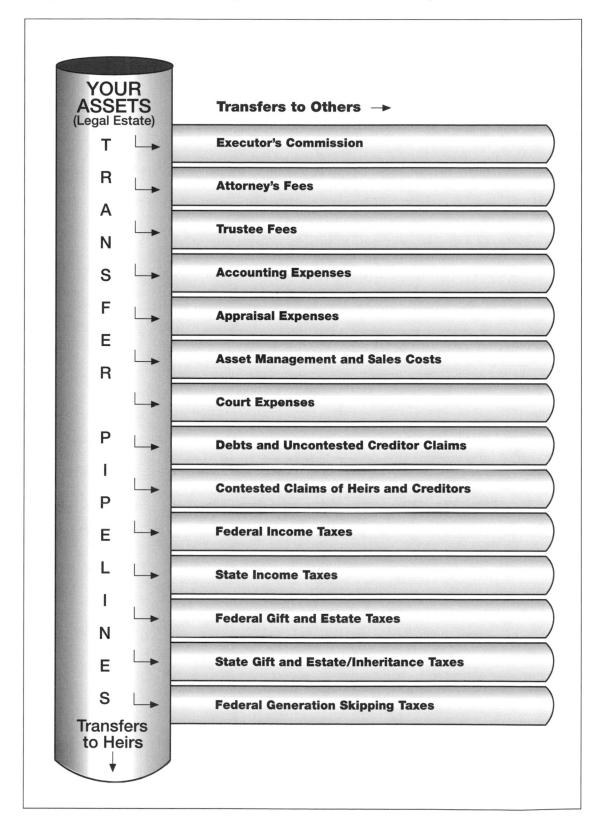

PROBATE AND LIVING TRUST ASSET TRANSFER CHOICES

Advantageous estate and tax planning, as well as personal security, will require you to retain sole title and ownership to certain assets. Presently, you have the choice of allowing these assets to transfer by the probate process, or the living trust process, at your death. Probate transfers require a court-empowered executor to transfer the assets through the probate estate while completing many court-dictated forms. Living trust transfers require you to empower a trustee to transfer the assets through a living trust estate. Probate estate legal work occurs after death, while the majority of living trust estate legal work occurs before death unless you have a complex or taxable estate.

Note: I support new laws to make estate planning and administration faster and easier by elimination of the need for probate or living trust estates in most testate cases. Please see epilogue for proposed Alternative Estate Administration (AEA) which, if adopted in your state, would save you money and time while reducing paperwork in our overburdened court system.

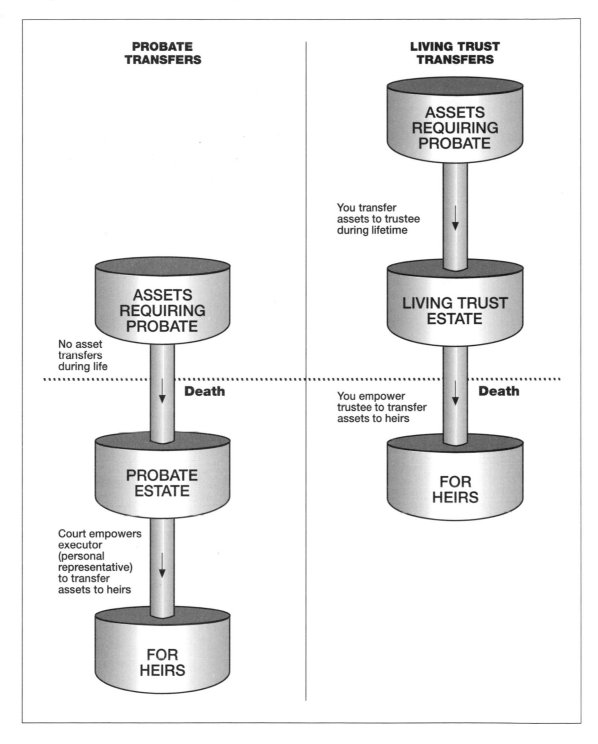

PROBATE
TRANSFERS

LIVING TRUST
TRANSFERS

ASSETS
REQUIRING
PROBATE

You transfer
assets to trustee
during lifetime

ASSETS
REQUIRING
PROBATE

No asset
transfers
during life

LIVING TRUST
ESTATE

Death

Death

You empower
trustee to transfer
assets to heirs

PROBATE
ESTATE

FOR
HEIRS

Court empowers
executor
(personal
representative)
to transfer
assets to heirs

FOR
HEIRS

LIVING TRUST FUNDING VARIATIONS
Chart

If you choose a living trust design for your estate planning documents, there are three funding variations. You should make a conscious decision as to which variation will achieve your present goals. Factors to consider include your age, health, family, asset ownership and location, changing financial conditions, and required paperwork. In a fully funded trust, all property interests in your name that would otherwise pass through probate are transferred into the trust during your lifetime. Upon your death, there will be no probate of these assets. In a partially funded trust, selected property is transferred into the trust, such as out-of-state property to avoid ancillary probate in another state. In an unfunded standby trust, no property is transferred into the trust at the time of its creation. The trust stands by, available for future funding.

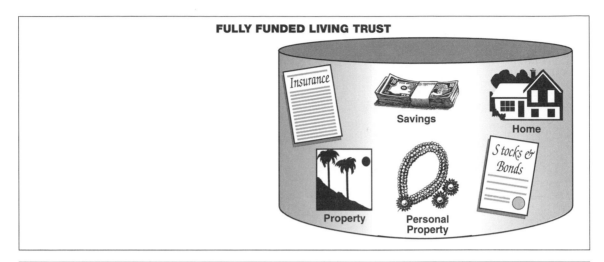

LIVING TRUST FUNDING METHODS

Living trusts are funded by the transfer of assets to the trust. Assets must be titled in the name of the trust, or trustee with trust identified, pursuant to state law, to achieve probate avoidance goals. Funding of the living trust is often called *implementation of the plan*. If you adopt a living trust plan, but do not fund it, it is referred to as a *standby trust,* meaning that it is standing by waiting to receive assets at a future time. Living trusts do not save estate taxes unless additional tax planning is included.

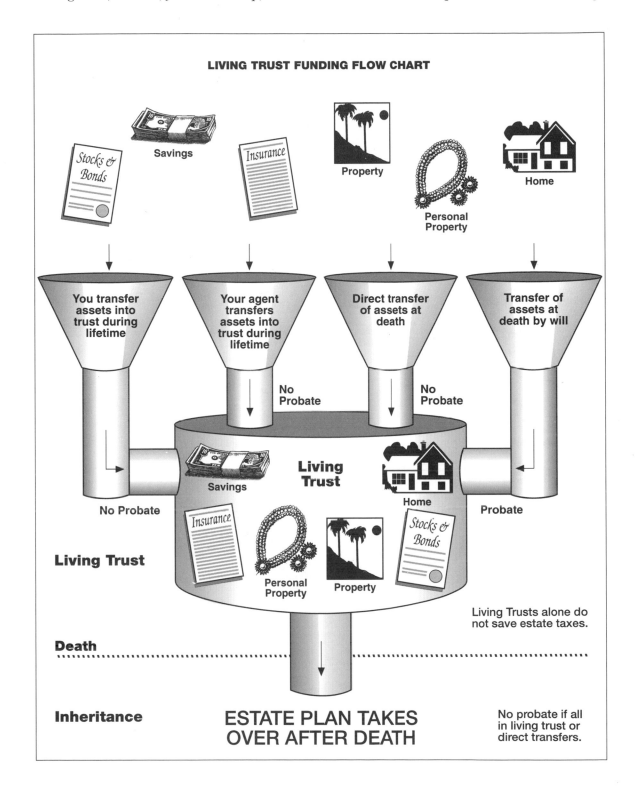

LIVING TRUST ASSET FLOW
MARRIED COUPLE EXAMPLE

This Flow Chart illustrates the flow of assets through a living trust for a married couple using a bypass trust and descretionary marital trust.

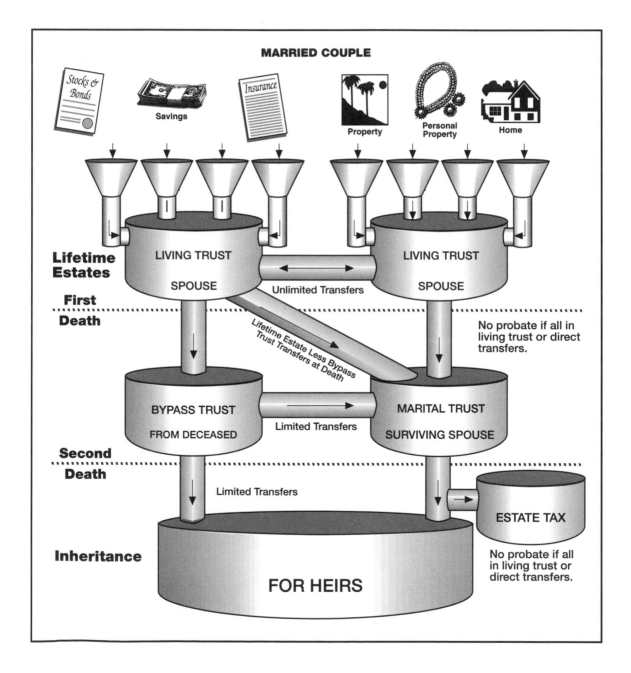

How to Avoid Probate with a Living Trust
❖ ❖ ❖

A trust is a form of contract in which the ownership of property is separated into two parts. The legal title and management of the property are vested in one person, and the beneficial or economic ownership of the property is vested in another. There are two broad categories of trusts—the living trust and the testamentary trust. A living trust is created during the maker's lifetime; a testamentary trust is created upon the maker's death by the maker's will. In recent years the revocable living trust as an instrument in estate planning has become increasingly popular as a way to avoid probate.

Before going further, there are several terms used in connection with trusts that you should know. If you create a trust you may be called the *trustmaker, grantor,* or *settlor* of the trust. The person or bank who is given legal title, possession, and management of the trust assets is the *trustee,* and the person who is entitled to the income and other benefits from the trust is the *beneficiary.*

In creating the trust, the trustmaker desires to provide financial benefits to the beneficiary. However, for tax or other reasons, rather than transferring the trust property directly to the beneficiary, the title is transferred to the trustee to hold and manage for the beneficiary.

Terms of a Typical Revocable Trust

In the typical revocable living trust, a trustmaker transfers property to a trustee under a written agreement. The agreement provides for the trustee to pay the trustmaker all the income from the trust during the trustmaker's lifetime, together with such amounts of principal as may be requested by the trustmaker. It also provides that the trustmaker can amend or revoke the trust or change the trustee at any time.

Upon the death of the trustmaker, the trust becomes irrevocable, meaning that the terms of the trust cannot thereafter be changed. The trust property is held, administered, and distributed as if it had passed under the trustmaker's will through probate and into a testamentary trust. The provisions of the trust agreement that apply to the administration and distribution of the trust assets after the death of the trustmaker become operative and are carried out immediately. There are no probate delays, and the publicity normally necessary to the probate of a will is dispensed with.

Ten Advantages of a Living Trust
❖ ❖ ❖

A revocable living trust has a number of advantages and disadvantages when compared with a will requiring probate.

Advantage 1: Management Uninterrupted by Incapacity

If a bank or an experienced person is selected as trustee of a revocable living trust, and a large part or all of the trustmaker's assets are placed in the trust during the trustmaker's lifetime, the revocable trust can afford continuous experienced management of the trust assets regardless of the trustmaker's physical or mental incapacity. This avoids the necessity of a court declaration of incompetence and the management of the assets by a court-appointed guardian or conservator. If the trustmaker of the trust desires to retain investment control of the trust assets, the trust agreement can provide that while the trustmaker is alive and remains competent, the trustmaker will serve as trustee. If someone other than the trustmaker is serving as trustee, the trust can provide that no purchases or sales of the trust assets or any other important actions can be made without the trustmaker's approval. Should the trustmaker become unable to manage assets and financial affairs, either through mental or physical disabilities, the revocable trust is the ideal instrument for continuing proper management.

In contrast, a power of attorney given to another person to manage the trustmaker's affairs will be automatically revoked upon the trustmaker's mental incapacity unless the power of attorney is a "durable power of attorney," which means that it specifically provides that it is to survive the incapacity of the person making it. Proceedings for the appointment of a guardian or conservator for the property of a person upon becoming senile or incompetent, or upon drifting in and out of lucid mental periods, can provoke unpleasant family quarrels. It certainly will involve court control of the assets of the incompetent, potentially large legal and bond fees, severe restrictions on investments, and much red tape.

The revocable living trust is an answer to these problems. The trustee can perform all the necessary management of the trust assets, including the collection of income, the purchase and sale of trust assets, and the management of a closely held business or real estate. In addition, the trustee can make payment of hospital, nursing and doctor bills, and other expenses of the trustmaker. When the period of temporary crisis ends, the trust can be revoked by the trustmaker if so desired, or the trustmaker may again take up active management of the trust assets. If the trustmaker dies, the trust can act as a substitute for the trustmaker's will insofar as the distribution of the assets of the trust are concerned.

Advantage 2: Time Management for the Busy Executive or Professional

A revocable trust is a valuable aid to the busy executive or professional person who does not have time to study the stock market or to do the many other things that are involved in managing the investment of valuable trust assets. A bank or other qualified trustee can supply experienced investment guidance and free a busy executive or professional person from worries that might interfere with the pursuit of such person's business or profession, while at the same time assuring the continuous expert investment management of the trust assets.

Advantage 3: Segregation of Assets

A revocable trust also has the advantage of preventing certain properties from becoming commingled with other property. For example, if a wife has inherited property from her parents, and she desires that the property be kept separate from the property of her husband, she can place her separate property in a revocable trust. The trustee, which can be the wife, can then maintain adequate records to keep that property segregated from the husband's assets.

Advantage 4: Trial Run for the Trustee

The revocable living trust allows the trustmaker to observe the operation of the bank or person that the trustmaker desires to manage the estate upon the trustmaker's death. The trustmaker can then be satisfied as to the manner in which the assets will be managed and administered after death. This will also allow the surviving spouse to become familiar with the trustmaker's trust officer and lawyer, so that old friends, instead of strangers, will be there to take care of the surviving spouse and children at death. If the surviving spouse or a surviving child is to become the trustee upon the death of the trustmaker, the spouse or child will be able to familiarize himself or herself with the operation of the trust while the trustmaker is available to assist the trustee.

Advantage 5: Privacy

Another advantage of the revocable trust is the privacy afforded the trustmaker for the disposition of the estate at death. Assets placed in a revocable living trust do not become a matter of public court record as may be the case with a probated will. New probate laws are moving toward more privacy.

Advantage 6: Less Expensive, with Fewer Delays, than Probate

A revocable living trust will result in the reduction of probate expenses. Executors' commissions, attorneys' fees, accounting fees, appraisers' fees, and other charges arising from the administration of a deceased person's estate are required by statute to be reasonable (although in some states they are still determined by percentage fee schedules), but to a certain extent such fees are based on the value of the assets passing under the decedent's will. Keeping property out of the probate or testamentary estate of the trustmaker can reduce such charges. If all a trustmaker's assets are in a revocable trust at the time of death, it will not be necessary to go through probate at all. However, if a banker or nonfamily member is the trustee, this reduction may be offset to some degree by the cost of administering the trust assets during the trustmaker's lifetime. When the trustmaker owns property in more than one state, the avoidance of multiple probates can save substantial fees that would be duplicated in each state where property was located. More important than costs to some people is the delay that results from probate. During the period of court administration, that may last several months or several years, there may be substantial restrictions on access to assets of the decedent's estate. The living trust avoids this delay.

Advantage 7: Less Vulnerable to Attack than a Will

A revocable trust is less vulnerable to attack by disgruntled heirs than is a will. It is rather easy for a relative to attack the probate of a will, even when the attack is based on flimsy reasons. It is quite expensive and time consuming for the executor to win a total victory in such a contest.

An attack can be made on a revocable living trust on the same grounds used to contest a will, for example, lack of capacity or undue influence. However, such a contest does not tie up the trust assets in the same manner as a will contest ties up the probate assets. The burden of proof seems to lie more heavily with the trust contestor, as the attacks are more often successful with wills than with living trusts. The reason for this is that a will is merely a piece of paper until the testator's death. Nothing in a will has any effect or substance until after the will has been admitted to probate by a formal court order, and all assets are tied up until the will is settled. By contrast, a trust is in full force and effect from the time it is executed during the trustmaker's lifetime, and if there is a contest of the trust, the trustee has assets at hand with which to pay for a defense of the trust.

Advantage 8: Uninterrupted Management at Death

A revocable living trust provides a means for avoiding any interruption in the management of the trust assets upon the death of the trustmaker. Stocks, securities, real estate, and so on can continue to be managed, and debts, expenses of last illness, funeral bills, taxes, and so on can be paid without interruption. Further, there is no delay incurred in providing for the trustmaker's family immediately after death. This elimination of delay is especially important when the trust property consists of assets that require day-to-day handling to avoid loss, or when the family has immediate financial requirements upon the death of the trustmaker.

Advantage 9: Avoidance of Probate in Other States

If the trustmaker owns property physically located in different states, it is possible to avoid expensive and time-consuming probate proceedings in these states by conveying the property to a trustee during the trustmaker's lifetime. However, if real estate in other states is to be placed in a revocable living trust, it is important to make sure that the laws of the state where the property is located allow a trustee from another state to act within that state.

Advantage 10: Tax Treatment of the Revocable Trust

Assets in a revocable living trust are taxable under the federal income tax, estate tax, and gift tax laws in much the same manner as property owned outright by the trustmaker. No gift tax is payable when a trustmaker creates a revocable living trust and transfers property to it. During the trustmaker's lifetime, all the income of the trust is taxed to the trustmaker. At death, all the property in the trust is included in the trustmaker's estate for federal estate tax purposes. After death, the trust becomes irrevocable, and the same tax advantages available to a probate estate are available to the trust. These include the use of the unlimited marital deduction, the avoidance of a second federal estate tax upon the spouse's estate, and the advantage of providing different tax entities for federal income tax purposes. At the election of the trustee and executor, a decedent's probate estate and living trust may be combined for income tax reporting purposes. Both trusts and estates are able to make elections to treat distributions made in the first 65 days of a taxable year as if they were made in the previous year.

SEVEN DISADVANTAGES OF A LIVING TRUST

❖ ❖ ❖

Disadvantage 1: Expense of Drafting and Funding a Revocable Living Trust

Drafting and funding a comprehensive trust agreement is initially more expensive than alternatives utilizing probate. There is the expense of properly transferring title of a person's assets to the trust. Only assets transferred by the owner into the revocable living trust avoid probate.

Disadvantage 2: Lack of Automatic Revocation in the Event of Divorce

A disposition to a spouse in a will is automatically revoked if there is a divorce, whereas with a revocable living trust this is not the case. Under the common law, a trust must be amended to terminate provisions for an ex-spouse. If making such an amendment is put off, the issue can become a serious problem at the death of the trustmaker or upon his or her incapacity.

Disadvantage 3: Memorandum Disposition of Personal Property

If a will contains permissive language, memorandum disposition of personal property is permitted. Disposition by memorandum allows you to modify a portion of the will that directs distribution of personal property without incurring any legal costs. A revocable living trust may incorporate a memorandum provision but often does not. This matter is easily resolved, since a revocable living trust should be accompanied by a pour-over will incorporating the memorandum disposition of personal property.

Disadvantage 4: Financing Property

If you are borrowing money personally, and use assets in your living trust as security for the loan, the lender may require you to transfer the property to your own name during the financing process. After the loan paperwork is complete, most lenders have no objection to transferring the property title back to the living trust. Some mortgages include "due on transfer" language which could hypothetically be triggered by transferring encumbered property to a trust. If this is a concern, ask the lender for written consent for the transfer, which is invariably granted.

Disadvantage 5: Claims of Creditors

One of the principal purposes of probate is the identification and payment of creditors of a decedent. The claims of creditors are filed with the court and may be contested by the estate. Where a revocable trust completely avoids probate, there is no assurance that all legitimate claims have been paid and discharged. Any well-drafted trust should, however, provide for the payment by the trustee of the trustmaker's legitimate claims.

Disadvantage 6: Liability and Title Insurance

If an asset transferred to a trust is insured, such as an automobile or real estate, it is wise to notify the insurance company and request a change to the trust as named insured. While most insurance companies will pay claims without this added paperwork, there has been some litigation on this issue relating to title insurance on real estate. Use warranty deeds when transferring real estate to a living trust to give the trustee warranty claims on title insurance covering real estate previously titled to the trustmaker.

Disadvantage 7: Formalities of Operation

If the trustmaker is to serve as the trustee, it is clear that some effort must be made to learn how to manage assets in this new capacity. Although this may be slightly more complicated, most people find that serving as a trustee is not all that difficult. The alternative, of course, is to have a bank or trust company serve as trustee, subject to the direction of the trustmaker. The accounting and keeping of records for a trust should not be materially more complicated than the same activities on behalf of any other entity such as a partnership or corporation.

HOW TO AVOID PROBATE WITH DIRECT TRANSFERS
◆ ◆ ◆

The principal nontax uses of the revocable living trust are the avoidance of probate at death and the avoidance of an incompetency adjudication requiring the appointment of a court-supervised guardian in the event of lifetime disability. The main objections to probate are cost and delay. Direct transfers may be used without a living trust and often avoid probate. Direct transfers are often an integral and important part of planning most estates, regardless of size or complexity. If your estate is modest or uncomplicated, one or more of the following direct transfer techniques may be an appropriate means for transferring all your estate assets.

Joint Ownership with Rights of Survivorship

Ownership of real and personal property in joint tenancy is the most common method of avoiding probate. Joint tenancy is an estate in real or personal property held by two or more persons jointly with rights to share in its enjoyment. In other words, all joint tenants own an undivided interest in the property. Upon the death of a joint tenant, the entire estate passes immediately to the surviving joint tenant or tenants. The survivor(s) automatically own(s) the entire asset without the need for probate or any other form of court intervention. The death certificate of the deceased joint owner is all that is normally necessary to establish the title of the surviving joint tenant(s). Many state statutes have been passed creating various forms of joint tenancy. Some states have a form of joint ownership called *tenancy by the entireties,* which is permitted only between spouses and which has the same survivorship characteristics as joint tenancy.

Often there is a presumption against the creation of a joint tenancy in real or personal property other than bank accounts, unless the legal instrument transferring the property states that the property is conveyed or transferred in joint tenancy. The safest way to establish joint tenancy is to state clearly on the deed, assignment, or other document creating title, "in joint tenancy," "as joint tenants," or "as joint tenants with right of survivorship and not as tenants in common." The absence of such language will ordinarily create a tenancy in common, which does not have the survivorship feature.

A joint tenant's share of the estate may be conveyed by the joint tenant at any time, thereby terminating the joint tenancy. If the joint tenants cannot agree on how to divide the property, either may bring a partition suit and ask the court to divide the property. No will can destroy or affect the joint tenancy or prevent the entire interest owned by the deceased joint tenant from passing to the survivor.

Before creating a joint tenancy with your spouse, consider the following advantages and disadvantages.

Advantages

1. Joint tenancies are easily understood.

2. Joint tenancies often represent a relationship commitment.

3. Joint tenancy can be used to avoid probate, although joint tenancy property is required to be included in the estate tax return.

4. Joint tenancy property is often free from the claims of creditors of the deceased joint tenant if no prior lien was attached.

Disadvantages

1. Joint tenancy property cannot be passed by the will of the joint tenant dying first; instead, the property passes to, and is subject to disposition by, the surviving tenant.

2. The estate may be deprived of liquid funds necessary to pay death costs, claims, and taxes.

3. Joint tenancy property may be caught up in discord between spouses because of the inability to reach agreement on management of the property and the right of the noncontributing spouse to acquire one-half of the property through partition or severance.

4. If the joint tenancy property is subject to a mortgage, the property will pass to the surviving joint tenant, but the estate may be required to pay the mortgage out of the residue, thus frustrating the decedent's family giving plan.

5. Creditors of either joint tenant may attach the person's interest in the property during life.

6. There may be unfavorable tax consequences depending on the specific facts of each case. See following discussion.

Consider the example of a misplaced joint savings account created by Julia Strahle, a widowed mother of three. She transferred her life's savings into a joint account with one nearby daughter for convenience. Upon her death, her daughter received the entire account. It did not matter that her will provided all three children were to share the money equally.

Tax Issues and Traps of Joint Ownership with Rights of Survivorship

There are many tax issues and traps for the unwary that develop from joint ownership with rights of survivorship, including the following:

1. The creation of a joint tenancy between spouses does not create a taxable gift because of the unlimited marital deduction.

2. The creation of a joint tenancy with a nonspouse creates a taxable gift when the contributions are unequal. When a donor conveys to himself or herself and a donee as joint tenants and either party has the right to sever the interest, there is a gift to the donee in the amount of one-half of the value of the property. The gift usually occurs when the noncontributor claims or takes a portion of the joint interest.

3. The creation of a joint tenancy for convenience, often by a parent with one nearby child, will result in that child receiving the joint property upon the death of the parent.

4. If property is held in joint tenancy between spouses, only one-half of the value is included in a deceased joint tenant's estate. The descendant's one-half interest acquires a stepped-up basis. Compare this with community property states where both halves acquire stepped-up bases. This adjustment to the surviving spouse's basis is a major incentive for classifying property as community property, and creates complex tax issues when moving from a community property state.

5. If property is held in joint tenancy with a nonspouse, termination may trigger gift tax consequences. The entire interest of the property is included in the estate of the joint tenant first dying, unless the estate is able to prove the amount of consideration furnished by the survivor. The contribution of the survivor must not be traceable to the decedent. There is an exception where the property was acquired by the decedent through inheritance.

6. Use of joint tenancy may frustrate other tax planning. For example, use of joint tenancy can result in overqualification of the marital deduction, resulting in property being taxed a second time in a survivor's estate.

Correct Beneficiary Designations Avoid Disaster

Mistakes and neglect in properly designating and changing beneficiaries result in the most number of problems in estate administration. Forms are often filled out by untrained, inexperienced clerical staff with no consideration for individual goals, an integrated financial plan, or tax avoidance. Many beneficiary designations are made and forgotten in the files of insurance companies and banks. Later marriages, divorce, births, deaths, financial needs, and estate planning goals are not taken into consideration. Imagine the surprise when a former spouse turns up the beneficiary after a bitter divorce or an after-born child is forgotten.

Beneficiary designations should always be signed and reviewed when any family or planning changes occur. If no beneficiary designation exists, most policies, plans, or accounts have an automatic designation. If your estate is large enough to be subject to federal estate taxes, coordinate the designation with tax planning.

Payable-on-Death Accounts Are Quick and Easy

The Uniform Probate Code created various forms of ownership designed to avoid the need for probate. One of these is the payable-on-death (POD) bank or savings and loan account. Under this form of registration, the account remains the sole property of the depositor (unlike a joint account where some other person has authority to make deposits and withdrawals from the account). However, the account owner can designate a beneficiary to take the account at death. Such an account would typically read "John J. Doe, POD Mary J. Doe." Upon presenting proof of the death of the primary account owner, the funds would be delivered to the designated beneficiary. Great flexibility can be accomplished by creating a POD account and giving the designated beneficiary a power of attorney over the account. By combining the POD designation and the power of attorney, probate is eliminated, and lifetime incapacity would not require the appointment of a guardian or conservator.

Postmortem Assignments

This can be a particularly effective method of avoiding probate, but due to the unusual and somewhat controversial manner in which the statute is drafted, there may be occasions when, like the problems with assuring acceptance of a durable power of attorney by third parties, it may be difficult to convince a third party to accept such an assignment. The Uniform Probate Code and probate codes in most states seem to be broad enough to cover almost all types of transfers under a postmortem assignment, except real estate. For example, a provision can be inserted in a promissory note that, upon the death of the primary payee, the balance of the payments on the note would be made to a secondary payee. A stock assignment may contain a marginal notation that the transfer will be effective only at the death of the stockholder. Although it might be difficult to get a stock transfer agent to accept such an assignment easily, it should pose no difficulty with closely held corporations. If all securities are deposited in a custodian or "street name account," a postmortem assignment of the account will eliminate probate of all securities in the account as of the date of the death of the account holder, thereby eliminating the need to make separate postmortem assignments of each and every security. Postmortem assignments of street name accounts should be relied upon only if advance acceptance is obtained from the transfer agent.

Small Estates Act

Most states have some amount of property that can be transferred without a formal probate proceeding. For example, state law may allow the transfer by affidavit of assets of a decedent other than real estate which do not exceed a statutory aggregate value of $20,000–$50,000. These statutes were designed to eliminate the need for a court proceeding to transfer automobiles, tangible personal property, most bank accounts, and other assets. The size of the estate and type of assets which can be transferred under such statutes vary from state to state and may be quite small in some jurisdictions.

Unrecorded Deeds

In some states, it is possible to record a deed after the death of the property owner, and such recording will effectively transfer ownership to the grantee named in the deed. This is a useful alternative to avoid probate of real estate, since the title remains in the name of the property owner during his or her lifetime, but recording the deed after death eliminates the need for probate of that property. Since this type of deed can be challenged, it should not be used where there are conflicts in the family. It is not generally a satisfactory technique for property owned in joint tenancy. This method of avoiding probate should only be utilized after consulting your attorney.

RETIREMENT AND IRA ACCOUNT STRATEGIES
◆ ◆ ◆

Assets held in account-based retirement plans, such as IRAs and defined contribution plans, are growing at a phenomenal rate. Much of the growth can be attributed to individuals who roll over distributions from their defined contribution plans into IRAs when they separate from employment. Approximately 50 percent of the nation's estate tax returns include retirement account-based assets, comprising an ever-increasing percentage of reported wealth.

These assets are often not being consumed by the person who accumulated the account. Instead, these accounts are commonly rolled over tax free to a relieved surviving spouse. But that relief is short lived when the surviving spouse finds out that up to 77% of the account may have to be paid to the government in federal estate and income taxes when this account is transferred to the next generation. Yes, 77% or more may be paid to the Internal Revenue Service. The federal government is spending at the rate of $57,000 per second, twenty-four hours a day, which makes leaving a lasting legacy by paying taxes unlikely. To reduce or eliminate these alligator taxes on life savings, develop and maintain a smart plan for retirement account assets that will transfer to future generations.

PENSION, PROFIT-SHARING, IRA, 401(K), AND KEOGH RULES READ LIKE A FOOTBALL TEAM PLAYBOOK
◆ ◆ ◆

The rules governing the distribution of plan benefits during retirement and after death are comparable to the play book of an NFL football team. Written in code words; difficult to implement; always changing; subject to many complicated technical penalties. It is important to know the rules to score the most benefits and pay the least tax.

Income Taxes. When qualified plan benefits are distributed, which normally happens upon retirement, death, or termination of employment, the amounts received—to the extent that they are attributable to the employer's contributions—are taxable as income to the employee, or if deceased, to the employee's beneficiaries. The manner in which these amounts are taxed as income depends on the timing and form in which they are received, primarily as an annuity or as a lump sum. Roth IRAs are not subject to income tax at payout.

Estate Taxes. The general rule is that all death benefits receivable by a beneficiary from a qualified retirement plan on account of death are included in the decedent's gross estate. However, the benefit will not be subject to estate tax if the benefit flows to the surviving spouse because it will qualify for the marital deduction. The law requires employee's spouse to be the beneficiary of the employee's qualified plan benefits, unless the spouse consents otherwise.

Distributions during Lifetime. In order to limit the amount of tax deferral and to force accounts to be used for retirement income, the tax laws require payments to be made from these accounts to a participant beginning at age 70½. As a general rule, all of the assets in account-based plans must be distributed over the account owner's remaining life expectancy. However, a person can normally have payments extend over the combined life expectancy of the owner and successor beneficiary, subject to the minimum distribution incidental benefit limitation, and use the longer payout term to reduce each year's minimum distribution. Develop payout strategies in consultation with a retirement plan administrator or expert tax advisor.

Distributions at Death. The general rule is that all of the assets of a retirement account or IRA must be distributed within five (5) years after the account owner's death. Under some circumstances, all of these assets must be distributed within just one year of death. Although a surviving spouse can roll an inherited distribution over into a new IRA to defer tax, other beneficiaries will be forced to pay income tax upon receipt.

There are, however, two exceptions that permit distributions to be made over more than five (5) years. These exceptions have led several commentators to encourage the use of a "stretch-out IRA" that will make payments over the life expectancy of the decedent's child or grandchildren.

Generally, your spouse is the most desirable beneficiary for both income and estate tax reasons. A spouse can treat an IRA as the spouse's own IRA, and withdraw or roll over to a spousal IRA. On doing so, the spouse is treated as the owner of the IRA, with the right to make new elections. To achieve maximum deferral of distributions and income tax, the employee must have named a "designated beneficiary" as of the required beginning date or date of death, whichever occurs first. A designated beneficiary must be either an individual, or a trust that is irrevocable at the death of the account owner, such as a bypass trust.

Consider Who Should Be Named as Contingent Beneficiary. When designating your spouse, or other person, as a death beneficiary, consider specifying a contingent beneficiary in the event the primary beneficiary disclaims an interest. For example, at the time of the employee's death, the spouse beneficiary may not need the income and may prefer to have the death benefit paid to the bypass trust to avoid estate taxes on the spouse's death. By naming a spouse as a primary beneficiary and the bypass trust or children as the contingent beneficiary, the employee can preserve the needed flexibility to enable the spouse to select the best tax results by rolling over or disclaiming all or a portion of the account. In a disclaimer situation, a new life expectancy choice must be made to determine the minimum required distributions.

Multiple Accounts and Beneficiaries. If more than one beneficiary is named, consider dividing the benefits into separate accounts, or segregated shares, naming a separate beneficiary for each share. This way, each beneficiary will be able to use his or her own life expectancy for distribution purposes, and will not be saddled with using the life expectancy of the oldest beneficiary. Single accounts can even be divided into separate shares for each beneficiary after the death of the participant. As a part of income tax planning, consider having the death benefit divided among as many recipients as possible. The death benefits (less the deduction for the portion of the estate tax attributable to the death benefits) will be taxed as income in respect of a decedent. Therefore, by having the payments go to as many taxpayers as possible, the beneficiaries' income tax bracket may be lower.

Charity as Beneficiary. Consider the designation of a charity as a recipient of the death benefit. When the payment goes to a charity, income and estate taxes will be avoided. The estate owner may then leave other assets that are not subject to income tax to noncharitable beneficiaries.

FIVE ESSENTIALS OF TRANSFERRING IRA OR RETIREMENT PLAN ACCOUNTS TO INHERITORS

◆ ◆ ◆

1. PLAN FOR INCOME TAXES. The account payments received by beneficiaries are subject to income tax at the beneficiaries' rate in the year received, less an itemized deduction for a proportionate amount of any federal estate tax previously paid on the same account. The new Roth IRA is the exception.

2. PLAN FOR ESTATE TAXES. The value of the account is included at death for estate tax purposes, even though the account will be reduced by the amount of the income tax paid when the account is distributed. To make matters even worse, the estate tax is an inclusionary tax, which means you pay an estate tax on the amount of the estate tax paid to the government.

3. CAREFULLY DESIGNATE BENEFICIARIES. Name beneficiaries of each account. If you name a spouse, taxes will be deferred during the spouse's lifetime. The spouse will have the power to rename beneficiaries and change payouts. If children are named beneficiaries, a longer payout period is permitted, further deferring income tax assessments. New IRS regulations allow a trust to be effectively designated a beneficiary if the trust

INHERITANCE DISCLAIMED BY PRIMARY HEIRS
PASSES TO SECONDARY HEIRS

Heirs may decline to accept inheritance to pass assets to other heirs and save taxes. If a primary heir satisfies the legal requirements for a disclaimer, the assets will pass as if the heir died before the deceased person. The inheritance disclaimed will pass to the secondary heirs named in the will, or if the will does not provide for secondary heirs, by state law.

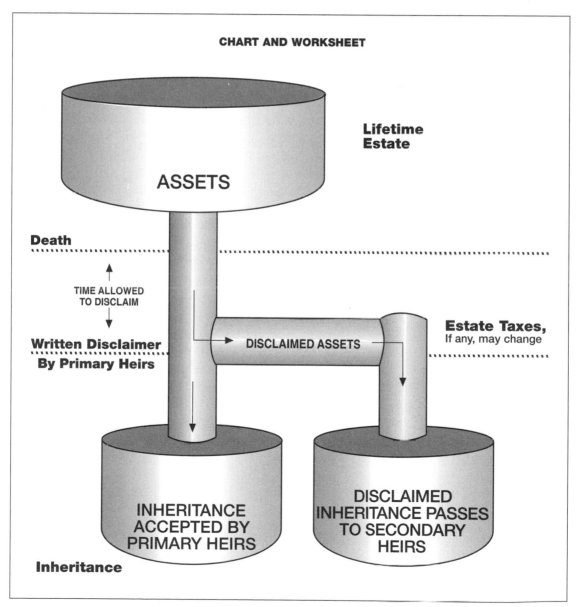

CHART AND WORKSHEET

Lifetime Estate

ASSETS

Death

TIME ALLOWED TO DISCLAIM

Written Disclaimer By Primary Heirs

DISCLAIMED ASSETS

Estate Taxes, If any, may change

INHERITANCE ACCEPTED BY PRIMARY HEIRS

DISCLAIMED INHERITANCE PASSES TO SECONDARY HEIRS

Inheritance

becomes irrevocable at death. This means the bypass trust can now be a beneficiary of a retirement account.

4. CHOOSE IRA OR RETIREMENT PLAN ACCOUNTS FIRST FOR CHARITABLE BEQUESTS. If you are planning to make charitable bequests, give IRA and retirement plan accounts first. By making a charity a beneficiary at death, all taxes can be avoided and 100% of the asset will be transferred to your favorite charity, rather than 77% to the government. Attractive charitable options to continue family participation include a donor-advised fund at a community foundation or a private foundation.

5. CREATE MULTIPLE ACCOUNTS FOR MAXIMUM FLEXIBILITY. Consider dividing retirement and IRA accounts into multiple separate accounts, or segregated accounts, naming a separate beneficiary for each share. Each beneficiary will be able to use his or her own life expectancy for distribution purposes. Single accounts can be divided into separate shares for each beneficiary after the death of the contributor. Tax deferral can be extended and marginal income tax brackets may be lower.

WHEN TO TURN DOWN AN INHERITANCE

◆ ◆ ◆

Can you imagine turning down an inheritance? Think twice before you answer "no." There may be times when it is family- or tax-wise to "disclaim" your right to property.

A disclaimer is the refusal to accept benefits conferred by will or by operation of law. If you do not wish to receive your share of your parents' estate because your income, estate, or both will be increased, you should consider disclaiming some or all of the interest. For example, if you are elderly or already possess a large estate, you may wish to have your inheritance pass directly to your children. This may save income, estate, gift, and even generation-skipping taxes on large estates. If state law and federal tax law requirements are met, the disclaimed interest for all transfer tax purposes will bypass the estate of the disclaiming heir.

There must be an irrevocable and unqualified refusal to accept an interest in property that satisfies four conditions under the Internal Revenue Code. First, the refusal must be in writing. Second, it must be made within nine months of the time that the interest is irrevocably transferred, which, for example, in the event of an inheritance, would be nine months from the date of the decedent's death. If the disclaiming party is under age 21, the time will be extended until nine months after he or she reaches age 21. Third, the disclaiming party must not have accepted the interest or any of its benefits before making the disclaimer. Fourth, the interest must pass to a person other than the disclaiming party without any directions on the part of the disclaiming party.

A disclaimer may be made of an undivided portion of an asset and also of a separate interest in property. Surviving joint tenants may file a qualified disclaimer. Both state law and federal tax law must be satisfied.

Disclaimers can be an important tool in estate planning. They may be used to bypass a generation who does not need the inheritance. They may be used by a surviving spouse to increase the assets transferred to the bypass trust. They may be used to pay estate taxes upon the death of the first spouse and avoid stacking assets in the second spouse's estate at eventual higher death tax rates.

Chapter

5

SIXTY-MINUTE CHARITABLE PLANS

by Phillip A. Kendall

BENEFIT YOURSELF AND YOUR FAVORITE CHARITY

◆ ◆ ◆

Charitable giving is an often-overlooked estate planning vehicle. In addition to providing financial rewards to the charity, an appropriately planned charitable gift can provide significant rewards to you as well. In the discussion that follows, five ways of giving are explored:

- ◆ Outright Gift
- ◆ Bequest Under Will
- ◆ Gift to Charity Reserving Life Income
- ◆ Lead Interest to Charity with the Remainder to the Family
- ◆ Conservation Easements

In making your selection, consideration needs to be given to maximizing the benefit to the charity and minimizing the cost to you and your family. In fact, under certain

129

scenarios, you can significantly enhance your own financial position while at the same time greatly benefiting the charity. Each method has characteristics to be considered when deciding how you would like to give to your favorite charity.

PLAN C1:
OUTRIGHT GIFT

◆ ◆ ◆

An outright gift is a direct gift by you during your lifetime to the charity. An obvious advantage of such a gift is its simplicity. A disadvantage is that the gift, once made, is irrevocable. Other important benefits are the following:

Personal Benefits

- ◆ The charity benefits immediately.

- ◆ You, as donor, are recognized during your lifetime.

Tax Benefits

- ◆ Charitable gifts are deductible from income taxes.

   Deductible up to 50% of adjusted gross income if cash.

   Deductible up to 30% of adjusted gross income if appreciated property (real estate, securities, etc.).

- ◆ Capital gains tax is avoided (where gifting certain appreciated property).

- ◆ Federal estate tax is reduced (where there is a taxable estate).

There is a right way and a wrong way to make an outright gift. Consider the following comparison of a gift of appreciated assets and a gift of cash:

Assumptions

You, as donor, are considering a gift of $20,000 to a charitable organization. You have discretionary income to make the gift from current cash. Among your assets are some highly appreciated securities, namely, Coca-Cola stock, providing a low yield rate on present value (fair market value $20,000; your cost basis in the stock $2,000).

Alternatives

1. Give cash outright.

2. Give the appreciated Coca-Cola stock.

PLAN C1—CHARITABLE GIFT
Difference in Cost Between Gift of Cash and Appreciated Stock

	Cash Gift Outright	Give Appreciated Securities
(a) Gift (charitable deduction)	20,000	20,000
(b) Savings from charitable deduction (assuming tax rate of 36%)	(7,200)	(7,200)
(c) Cost after income tax	12,800	12,800
(d) Capital gains tax paid (saved) [20% of $18,000]	0	(3,600)
(e) Final net cost of gift	12,800	9,200
(f) Cost to you as donor per dollar received by charity e ÷ a	$ 0.64	$ 0.46

Note: Income and capital gains tax rates vary and change. Above-stated tax rates assumed for purposes of this example only. Higher tax rates increase economic advantages of charitable gifts.

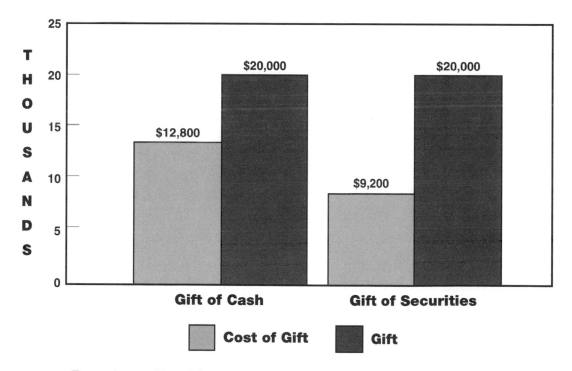

Based on gift of Coca-Cola stock with cost basis of $2,000

PLAN C2:
BEQUEST UNDER WILL

❖ ❖ ❖

The advantage of a bequest under a will, as opposed to an outright gift, is ability prior to death to change your mind. Although there is no current income tax deduction, if you have a taxable estate, all the assets passing to charity are 100% deductible against estate taxes otherwise owed. For example, if your estate is in a 55% tax bracket, by giving $1,000,000 to a charity, the charity would receive the full $1,000,000 and your estate would pay $550,000 less in estate taxes. Important characteristics of a bequest under a will include

- ❖ Revocability—you can change your mind

- ❖ No income tax deduction

- ❖ Estate tax savings through a charitable deduction in taxable estates

PLAN C3:
GIFT TO CHARITY RESERVING LIFE INCOME

❖ ❖ ❖

Under the current tax laws you may make a gift to a charity now, but reserve for yourself income from the gifted asset during your life. The device, which is known as a charitable remainder trust (CRT) can be advantageous for both you and the charity.

Operational Steps for a Simplified CRT

1. You gift highly appreciated securities or other assets to trustee of charitable remainder trust.

2. Trustee sells assets, and since the CRT is tax exempt, no capital gains taxes are due.

3. Trustee reinvests proceeds in high-income-producing investments.

4. Trustee pays to you during your life either (a) a fixed dollar amount each year (charitable remainder annuity trust) or (b) a fixed percentage of the value of the trust assets revalued each year (charitable remainder unitrust).

5. Upon your death, the remaining assets in the CRT pass outright to the charity(ies) you select.

Benefits

1. Highly appreciated assets are converted into increased lifetime income without paying any capital gains taxes.

2. There is an immediate charitable income tax deduction based on the present value of the charitable remainder interest which is based on your age, the payout rate and the IRS-required discount rate.

   a. Deduction up to 50% of your adjusted gross income results if you give cash.

   b. Deduction up to 30% of your adjusted gross income results if you give appreciated property.

   c. Excess deductions can be carried forward five years beyond the year of initial gift.

3. Estate tax savings result since assets gifted to CRT are excluded from your estate.

4. Benefits accrue your favorite charity.

How a Charitable Remainder Trust Can Benefit You Now

John and Mary Jones, ages 70 and 65 respectively, contribute $1 million of highly appreciated securities to a charitable remainder unitrust with a 7% payout. Their cost basis in the stock is $100,000 and the stock only pays a 2% dividend (i.e., $20,000 per year). If John and Mary sell their stock they would incur capital gains tax of $180,000, assuming they are in a 20% bracket. If they reinvested the net dollars after payment of capital gains taxes, they would realize an annual income of $41,000 at a 5% interest rate. The Joneses prudently decide to establish an intervivos charitable remainder unitrust naming several of their favorite charities as remainder beneficiaries. The $1 million of securities are transferred to the CRT with the CRT selling the securities and paying no capital gains taxes. The CRT then reinvests the proceeds (the entire $1 million) and earns income of 3.3% and capital appreciation at 6.57%. The Joneses receive an immediate income tax deduction of $288,260 which based on their blended income tax bracket of 42.6%, saves them $122,799 in income taxes. (These calculations assume an applicable federal discount rate, or § 7520 rate of 7.8%.). The unitrust then pays the Joneses 7% each year over the lives of both which amounts to $70,000 the first year, $50,000 more than they were receiving and $29,000 more than they would receive had they sold the securities themselves and invested them at a 5% interest rate.

PLAN C2—CHARITABLE REMAINDER TRUST
Chart and Worksheet

CHART AND WORKSHEET

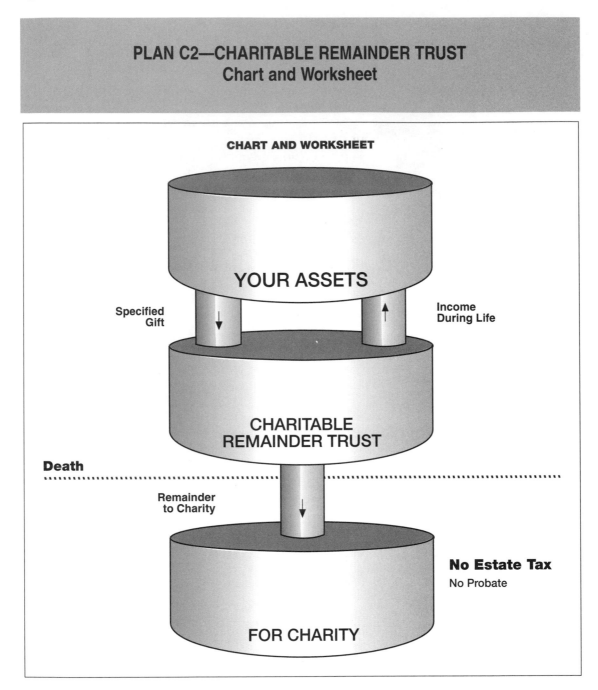

After both of the Joneses die, the $1,000,000 plus any appreciation passes to their favorite charities. Upon the second of Mr. and Mrs. Jones's death, if their estate is in a 50% tax bracket, $500,000 of estate taxes are avoided. In this scenario, the Joneses avoid capital gains taxes, save $500,000 in death taxes, save income taxes and at the same time increase their income.

Charitable Remainder Trust with Life Insurance Replacement Trust

You may decide on a charitable remainder trust in combination with a life insurance replacement trust (LIRT). One possible disadvantage of the charitable remainder trust is that the charity receives what would otherwise have passed to your children, although after taxes. A charitable remainder trust combined with a life insurance replacement trust allows you to provide for both your favorite charity and your children, sometimes even without paying any estate taxes. The following discussion compares this combination option with a stand alone charitable remainder trust.

Operational Steps

A. CHARITABLE REMAINDER TRUST

1. You gift highly appreciated securities or other assets to trustee of charitable remainder trust.

2. Trustee sells assets, and since the CRT is tax exempt, no capital gains taxes are due.

3. Trustee reinvests proceeds in high-income-producing investments.

4. Trustee makes payments to you during your life of either (a) a fixed dollar amount of income each year (charitable remainder annuity trust) or (b) a percentage of the value of the assets revalued each year (charitable remainder unitrust).

5. Upon your death, the remaining assets in the CRT pass outright to the charity(ies) you select.

B. LIFE INSURANCE REPLACEMENT TRUST

1. You also create a LIRT into which you transfer an existing policy or the trustee of the replacement trust acquires a new life insurance policy on your life.

2. Each year you contribute to the LIRT in an amount equal to the premiums due.

3. Immediately after each contribution, your trustee notifies your children of their right to withdraw their proportionate share of the amount from the trust. This is for the purpose of giving the children a "present interest" in your contribution gift to the LIRT, thereby qualifying the gift for the $10,000 annual gift tax exclusion per donee.

4. The children do not exercise their right to withdraw the gifted amount from the trust.

5. The trustee of the LIRT then uses the gift to make premium payments on the policy.

6. Assuming you survive three years beyond the establishment of the trust, then upon your death the life insurance proceeds are paid to your children estate tax free. The overall plan is designed such that the net dollars received by your children upon your death more than replace the amount that your children would have received had you made no gift to charity.

Benefits

1. Highly appreciated assets are converted into increased lifetime income without paying any capital gains taxes.

2. There is an immediate charitable income tax deduction based on present value of the charitable remainder interest, your age, and the payout you receive from the CRT.

   a. Deduction up to 50% of adjusted gross income results if you give cash.

   b. Deduction up to 30% of adjusted gross income results if you give appreciated property.

3. Estate tax savings result since assets gifted to CRT are excluded from your estate.

4. Benefits your favorite charity.

5. Benefits to your children are achieved through replacement trust in an amount equal to what they would have received had you made no gift to charity.

The Added Benefit of a CRT and a Life Insurance Replacement Trust

One of the drawbacks of a charitable remainder trust is that ultimately the family estate may pass to a charity instead of to your children. In most cases families are concerned most about providing for their children and secondarily about providing for charities. With a Life Insurance Replacement Trust both the charity and the family can be provided for.

Example: William and Margaret, ages 57 and 55 respectively, create a charitable remainder unitrust paying them 6% each year. They contribute $100,000. Upon creating the trust, William and Margaret receive a current charitable income tax deduction of $21,194. This saves them $8,690 in taxes assuming that their combined federal and state income tax rate is 41%. In addition to this initial tax savings, William and Margaret are now earning $7,000 per year, whereas they were earning only $3,000 per year with their highly appreciated securities which paid a dividend of only 3%. Since the assets had an aggregate fair market value of $100,000 and a cost basis of $10,000, they also avoided $90,000 of capital gains and a tax savings of possibly $18,000 assuming a 20% capital gains rate.

Since William and Margaret are now earning $4,000 more each year than they were previously, they can acquire a survivorship life policy using the tax savings in their first year and part of the incremental increase in earnings for several years thereafter. (A survivorship life policy pays out death benefits only after the death of both William and Margaret). Survivorship life in the face amount of $100,000 could be easily acquired with only a part of these excess dollars given William and Margaret's ages, assuming they are in good health. By having the insurance acquired in a life insurance replacement trust set up as an irrevocable life insurance trust, estate taxes can be avoided and as a result the irrevocable life insurance trust more than replaces what was contributed to charity, thereby providing even greater dollars to the children.

PLAN C3—CHARITABLE REMAINDER TRUST WITH LIFE INSURANCE REPLACEMENT TRUST
Chart and Worksheet

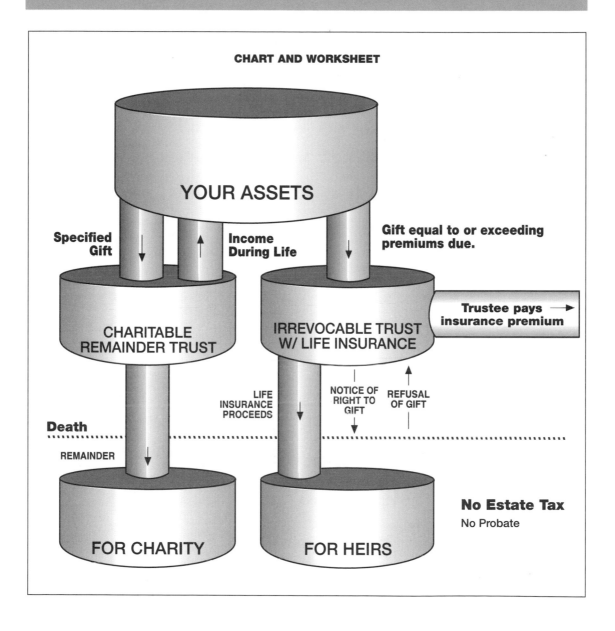

CHART AND WORKSHEET

YOUR ASSETS

Specified Gift

Income During Life

Gift equal to or exceeding premiums due.

CHARITABLE REMAINDER TRUST

IRREVOCABLE TRUST W/ LIFE INSURANCE

Trustee pays insurance premium

LIFE INSURANCE PROCEEDS

NOTICE OF RIGHT TO GIFT

REFUSAL OF GIFT

Death

REMAINDER

FOR CHARITY

FOR HEIRS

No Estate Tax
No Probate

There are some other things to remember about charitable remainder trusts, in general:

Personal Considerations

- ◆ CRTs are irrevocable.

- ◆ Trust portfolio is managed.

- ◆ Donor(s) receives an annual income.

- ◆ There are no probate costs.

Tax Considerations

- ◆ Charitable remainder gifts are partially deductible from income taxes:

    Deduction based on present value of the remainder interest passing to the charities and the donor age(s)

    Deduction up to 50% of adjusted gross income if cash

    Deduction up to 30% of adjusted gross income if appreciated property (securities, real estate, etc.)

- ◆ Capital gains tax is eliminated.

- ◆ Estate tax is reduced.

PLAN C4:
LEAD INTEREST TO CHARITY
WITH REMAINDER TO FAMILY

◆ ◆ ◆

Another method of addressing the concern of preserving your estate for your children while still making a gift to a charity is a charitable lead trust (CLT). A charitable lead trust is essentially the reverse of a charitable remainder trust. With a charitable lead trust, initially the income interest passes to a charity, then later the remainder interest passes on to family members of the grantor (the creator of the trust). Although no income tax savings is realized in a lead trust, significant gift or estate tax savings are achieved. A charitable estate or gift tax deduction is equal to the present fair market value of the guarantied annuity or unitrust interest passing to the charity. The trust may terminate and pass on to the family after a fixed term of years or upon the death of the individuals living at the time the trust is created.

There are two forms of charitable lead trusts, a grantor charitable lead trust and a non-grantor charitable lead trust. With a grantor CLT, the grantor, or creator of the trust, or his or her spouse retains a reversionary interest that exceeds 5% of the value of the trust. The grantor CLT trust is taxed under the grantor trust rules, meaning that the grantor remains taxable on all trust income. A non-grantor qualified CLT is significantly different. There is no up-front charitable income tax deduction to the grantor, rather the income is taxed to the trust which is a separate taxable entity. The trust offsets its income with charitable deductions it takes for the annual gifts to the charities. Income is taxed to the trust as a complex trust and is offset by the trust's unlimited charitable deduction. As a general rule, to avoid complexities and to secure the best tax benefits, a qualified non-grantor CLT is generally established.

A non-grantor charitable lead trust can be created either during the lifetime of the grantor or as part of the grantor's will. Under a lifetime non-grantor CLT, gift tax is imposed based upon the remainder interest passing to the children or grandchildren of the grantor. A charitable gift tax deduction is available in an amount equal to the present value of the income stream to the charitable beneficiary. Under a CLT created at death, which is a testamentary non-grantor CLT, the estate is entitled to an estate tax charitable deduction equal to the present value of the charity's annuity or unitrust interest.

Some of the benefits of a non-grantor qualified CLT are as follows:

◆ Immediate income is paid to your favorite charities.

◆ After a term of years or a time period measured by your life, property passes to your family at reduced estate or gift tax costs.

◆ There are no probate costs.

Operational Steps

1. You transfer highly appreciated assets to the charitable lead trust, thereby removing a portion of these assets from your taxable estate.

2. Trustee pays income either in the form of a fixed annuity or a unitrust amount to the charity for a term, which could be a fixed term of years or the term of your life.

3. At the end of the trust term, the remainder of the trust assets are distributed to your children.

Benefits

1. You realize a gift or estate tax savings based on certain actuarial calculations.

2. You benefit your favorite charity.

3. There are no probate fees.

Example: Let's assume that you create a non-grantor qualified charitable lead trust and you contribute assets with an initial value of $100,000. If you specify that a guar-

PLAN C4—CHARITABLE LEAD TRUST
Chart and Worksheet

CHART AND WORKSHEET

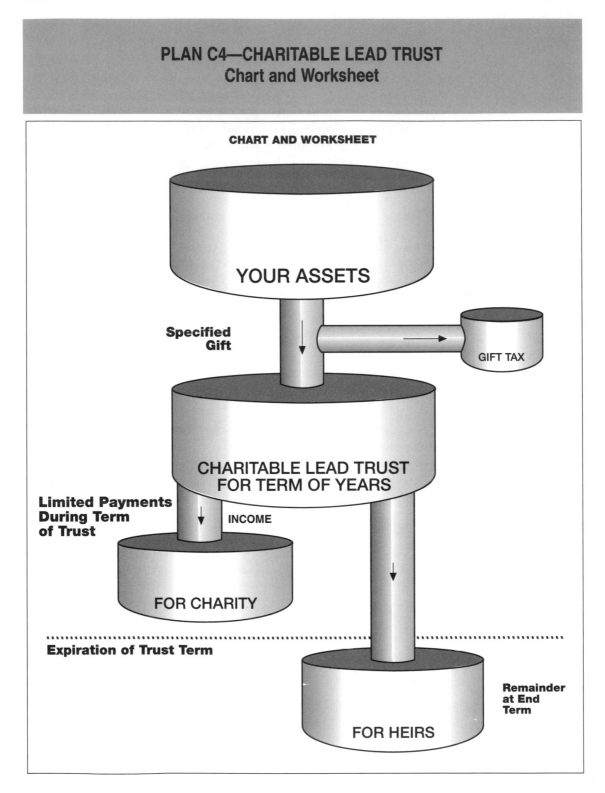

YOUR ASSETS

Specified Gift

GIFT TAX

CHARITABLE LEAD TRUST
FOR TERM OF YEARS

Limited Payments During Term of Trust

INCOME

FOR CHARITY

Expiration of Trust Term

Remainder at End Term

FOR HEIRS

antied annuity amount of $9,000 is to be paid to your favorite charity at the end of each year for a term of thirty years, then the CLT would have a charitable income interest equal to $99,438 (This assumes that the applicable federal discount rate, (the § 7520 rate) is 8.2%). After thirty years the remainder interest passes to your son. The net effect of this gift is that almost the entire remainder interest will pass to the son free of any gift or estate taxes. By comparison, if this same lead trust paid only $7,000 each year to a charity for a 20-year term, then the charitable deduction would be $67,716, with the remaining $32,284 being subject to a gift tax in the case where you set up the lead trust during your lifetime or an estate tax in the event you create a testamentary lead trust through your will.

PLAN C5: CONSERVATION EASEMENT

Conservation easements allow you to preserve your land for future generations while deriving current tax benefits. The conservation easement is a legally binding agreement with permanent restrictions on the future development or use of your land. You may choose to do this to preserve your land and maintain it in its current condition. Frequently, conservation easements allow for certain limited development, such as one or two additional homesites for members of your family.

A conservation easement is a legal document between you as a land owner (grantor) and a land trust (grantee). The signed conservation easement is then recorded with the clerk and recorder's office where the land is located. The land trust is typically a private nonprofit corporation which receives conservation easements and enforces the development restrictions set forth on the conservation easements. Typically, members of the land trust inspect your property on occasion to confirm that it is being used in compliance with the terms of the conservation easement. Public access to your land held under conservation easement is typically not required.

The tax benefits of a conservation easement are significant. Upon donating a conservation easement to the land trust, you obtain a charitable income tax deduction based on the value of the development rights which you forfeit through the conservation easement. The conservation easement also reduces the fair market value of the property for estate tax purposes. On occasion, a land trust will buy part or all of the conservation easement, as opposed to your making a complete donation. For tax purposes, this purchase is treated as a taxable sale.

A conservation easement is valued by an independent appraiser who takes a "before and after" approach. The value of the conservation easement is the difference between the value of the property before the conservation easement is in place and the value of the property after it is restricted by the conservation easement.

Operational Steps

1. You enter into a conservation easement agreement with a land trust placing permanent restrictions on the future development rights of your property.

2. You may reserve the right to develop a limited number of home sites.

3. An independent appraiser determines the value of the conservation easement by valuing your property both before and after the easement is in place.

4. You receive an immediate income tax deduction based on the value of the conservation easement. This income tax deduction may be used to the extent of 30% of your adjusted gross income in the first year and to the extent any excess remains may be carried forward for an additional five years.

5. The land trust periodically inspects your property to assure that you are not engaged in development or use of the property beyond that allowed by the conservation easement.

6. At the time of your death, the property is valued for estate tax purposes at the lower value since development rights have been gifted away.

Benefits

1. You realize an immediate income tax savings based on the value of the conservation easement.

2. You preserve your property for future generations.

3. You reduce your estate taxes, possibly enabling your family to retain the property which they otherwise might be forced to liquidate to pay estate taxes.

Example: You own a 1,000 acre ranch just outside of a ski resort with a value of $5,000 per acre. Because of the proximity to the resort, part of the land value is based on your ability to subdivide the property for residential and/or commercial development. You place a conservation easement on the property allowing only one additional home-site, reducing the property value of $5,000 per acre to $2,000 per acre. The value of the conservation easement in this example is the difference between the $5 million value before removing development rights and the $2 million value after removal of the development rights, resulting in a conservation easement value of $3 million.

You will receive a $3 million income tax deduction which may be used to offset 30% of your adjusted gross income in the year the conservation easement is created and may be carried forward over the next five years, again offsetting up to 30% of your adjusted gross income each year.

Under this example the property is valued for estate tax purposes at $2 Million rather than $5 Million. If your estate is in a 50% tax bracket, this could save you as much as $1.5 Million in estate taxes. This may enable your family to retain your ranch rather than be forced to sell the property to pay estate taxes.

Chapter 6

LIFE INSURANCE
AND ANNUITIES

BENEFICIARY DESIGNATIONS

❖ ❖ ❖

Incorrect beneficiary designations guarantee that the money will go to the wrong person and may increase estate taxes. When life insurance, pension, profit-sharing, Keogh, or IRA benefits are part of an estate plan family giving program, it is vitally important always to correctly designate and timely change beneficiaries in writing and submit it to the insurance company to assure that death benefits will be paid to the preselected beneficiaries.

Good intentions are not enough. Consider the following windfall to an ex-spouse after a bitter divorce. Jack Christensen received his engineering degree and married a month later. A desire for security led him to join the Air Force. He did not intend to make the military a career, but he found himself repeatedly extending his commitment.

His wife, Debra, a grade school teacher, found limited professional opportunities in the American schools at the Air Force base stations. Jack and Debra had no children, and Debra became frustrated with her life. She began to plan a new career in law. Jack completed his 20 years in the Air Force while Debra attended law school, and, after retirement, he searched for new directions in his life.

After passing the bar, Debra went to work full time for a small firm. Jack began to fly for a charter plane service. Debra eventually tired of Jack's lack of goals or financial success in life. Their marriage was dissolved. Shortly after the marriage breakup, Jack was killed in a tragic car crash.

Jack had a $100,000 life insurance policy naming Debra beneficiary in the event of his death. He intended to change the beneficiary designation after the divorce, but had delayed the paperwork because he had not yet decided whether to cancel the policy and receive the cash value or to pay the premiums and name his sister's two children as beneficiaries. The divorce settlement agreement made no reference to life insurance policies.

Debra made a claim for the life insurance death benefits, and the court ruled in her favor. Debra thus received an additional $100,000 tax free when Jack died because she was still the named beneficiary on the insurance policy. The law requires the policy owner to change the beneficiary of a policy, or the change must be incorporated into a separate agreement or court order to be effective.

The insurance was included in Jack's taxable estate. The estate tax rate was 40%. Jack's residuary probate estate paid $40,000 of federal estate taxes on the insurance death benefits and his unintended heir, Debra, enjoyed skiing at Aspen all winter long.

Are all your life insurance, annuity, profit-sharing, pension, Keogh, and IRA beneficiaries properly designated? Vicissitudes of life may cause you to change your mind about beneficiaries. Have you considered possible tax issues? Do you have copies of all signed beneficiary designation forms for review and reference? Do you know the proper agent and company names and addresses to contact for more information?

WHAT YOU NEED TO KNOW ABOUT LIFE INSURANCE
◆ ◆ ◆

Life insurance is often the first outside investment the head of a family makes. It is the only way to create an instant estate. Life insurance buys time. In fact, life insurance often represents the largest single continuing investment that the average person makes during the course of life.

Of all the estate-planning tools, life insurance is the most flexible. Although its first and most important use is to create an instant estate, other purposes make it of interest to the owner of the large estate as well as the small, to individuals and companies, to business owners as well as employees.

Insurance replaces a financial loss resulting from the death of an individual. It is used to supply money for business and estate settlement purposes. Often it is an investment, providing an opportunity for saving with safe, tax-deferred capital accumulation. Always, it generates liquidity for the survivors to pay taxes and debts and, it is hoped, ultimately, enjoy the financial freedom and security liquidity provides.

Will Rogers Did Not Want to Buy Something He Did Not Understand

Will Rogers had never owned stocks or bonds. He always said he did not want to buy something he did not understand. But there were two things he did understand—life insurance and real estate. He had sent money back from his travels in South Africa to take care of his life insurance, and he had added to the policies over the years.

At the time of his death, Rogers had accident insurance with Lloyds of London for the maximum they would issue to someone who flew in airplanes, $262,500. This was the sum paid to the estate following his death in an airplane crash in Alaska in 1935. Rogers also had two life insurance policies with The Penn Mutual Life Insurance Company, and one each with The Equitable Life Assurance Society of the United States and The Mutual Life Insurance Company. His total life insurance ran up to $482,500. But this was not all. He had endowment policies amounting to $200,000. There were annuities. He had U.S. savings bonds. And he had investments in real estate.[1]

Today, there are insurance policies to meet any insurance need and many investment objectives. As one piece of the estate plan, the insurance program should be designed to achieve your goals and objectives. Consider the following principal types.

Term Insurance

A principal quality of term insurance is that it is temporary insurance, which exists for a given period of time such as 1 year, 3 years, 8 years, 15 years. You pay a fixed amount in premium for the period of its term. If you don't die in that term, the policy expires and protection ends. Most policies include a renewal option. On each renewal, the premium rises for the same amount of insurance, and usually the renewal options expire at age 65 or 70.

Term insurance requires the smallest outlay of cash. But in the long run, term is not inexpensive. Over a period of years, your total net cost for term will exceed the total net costs (net premium less cash value) of permanent insurance. There are many situations where term insurance is a useful solution, such as mortgage insurance and many business and investment situations.

Whole Life Insurance

Whole life insurance generally includes ordinary life and limited payment life. These differ mainly in the length of time premium payments are to be made.

When you buy ordinary life, both your policy and your premium payments are divided into two parts: risk protection and investment. The risk part represents term insurance. The investment part represents your savings account in the policy and forms a cash value. During the early years of your policy, much of your premium goes toward risk and the "loading" cost of putting the policy in force. Over time the cash value rises, the risk cost decreases, and a larger share of the premium is consequently added to the

---

[1] Paula McSpadden Love, *The Will Rogers Book* (Waco, TX: Texian Press, 1971), p. 166.

cash value, which has a built-in annual earning factor. The buildup of the cash value is free of income tax during the existence of the policy. This value may be used as a potential source of investment capital. When you terminate a policy and take the cash value, you pay an income tax only on the amount you get back which exceeds the total amount of premiums you have paid less dividends you received.

Limited payment life is like ordinary life, except the period of premium payments is limited to a certain number of years, such as 10 or 15 years, or until you reach a certain age. After that your policy is paid up and remains in full force with no further premium payments. Premiums are often high because of the shorter payment period. Limited payment life is good for a person who has a high income in early years such as professional athletes, artists, and entertainers. If the entire premium is paid in one installment, it is called paid-up permanent life insurance.

Variable Life

This variation to whole or ordinary life is based on the payment of a fixed annual premium, establishment of a cash value, and the guarantee of a minimum death benefit. It differs in that the insured may elect to have the cash value invested in stocks, bonds, money markets, or other types of investments. Investments may be changed free of taxes. The cash value of the policy will depend upon the success or failure of the investment program. The death benefit is guaranteed at its full amount. If the cash value has increased beyond the policy's assumed rate of growth, the amount of increase will be added to the full amount of the policy and will be received tax free by beneficiaries as life insurance death proceeds.

Universal Life

Universal life is a policy that includes an investment program and a term insurance contract. For income tax purposes, it enjoys the tax advantages of life insurance. It differs from other forms of insurance because once the initial premium is paid in the amount necessary to pay the costs of establishing the policy, paying the term insurance rate, and setting up a cash value account, annual fixed premiums are no longer required. The policyholder may invest selected amounts when he or she wishes into the cash value account within certain tax restrictions to avoid becoming a modified endowment contract. The annual term insurance cost is taken out of the cash value account. The death benefit will amount to the term insurance in force plus the cash value account and will be received tax free by the beneficiary.

Variable Universal Survivorship Life

Variable Universal Survivorship Life is insurance protection packaged with stock investments to provide flexibility and control, tax advantages, and potential investment opportunities. This new economic tool is similar to traditional and universal life products in that it (1) insures two lives; (2) pays the death benefits upon the second death; (3) guarantees that the death benefit is not less than the initial face amount, provided there is sufficient cash value to pay monthly charges; (4) builds cash value; (5) provides for flexible premium payments, including single premium deposits; and (6) provides liquidity for payment of taxes upon the second death. This product seeks to outperform fixed survivorship life policies. The market value of the Variable Universal Survivorship Life policy will fluctuate with changes in market conditions. Many options exist in this hybrid product.

Second-to-die, or survivorship, variable universal life insurance is a single policy insuring two lives that pays off at the second death only, just when estate taxes create the need for cash. Because the face value of the policy isn't paid until the second death, the premiums are lower than two separate whole life policies. After the first death, the dividends and cash value increase and the death benefit goes up, an advantage to estates appreciating in value. This policy is a very effective estate-planning tool insuring husband and wife. The unlimited estate tax marital deduction shifts all the estate tax payments to the estate of the second to die.

"These policies have always been around, but they have never been sold to the extent they are now," says Barry Kaye, president of Barry Kaye Associates, a Los Angeles insurance brokerage that sold such policies to Malcolm Forbes's family before the patriarch's death in 1990. Second-to-die policies are a hot product in the life insurance industry.

How much insurance and what kind of insurance are the most perplexing questions for most people. But no one, except you, can really answer that question. The only realistic view to arrive at a proper figure for life insurance coverage is to assess it in terms of your family's or business needs, now and in the future. How much income or capital will be needed if you die? The difference between the income or capital expected and the income or capital needed is the deficiency. The amount and type of insurance you select should be sufficient to realistically make up that deficiency. If you have a business, professional practice, farm or ranch, or substantial debt, additional and other types of insurance will be needed. Insurance is a vital economic tool with many uses.

IRREVOCABLE DEMAND TRUST SAVES ESTATE TAXES
◆ ◆ ◆

You may be shocked to find that life insurance on your life and owned by you will be included in your taxable estate regardless of the named beneficiary. For example, if you are single with assets of $400,000 and insurance of $500,000, your total estate on your death would be $900,000. After subtracting the maximum exclusion, you will have a taxable estate until the year 2005.

An irrevocable demand trust owning one or more life insurance policies is a powerful and common estate-planning technique to permanently exclude life insurance death benefits from your taxable estate. It must be properly designed, funded, and managed on a regular basis to achieve its goals. Ask your planner for details before proceeding. Consider the following advantages, disadvantages, and cautions.

Advantages

- ♦ The irrevocable trust enables both your estate and your spouse's estate to avoid estate taxes on insurance death proceeds.

- ♦ Liquidity for estate needs can be provided if the trustee is authorized to purchase assets from your estate.

- ♦ Death benefit proceeds are not included in your probate estate.

- ♦ Your surviving spouse can receive some or all of the annual income from the insurance trust and distribution of principle under certain conditions.

- ♦ A substantial sum of money after your death may be available for the benefit of your surviving spouse and children.

Disadvantages and Cautions

- ♦ The trust is irrevocable in order to accomplish the desired tax savings objective. This means that once it is established, it cannot be changed or revoked. However, the trustee may be given substantial flexibility in distributing income and principal. The trustmaker cannot be the trustee.

- ♦ There will be legal fees required to set up a trust and annual tax return filings that will require preparation fees and tax payments. There may be material trustee fees if a professional trustee is utilized.

- ♦ The best design is for policies to be owned by the trust from inception, and for the insured to have no interest in or control over the trust. If existing policies are transferred into the trust, your estate-planning counselor should be consulted so that you understand the conditions under which the policy transferred may be recognized for tax purposes.

- ♦ Substantial paperwork is required to satisfy the paper trail requirements of a demand-type trust intended to allow the annual premium payments to fall within the $10,000 or more annual gift tax exclusion.

Life insurance is a vitally important part of estate planning. It is a universal estate building block and the first outside investment the head of a family should make. Life insurance buys time; it is the only investment that does.

IRREVOCABLE LIFE INSURANCE TRUST OF SINGLE PERSON OR SPOUSE OF MARRIED COUPLE WITH ANY SIZE ESTATE
Chart and Worksheet

The irrevocable demand trust is often called a Crummey Trust, which is the last name of a successful tax litigant. By providing in the trust that the beneficiary is allowed to withdraw during each year the lesser of the amount of the annual exclusion of $10,000 or the value of the asset transferred to the trust during that year, the annual exclusion will be allowed. The irrevocable demand trust may also be used without life insurance. This planning tool is very effective if you follow the complex tax rules and create the paper trail necessarily required by the trust terms.

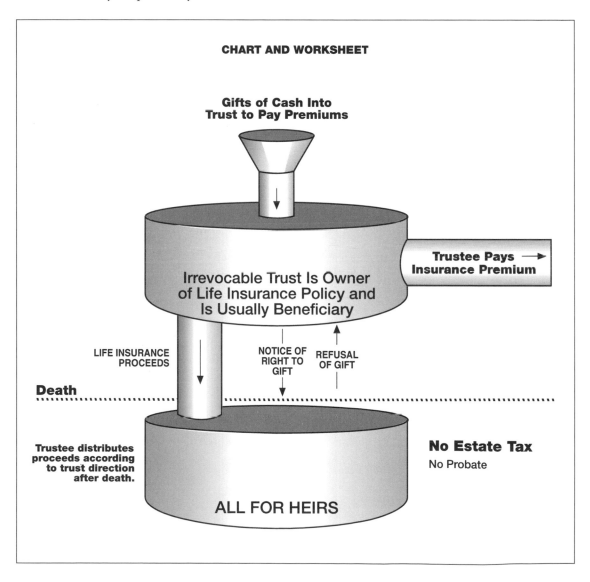

CHART AND WORKSHEET

Gifts of Cash Into
Trust to Pay Premiums

Irrevocable Trust Is Owner
of Life Insurance Policy and
Is Usually Beneficiary

Trustee Pays →
Insurance Premium

LIFE INSURANCE
PROCEEDS

NOTICE OF
RIGHT TO
GIFT

REFUSAL
OF GIFT

Death

Trustee distributes
proceeds according
to trust direction
after death.

No Estate Tax
No Probate

ALL FOR HEIRS

ANNUITIES PRODUCE PAYMENTS FOR LIFE AND TAXES AT DEATH

◆ ◆ ◆

An annuity may guarantee the payment of fixed amount periodic payments for your life or other specified period. There is no hazardous guessing about life's length. It allows you to consume both income and principal, and if geared to your lifetime, you will always have that financial support available while alive. Of course, to obtain an annuity contract, you must pay over your capital and receive only a contract right. You must rely on the financial soundness of the company issuing the annuity. You will be relieved of the duties of investing and managing assets you use to purchase the annuity, while gaining the advantage of a steady flow of money.

The death of the annuity holder may trigger a payoff of the contract to the beneficiary. The beneficiary is responsible for paying ordinary income tax on the earnings at the beneficiary's income tax rate. Even though a spousal beneficiary can elect to continue the contract, at some point, income taxes will have to be paid. As a general rule, a nonspouse beneficiary can wait up to five years before taking all the money out of an annuity. In addition, the entire value of the annuity is included in the estate for estate tax purpose. The net result is two levels of tax: income taxes on the deferred income and estate tax on the entire amount. The combination of income and estate tax can be an alligator that significantly reduces the net amount received by beneficiaries.

A few points should be considered before ever placing an annuity in the trust:

1. Once the annuity is placed with either a trust as owner or beneficiary, a spouse may lose planning options.

2. If annuity income is taxed at the trust level, progressive income tax brackets are often higher than the beneficiary's income tax bracket.

3. Annuities are not good funding tools for bypass trusts because with an annuity in an irrevocable trust, the gains may be taxable each year as ordinary income.

An annuity is a contract and can appear in many forms. Consider the following principal types:

Straight Life Annuity

A straight life annuity ceases on your death. There is no value that passes to another at your death and, therefore, no estate tax. No one else receives any benefits following your death.

Joint and Survivor Annuity

A joint and survivor annuity does not end upon the death of the first annuitant to die, as does a straight life annuity. There is value continuing after the first annuitant's death for the benefit of the surviving annuitant, which may be your spouse. If you die, the value to be included in your gross estate is what it would cost at your death to buy a straight life annuity for the survivor's age as of the date of your death. Special rules apply depending on who contributed to the total purchase price. Upon the death of the survivor, there is no estate tax because there is nothing of value remaining. Annuities may be purchased either for immediate or deferred payments.

Variable Annuity

A variable annuity provides for regular payments. The payments are not made in a set amount. If you purchase a variable annuity, you will buy units of a fund at their cost at the time of purchase. When your deferred annuity begins, the number of owned units will determine the amount of your periodic payments, and the payments will vary according to the fluctuation in value of the units during the period you are entitled to payments. Thus, the amounts of the payments are not guaranteed.

Employee Annuity

An employee annuity could be any type of annuity previously mentioned, or a combination, classified separately only because of a wide use by employers, usually on a group basis, to provide for an employee's retirement. It customarily provides for a refund feature geared to the employee's total contributions during his or her working career.

Private Annuity

An annuity issued by an insurance company in the business of selling annuities is a commercial annuity. An annuity purchased from anyone else, such as a member of your family or a business corporation, is a private annuity. This classification has its significance in determining when gain is realized for income tax purposes, and it has other tax ramifications. Private annuities are difficult to use because of the risk to the individual or corporation issuing the annuity.

Annuities may be very helpful to provide continuing security for one or two lifetimes. Income, gift, and estate tax issues arise and should be considered when you are purchasing an annuity contract. Integrate your annuity purchases into your complete estate plan. Your estate can be expanded through good planning.

KEY POINTS TO REMEMBER: LIFE INSURANCE, ANNUITIES, AND BENEFICIARY DESIGNATIONS

❖ ❖ ❖

1. Consider life insurance as a vital economic tool. Life insurance buys time and creates instant estates. It can generate assets, provide liquidity, fund agreements, and pay fringe benefits for employees.

2. Review all life insurance, annuity, profit-sharing, pension, Keogh, and IRA beneficiary designations when you prepare or change your estate plan, marry, divorce, have children, or change the purpose of the life insurance policy.

3. Obtain tax advice when changing insurance, annuity, and retirement plan beneficiaries in large estates or when income taxes may become payable.

4. Consider an irrevocable life insurance trust if you have one or more large life insurance policies and a taxable estate. You may permanently remove the death benefits of this life insurance from estate taxes. An alternative is to gift ownership of the policies directly to the beneficiaries. Remember, if you continue to pay premiums, the amounts of the payments are gifts.

5. Make all beneficiary designation changes on forms approved by the life insurance company issuing the policy or the institution or organization administering the benefit. Use wording approved by your attorney that will achieve your family-giving and estate-planning goals and be consistent with your executed documents.

6. Review your life insurance on a regular basis with a qualified person who will honestly and accurately discuss your needs and alternatives.

7. Annuities are economic tools to defer income tax and generate security and independence for the beneficiaries.

8. Annuity contracts are generally not good candidates for funding bypass trusts.

Chapter

PROTECTION OF FAMILY BUSINESSES, INVESTMENTS, FARMS, AND HOMES

"Don't take simple things for granted. Make sure there are good records—wills, trusts—even at a young age"[1]

Stephen and Alan Hassenfeld were the third set of brothers to run Hasbro, Inc., the toy manufacturing company based in Pawtucket, Rhode Island. The founding brothers, Polish immigrants Henry and Hillel Hassenfeld, expanded their rag business to cloth-covered pencil boxes, pencils, and school supplies. During World War II, under Stephen and Alan's father, Merrill, and his brother, Harold, the company began making toys (nurse and doctor kits). Stephen and Alan led the company to its position as the world's largest toy manufacturer.

The succession was not entirely orderly; the second set of brothers had a falling-out when Merrill appointed his son Stephen president in 1974. Harold thought the appointment was premature, and the feud continued until, after Merrill's death in 1979, Harold's part of the company, Empire Pencil Corp., separated completely from Hasbro.

---

[1] *Family Business,* Vol. 1, no. 4, April 1990, pp. 20–25.

The relationship between Stephen and Alan was much more harmonious—the brothers were best friends and housemates (until Alan's marriage), as well as business partners. "We were as close as two brothers can be," Alan recalled. "We were seven years apart, so there was no sibling rivalry. I don't ever remember having an argument with him. We disagreed, but we always tackled problems together."

The brothers' management styles, though different, were complementary. Stephen, who joined the company first and brought his brother on board in 1970, was quiet and disciplined, and dealt with the meat-and-potatoes issues—finance, product development, marketing. Alan, more relaxed and outgoing, spent most of his first decade with the company traveling the world, setting up Hasbro's international operations. Later, he ran the company's sales and marketing groups. Although Stephen announced corporate decisions and was titular head of the company, decisions were jointly made as a result of constant communication between the brothers.

In 1984, when Alan was in his midthirties and Stephen in his early forties, Stephen named his brother president of the company; Stephen became chairman and CEO. The move echoed his own appointment as president at the age of 32, based on his father's learn-by-doing philosophy.

It was to be expected that the brothers would jointly run the company for at least two more decades. But in 1987, Stephen contracted pericarditis, an infection of the lining of the heart, and required ten weeks to recuperate. When he returned to work, it was announced that he was fully recovered. But in May 1989, Stephen was hospitalized again, this time with pneumonia. After a month in intensive care, he died. He was 47 years old.

Following his first hospitalization, the brothers took steps to protect the company in the event of his death. They assembled a strong, independent board of directors and instituted a stock purchase plan to enable existing stockholders to thwart hostile takeover attempts. Most important, in 1988, six months before Stephen's death, they announced a reorganization of Hasbro's management. Three new operating divisions, headed by veteran company executives, were created, and long-term planning was delegated to the company's executive vice president. "Stephen and I talked long and hard for six or seven months" about the reorganization, Alan said. Without it, when Alan succeeded Stephen as chairman and CEO, retaining his title as president, "things would have been more difficult."

The Hassenfelds' experience illustrates the need for a family-run company to prepare for the unexpected loss of a key family member. Alan suggested these minimum steps:

"Don't take the simple things for granted. Make sure there are good records—wills, trusts—even at a young age. Stephen and I were as close as two brothers could be, and we instinctively did many things jointly. But when you see how fragile life can be, it forces you to communicate. You must delineate the separation in case something happens."

"If you're next in line for the CEO's job, organize your personal affairs sooner rather than later. When you're a CEO, you spend time worrying about everything but yourself. If something were to happen to me, I would feel better that at least things were organized."

"Have a good outside board of directors, and clean your ears so you can listen."

Have you taken simple planning and decisions for granted? Have you made choices required in the event of an unforeseen tragedy? Do you have knowledgeable family and outside advisors you can rely upon? Are you procrastinating?

DESIGN YOUR PLAN TO GIVE CONTROL TO CHOSEN HEIRS

◆ ◆ ◆

Malcolm Forbes was chairman and editor-in-chief of *Forbes* magazine when he died February 24, 1990. Readers and advertisers saw the biweekly publication, which had a circulation of 735,000 in the United States, as an extension of its flamboyantly successful founder. When he died, all 750 employees received an extra week's pay and forgiveness of all personal loans from the company up to $10,000.

Forbes's life-style and values offended some and were envied by others. He was an entrepreneur and exercised his individual prerogatives. He also knew how to run an organization. To that end, he made sure that there would be no sibling feud over the family business by leaving controlling interest to just one of his children. He had prepared his son, Steve, for the responsibility, and so it did not come as a surprise to his other children that that was what he did. There were no public complaints, and the next generation of Forbeses moved forward together.

There is nothing more destructive than family feuds over money and control of a business. Give your heirs opportunities, not battlefields. If you own a business, farm, or complex investments, train your heirs to take over; then give them encouragement and responsibilities. Develop a plan of management.

TIGER TOOLS FOR BUSINESS, INVESTMENT, AND FARM TRANSFERS—
Chart and Worksheet

Limited partnerships, corporations, and limited liability companies should always be considered a part of your estate plan if you own a business, significant investments, or a farm. They are called "tiger tools" because they are quiet, powerful, swift, and sure planning tools to transfer interests, reduce taxes, and protect assets. Each has its own unique legal and tax implications that require evaluation before selection. Use the accompanying chart and worksheet to hypothesize how you might transfer ownership of your business, investments, or a farm.

CHART AND WORKSHEET

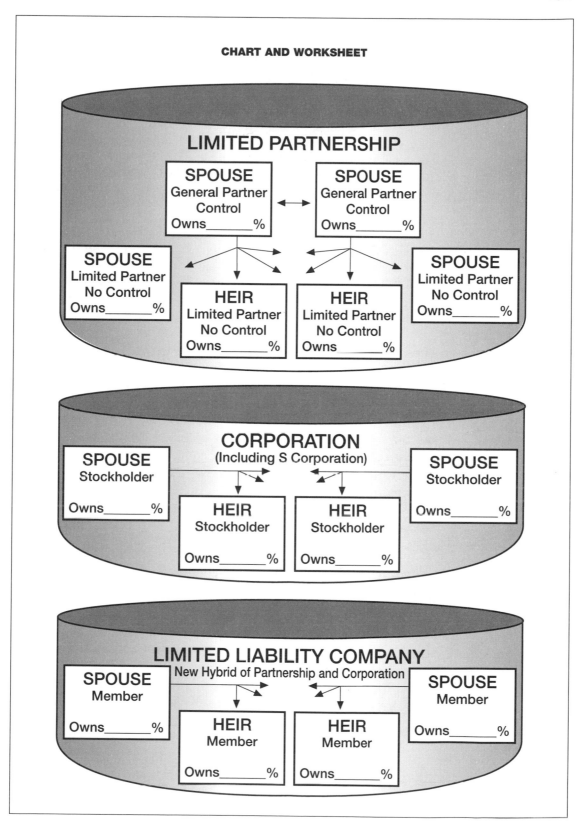

LIMITED PARTNERSHIP

SPOUSE
General Partner
Control
Owns_____%

SPOUSE
General Partner
Control
Owns_____%

SPOUSE
Limited Partner
No Control
Owns_____%

HEIR
Limited Partner
No Control
Owns_____%

HEIR
Limited Partner
No Control
Owns_____%

SPOUSE
Limited Partner
No Control
Owns_____%

CORPORATION
(Including S Corporation)

SPOUSE
Stockholder

Owns_____%

HEIR
Stockholder

Owns_____%

HEIR
Stockholder

Owns_____%

SPOUSE
Stockholder

Owns_____%

LIMITED LIABILITY COMPANY
New Hybrid of Partnership and Corporation

SPOUSE
Member

Owns_____%

HEIR
Member

Owns_____%

HEIR
Member

Owns_____%

SPOUSE
Member

Owns_____%

BUY-SELL AGREEMENTS AND OTHER BUSINESS TRANSFER ARRANGEMENTS

◆ ◆ ◆

If you own a sole proprietorship, or a business interest in a partnership, closely held corporation, or limited liability company, special planning is needed. You must give consideration to the value of your business at the time of your death, who will receive the interest, and who will control the business after you are gone.

If the business interest is not complex, you may choose to transfer it by identifying it in your will or living trust, and designating the heir to receive it. If your spouse receives the full interest, there will be no estate taxes because of the unlimited marital deduction. However, you may be creating a tax monster later when your spouse dies. If one child receives the interest, make sure that there are no conflicts with other children. If more than one child receives an interest, are there potential family feud situations? If no one has a controlling majority interest in a business, watch out for destructive management conflicts.

Specific problems often arise if one or more of the children is active in the business while other children are not. If you would like to leave the business to your child who is most active in the business, consider allocating as much of the business as possible to the active child's share and then require that child to buy the other children out, or at least give the active child the first right of refusal. Selection of the proper executor or trustee can also be critical to fair dealing and cooperation when dividing business interest.

When there is more than one owner of the closely held business, the use of a buy-sell agreement will be helpful in solving many estate-planning problems. A buy-sell agreement is an agreement that provides that on your death, your interest will be purchased. If your interest is to be purchased by the surviving owners, the agreement is called a cross-purchase agreement. If the interest is to be purchased or redeemed by the business, it is referred to as an entity or redemption agreement.

Buy-sell agreements, whether of the purchase or entity type, have certain purposes in common:

◆ To provide a sure and uninterrupted, conflict-free continuation of the business after your death. By purchasing your interest, the surviving owners will eliminate conflict with your estate and heirs.

◆ To provide a method whereby your estate will receive cash or other liquid assets on your death rather than an unmarketable interest in a closely-held business. Many businesses do not pay profits or dividends. Often the business interest may not only be unmarketable, but for all intents and purposes, it may be next to worthless to your family, and yet, for death tax purposes, it may have a substantial value.

◆ To fix the estate tax evaluation of your business interest.

Absent such an agreement, your estate will be faced with the very difficult problem of ascertaining the value to be fixed on your business interest and having the value accepted by the taxing authorities. Valuation questions, particularly when the estate is not liquid, should be avoided if at all possible.

There are three major alternative methods which owners of a closely-held business frequently use to set the price in a buy-sell agreement. These methods are (1) a predetermined price, perhaps subject to periodic review, (2) a price determined by appraisal or arbitration, and (3) a price determined by formula. Each of these alternatives has advantages, disadvantages, and trade-offs and should be discussed thoroughly with your business partners and advisers.

The buy-sell agreement should prescribe the method of payment upon your death. Funding the payment, in whole or in part, with life insurance on the lives of all owners should always be considered. In this way, when an owner dies, the estate will receive immediate payment, and the purchaser will not have to raise funds. When the owners are insurable, this method is in most cases the most advantageous. Various insurance funding alternatives cause different income, estate, and gift tax results. Plan the insurance program carefully.

Although buy-sell agreements are beneficial more often than not, disadvantages in a given situation should always be considered. It may be possible for the estate, at no increased costs, to receive both the business interest and the value. Instead of entering into a buy-sell agreement to be funded with life insurance, each business owner could obtain the desired amount of life insurance on his or her own life and select a beneficiary or place the policy in an irrevocable life insurance trust. Upon the owner's death, his or her family will have both the business interest and a greater amount of insurance proceeds. There are trade-offs. Your lifetime rights in the business interest are restricted. The price described in the buy-sell agreement may become unrealistic. Upon your death, it may be preferable to liquidate the business. You may wish your business interest to continue for the benefit of your family rather than be sold.

A family business is a treasure. Americans dream of becoming entrepreneurs. Most folks work hard so that their heirs will enjoy a bountiful inheritance. Acquiring, building, and planning the disposition of your business interest require maximum efforts, but often different knowledge and advice.

DISCOUNTED VALUE TRANSFERS

◆ ◆ ◆

Another technique useful in disposing of any interest in a closely-held business is transferring the business on a "discounted" basis. This method, if successful, will accomplish two objectives. First, posttransfer appreciation will be eliminated from the giver's estate. Second, it may be possible to structure the transfer so that even the present value is not fully subject to either gift or estate taxation. Discounts generally vary from 15% to 50%.

Court decisions have permitted minority interest discounts for unmarketability, lack of control, and blockage to be taken in valuing the shares of stock in a family-owned corporation for both gift and estate tax purposes. These decisions create an excellent planning opportunity. An owner of a business, over a period of time, may make sufficient minority interest gifts to several children so that the owner at the time of death will no longer own the majority interest. Each of these gifts may be valued after applying the minority interest discount. Upon the owner's death, the remaining interest may also be valued as a minority interest. In this way, the entire business interest may be transferred, and none of it will be taxed at full value.

For example, assume the present value of a business is $2,000,000. The owner transfers 30% of the stock to each of two children, retaining 40%. If a minority interest discount of 25% is appropriate, then 60% of the business will have been gifted at a value of $900,000, instead of $1,200,000. On the owner's death, assuming the business is still worth $2,000,000, his or her 40% interest should also be valued after applying the minority discount. If the appropriate discount is still 25%, then the estate value of the 40% interest will be $600,000, instead of $800,000. As a result, the total business interest will have been transferred at a value of $1,500,000 instead of $2,000,000.

ASSET PROTECTION IS A THEME WITH MANY DIMENSIONS

❖ ❖ ❖

Offshore bank accounts and "asset protection" trusts once were money-hiding gambits preferred by financial criminals and con men. But in today's environment of rising taxes and rapidly escalating litigation risks, more and more individuals are searching for legal methods to protect their assets.

Lawsuits are mushrooming in the United States. Jury awards have hit new records. Liability has been expanded to ensnare many people who previously would not be considered culpable according to the Insurance Institute in New York. In some cases, litigants look for deep pockets, which may be a business, savings, or a home.

U.S. courts do not encourage financial criminals to manipulate the system to hide their assets from legitimate claims. Judges generally void any technique that was used solely to protect assets from existing creditors and litigants. For example, if you try to put your assets out of reach of creditors while you are being sued or threatened with a lawsuit, courts are inclined to find you engaged in a "fraudulent conveyance" and reverse everything you have done. But they are hesitant to dismiss techniques that were employed for legitimate estate planning reasons years before lawsuits or creditor problems were on the horizon.

Asset protection involves often unacceptable trade-offs. The main asset protection effort involves giving your assets away to family, friends, or charities. Some strategies give you substantial control over those assets, but others do not. If you later change your mind about who is to receive your property, you may be out of luck.

Asset protection is a new industry buzzword. The legal and tax planning tools used have been around for a long time (except for limited liability companies—a new form of business entity which is a hybrid between a partnership and a corporation). Commonly used planning recommendations include the following:

Family Limited Partnership—This has long been an excellent estate- and inheritance-planning strategy and should be considered in every estate plan where it fits. Often, a husband and wife are the general partners, and the husband and wife and children are limited partners. Parents make gifts of partnership interest to reduce their estate and distribute income. Minority interest and unmarketability discounts may reduce the value of the gift.

For asset protection, the partnership should include a provision that states that distributions from the partnership will be made only at the general partners' discretion and that the general partners can be removed only by a supermajority vote, such as 90–100%. A general partner should be allowed to resign and become a limited partner. A creditor generally cannot force the partnership to make distributions or attach its assets. A creditor historically can only obtain a charging order which only allows it to receive distributions from the partnership if and when made, although this limitation is under attack in our courts. Further, if the partnership earns income, the creditor may then be taxed on the income, even if not distributed.

If you have various assets you wish to place in limited partnerships, consider creating a partnership for safe assets, such as stocks and bonds, and one for risky investments, such as real estate. A partnership interest may be transferred to a living trust. Many states now allow limited liability limited partnerships which give the general and limited partners protection from creditors.

Family General Partnerships—General partnerships allow more participation and decision making by all partners. A managing partner may be designated. Many states now allow limited liability general partnerships which give all partners protection from creditors. General partnerships may give more tax predictability than limited partnerships.

Family Corporation—Again, this has long been an excellent planning entity. Use a corporation if there is substantial liability risk or an operating business with employees. Stock may be gifted to the next generation. Buy-sell agreements and transfer restrictions help control ownership. Majority voting stockholders control management. S corporation tax elections eliminate the risk of income tax at the corporate level.

Family Limited Liability Companies (LLC)—This fast-developing hybrid cross between a partnership and corporation requires close watching and consideration. Owners are called members and individuals in charge of management are logically called managers. LLCs provide the risk management advantages of a corporation and the tax advantages of a partnership. There must be more than one owner.

Irrevocable Life Insurance Trusts—Irrevocable life insurance trusts remove the death benefits from the insured's estate. Therefore, the death benefits are not taxable and beyond the reach of creditors.

Dynasty Trust—A dynasty trust allows you to protect as much as you can for as long as you can. It is a protective shield against creditors, and it provides benefits to successive generations without initial payment of gift, estate, or generation-skipping taxes (GSTs) by taking advantage of the exemption equivalent and the $1,000,000 GST exemption. Eventually, as the trust property vests in the final beneficiaries, transfer taxes may be payable at rates as high as 55% federal, plus possible state tax. Principal and income may be distributed for successive generations. Income taxes are an issue. The dynasty trust may be used to accumulate wealth or protect special assets, such as vacation homes or artwork.

Special Needs Trust—Much has been written about special needs trusts to insulate inheritance from government claims under Supplemental Security Income (SSI), Medicaid, and other government support programs. The plan includes transferring assets to an irrevocable trust that provides benefits only for special needs, thus qualifying the trust beneficiary also for government entitlements. There are three major disadvantages: (1) plans require loss of asset control and security, (2) recent changes in federal and state laws and regulations as well as court decisions requiring entitlement waiting periods up to 5 years after transfer of property to a trust and criminal sanctions for law violations, and (3) Medicaid places the recipient in a permanent public welfare status.

Foreign Trusts—Various foreign account arrangements have long been inextricably linked to drug dealing, organized crime, money laundering, and tax evasion. Thus there is an inherent prejudice against use of foreign trusts. The list of countries which solicit foreign trust business reads like a vacation wonderland. The Bahamas, Bermuda, Barbados, the Cayman Islands, the Cook Islands, and Gibraltar. Don't let these exotic places fool you. The risks of losing control of your assets, a U.S. court declaring the trust and transfers in defraud of creditors, adverse tax consequences, new laws, big legal and accounting fees, and unending paper trails are unacceptable trade-offs for most people. Nevertheless, the added barriers to creditor collection efforts have frustrated some creditors into agreeing to discounted settlements in unusual circumstances.

KEEPING THE FARM IN THE FAMILY USING SPECIAL VALUATION

◆ ◆ ◆

Family farms and ranches are businesses and more. Usually, they are family operations, and increasingly inherited. Farm- and ranchland is simply too expensive to purchase and does not offer a reasonable return on capital for new investors. All the challenges and issues of business are inherent in agriculture.

Since inheritance will be the primary method for the next generation of farmers and ranchers, planning is absolutely essential to assure your heirs of a reasonable chance of success. Prices, management, government programs, and the global economy will be enough of a challenge. Family feuds and unmanageable taxes can become surprise tornadoes that destroy several generations of backbreaking work and worry.

In 1976, Congress passed a tax relief provision for the special valuation of family farm and ranch property, and for real estate used in other types of family businesses as well. This relief provision is called "special use valuation."

Special use valuation allows farm- and ranchland to be valued at a low agricultural value instead of its value for other purposes. This may save substantial federal estate taxes. Special use valuation is not for everyone because of its requirements. Nevertheless, it should be discussed and considered during planning, or after the death of a farmer or rancher.

Special Use Valuation Saves Estate Taxes

The IRS has set strict requirements for the use of special use valuation, including the following: (1) the value of all farm assets, less debt, must be at least 50% of the deceased owner's estate; (2) the value of the farmland must be at least 25% of the deceased owner's estate; (3) the property must have been actually managed by the deceased owner for five out of the eight years prior to death and must have been used for farming during that period; (4) a qualified heir must actually manage the property after the owner's death; (5) the land must be used as a farm for ten years after the owner's death; (6) the land is subject to a federal tax lien; and (7) the land value can be reduced to a special use valuation by as much as $750,000, indexed annually for inflation.

A federal tax lien on property makes it difficult for its current owners to mortgage the property. As a result, family members actively engaged in farming may find it difficult to borrow money to keep the farm or ranch going. Like many provisions of the Internal Revenue Code, it has its trade-offs. Because of the unlimited marital deduction, special use valuation serves no useful purpose if all the property is passed to a surviving spouse. However, upon the death of the second spouse, it may save estate taxes. Special use valuation may also apply to other types of family businesses.

Estate Tax Exclusion for Qualified Family-Owned Businesses Is an Apple Seldom Picked

If more than 50% of the estate of an individual consists of qualified family owned business interests, the executor may elect to exclude up to $675,000 in value of the interest from the gross estate. This business exclusion, however, goes down each year. This is because the business exclusion may not exceed the excess of $1.3 million over the maximum exclusion flowing from the unified credit. Thus, an estate electing the business exclusion is limited to a total exclusion of $1.3 million.

For example, in 2006, the exclusion is elected for the Conley Estate holding a $300,000 business and for the Winter Estate holding a $1 million business. In each case, the estate is allowed a qualified family owned business exclusion of $300,000 and a maximum exclusion amount of $1 million flowing from the unified credit, because total exclusions can not exceed $1.3 million.

The amount of the exclusion can be as much as $675,000 after 1998 and can be used to offset an equal amount at estate's highest tax bracket. Congress continues to modify this break. This tax exclusion has many conditions which severely limit its usefulness. Family ownership percentages, valuation limitations, years of consecutive material participation, and specific recapture events within ten years of death are worms in this tax savings apple. Coincidence, rather than planning, will produce the most tax savings from this political apple. This is how the law originally looks on paper:

Year	Applicable Exclusion Amount	Unified Credit	Exclusion for Family Business
1998	$625,000	$202,050	$675,000
1999	650,000	211,300	650,000
2000/2001	675,000	220,550	625,000
2002/2003	700,000	229,800	600,000
2004	850,000	287,300	450,000
2005	950,000	326,300	350,000
2006	1,000,000	345,800	300,000

Pay Estate Taxes on Closely Held Businesses in Installments to Save Money

A fiduciary may elect to pay estate taxes attributable to a closely held business interest in installments over a maximum period of 14 years. If the election is made, the estate pays only interest for the first four years, followed by up to ten annual installments of principal and interest. A special 2% rate applies for the deferred estate tax attributable to the first million in taxable value of the closely held business (i.e., the first $1 million above the maximum exclusion). Thus, for example, in 1999, when the maximum exclusion is $650,000, the amount of estate tax attributable to the value of the closely held business between $650,000 and $1,650,000 will be eligible for the 2% interest rate. Interest rates on additional deferred taxes are reduced according to a formula. The interest paid is not deductible for estate or income tax purposes.

WOULD YOU DARE GIVE YOUR EXPENSIVE HOME AWAY?

◆ ◆ ◆

A personal residence trust (PRT) and qualified personal residence trust (QPRT) are specialized grantor retained income trusts (GRITs). These two planning tools may be used in giving away a high-value personal residence if the trade-offs fit your situation.

The PRT and QPRT allow you, as a homeowner, to establish a trust to irrevocably transfer a personal residence and retain, for a fixed period, a term interest in the trust. You retain the right to occupy the residence during the term interest. At the end of the term, the residuary passes to the remainder heirs.

The advantage of a PRT or a QPRT is that you make a completed gift at a reduced gift tax value and remove it from your estate. For example, assume that your residence is valued at $1,000,000, the selected term is 12 years, you do not retain a reversionary interest, you are 65 years old, and the applicable Internal Revenue Code interest rate is 7.4%. Based on this example, your taxable gift would be valued at $497,700. If your interest further provides that if you fail to survive the 12-year term, the trust property will pass as you direct by will or through your estate, then the value of the contingent reversionary interest further reduces the value of the gift from $497,700 to $284,120. If you survive the term, the value of the retained interest plus all posttransfer appreciation will be excluded from your gross taxable estate.

As in every planning decision, there are trade-offs. Use of a PRT or QPRT eliminates the step-up in basis. At the end of the term, continued use of the residence may cease. The QPRT or PRT may also be used for a second home or for a fractional interest in a residence.

The QPRT and PRT have different requirements. A PRT is a trust that cannot hold, during the term interest, any asset other than one personal residence for the term holder. A PRT allows commutation of a term holder's interest, which could be useful if you were likely to die during the term. The QPRT allows the trustee more flexibility than the PRT in what can be done with the residence. Changing laws and rulings require expert tax advice when selecting a PRT or QRT.

KEY POINTS TO REMEMBER: SPECIAL PROTECTION OF FAMILY BUSINESS, INVESTMENTS, FARMS, AND HOMES

◆ ◆ ◆

1. Prepare for an orderly succession in management and control. Your choice of a successor will determine whether your business will survive your demise.

2. Require that each member of the next generation earns a favored position of management or ownership in a family business or farm before transferring control to these prospective successors.

3. Seriously consider giving controlling interest in a family business or farm to one person in the next generation to avoid divisive management problems.

4. A buy-sell agreement may be the most important document to a business owner. A good buy-sell agreement should address what will happen in the event of death, disability, retirement, or change in relationship to the business. A buy-sell agreement guarantees that a decedent's beneficiaries will receive fair market value for the business and allows the remaining owners to own the business without undesirable or unqualified business associates. Disadvantages of a buy-sell agreement may be

foreclosing the alternative of retaining the business interest for family members and the risk of being locked into an unrealistic value.

5. Discounted value transfers may permit an interest in a closely held business to be gifted during life, or transferred at death, on a "discounted" basis. This planning method, if successful, will reduce estate value and taxes. Recent court decisions have permitted minority interest discounts of 25% and more in valuing the shares of stock in family-owned corporations for both gift and estate tax purposes.

6. Family limited partnerships, corporations, and limited liability companies are "tiger tools"—quiet, powerful, swift, and sure methods to transfer business, investment, and farm interests. Tax savings and asset protection may follow. Use requires irrevocable transfer of some ownership.

7. "Asset protection" is a theme with many dimensions. Irrevocable life insurance trusts often make sense to remove life insurance death benefits from your taxable estate and beyond the reach of creditors. Special needs trusts to insulate inheritance from government claims and qualify a person for Medicaid require transfer of control and loss of security and may be blocked by legislation or the courts. Foreign trusts may not work and require trade-offs which are generally unacceptably complex and unpredictable.

8. Special use valuation may save federal estate taxes when transferring farms and ranches. The Internal Revenue Code requires compliance with qualifying conditions before this tax relief is available.

9. The dynasty trust is a protective shield against creditors, serving to preserve as much as you can for as long as you can. Depending on state perpetuities laws, by the use of gift, estate, and generation-skipping tax exemptions, transfer taxes may be avoided upon creation. Eventually, when the trust property vests in the final beneficiaries, federal transfer taxes at 55% may be payable. Trustees may be given discretionary powers concerning distribution of income and principal. Income tax issues exist.

10. The 1997 tax act created an estate tax exclusion for Qualifying Family-Owned Businesses that is an apple seldom picked. Qualifying conditions limit its usefulness. Coincidence, not planning, will produce the most tax savings.

11. Pay estate taxes on closely held businesses in installments to save money.

12. The grantor retained income trust (GRIT) including the Personal Residence Trust (PRT) and Qualified Personal Residence Trust (PRQT) is an irrevocable trust created during your lifetime, in which you continue to receive the benefit for a term of years. If you live beyond the term, the asset will be excluded from your estate because you no longer own it. It is occasionally used in transferring a valuable home, vacation property, or artwork, but special conditions, limitations, and trade-offs exist.

Part
III
***

INHERITANCE PLANNING ALWAYS INCLUDES PERSONAL VALUES

Chapter 8

How to Determine and Carry Out Your Goals

Inheritance Planning

❖ ❖ ❖

Historically, the word *inheritance* has been of much more importance than the word *estate*. For example, in modern translations of the Old and New Testaments of the Bible, the word *inheritance* is written 233 times. The word estate does not appear once.

Typically, estate refers to your assets and liabilities at time of death. Your estate is basically your current financial statement. It is a legal- and tax-centered term devoid of human caring.

Inheritance refers to what your heirs receive. The word inheritance includes people. Inheritance is property and much more, such as the right to die, family business, retirement planning, life insurance, asset protection, guardians for children, inspirational bequests, anatomical gifts, values, and the organization of your life and death.

You are encouraged to expand your estate plan by considering other related issues. Inheritance planning applies a people-centered approach. The focus of Part Three tilts toward what the next generation of heirs will receive individually and collectively across the United States. How do other Americans plan? What works? What doesn't work? Inheritance is more than financial statements. Can you make a difference? Some personal vignettes are included to help direct your choices—and make planning an adventure in relationships.

WHY THE INHERITANCE BOOM IS IMPORTANT TO YOU
◆ ◆ ◆

Inheritance of property by the next generation will be the greatest wealth transfer in the history of the world—more than $11 trillion.

Many Americans of the World War II generation, ages 50 to 75, did well for themselves—very well. Hard work and perseverance were the commitments of the generation who fought on foreign shores. They came home and built the wealthiest nation in the world. According to economist Robert Avery of Cornell University the estimated personal net worth of Americans over 50 years of age is more than $8 trillion, not counting pensions and Social Security. Longer life, retirement accumulations, and inflation continue to increase the reservoir of wealth accumulations.

Currently nearly 70% of all wealth is in the hands of people over 50 years old. As these people die, their wealth will pass to a generation struggling to find and retain good jobs, or save money for their future. Thus inheritance becomes key in planning for both parents and children. Estate planners should include the children of their retired clients in estate-planning sessions. Never has the next generation had so much to gain or lose through the inheritance process.

The inheritance of this generation's property by the next generation will be the greatest wealth transfer in the history of the world. Never before have so many people of one nation stood to inherit so much. A family residence, jewelry, coin collections, vehicles, land, securities, and savings all become inheritance upon the death of the owner.

The very prosperity of America has created a new class of well-to-do families capable of passing along their good fortune to their children. Where once only the top 10–15% of families had significant wealth to bequeath, today it is the upper quarter or third of families. That means about twice the percentage of younger Americans now have a chance to inherit wealth than was the case in the 1950s and 1960s. Families with high incomes dominate this expanded upper-middle wealth class. But also included are some with only modest incomes: barbers and factory workers who saved diligently, invested wisely, or happened to own homes in cities with hot real estate markets.

To top it all off, the older generation also received a generous windfall from government entitlement programs. According to government estimates, people who retire now will receive from Social Security 2.5 times their contributions, and from Medicare 7 to 12 times their contributions. Baby-boomers may not make out nearly as well.

Another aspect of the inheritance boom applies to investors in stocks and bonds. The 1980–1990s stock price run-up has benefited a wide portion of the upper middle class, but especially older Americans in the top 1% wealth bracket who own about two-thirds of corporate equities held by households. The number of millionaires and decamillionaires (those worth $10 million) tripled between 1980 and 1998. Moreover, thanks to Reagan-inspired 1981 tax breaks, the number of estates subject to tax plummeted by two-thirds while estate tax rates on the wealthiest fell. (New tax proposals should be followed closely. Undoubtedly some will impact inheritance.)

As a result of these changes, today, wealth is becoming increasingly concentrated among the elderly (rather than those under 45). A great deal of wealth which younger families do have comes from transfers from living parents. Inheritance will constitute an increasing portion of the wealth of U.S. households because of the high concentration among the elderly. However, due to longer life spans, many children will inherit from their parents when they themselves are in their sixties or seventies.

Economists Edward Wolff of New York University and Daphne Greenwood of the University of Colorado looked at changes in the pattern of wealth among different age groups.[1] Wealth transferred to younger family members while the parents or grandparents were still alive comprised over 50% of the total wealth of all households under age 50. As the study indicates, inheritance and intergenerational transfers among the living are becoming increasingly important sources of wealth as we move to the close of the twentieth century. Demographic and economic trends suggest that their importance will only increase over the next few decades.

Another impact of these changes is that grandparents are skipping a generation and giving property directly to the grandchildren. Knowing that their children do not really need their patrimony, grandparents are cutting out the middleman and investing directly in their grandchildren. Some states have even set up special education investment schemes to capture the giving trend among the grandparents and parents. States such as Michigan, Wyoming, Wisconsin, and Florida have sold prepaid tuition packages for in-state public colleges and universities. A survey by Richard Anderson of Columbia University found that 25% of all those prepayment plans—and nearly 100% of them for kids under 12—were paid for by grandparents, over half of whom had incomes above $50,000. Fourteen percent of the tuition at private elementary and secondary schools is also paid for by grandparents.[2]

Many well-to-do grandparents take advantage of the annual gift tax exclusion to give property directly to adult grandchildren and into bank accounts under the Uniform Transfer to Minors Act for those not yet of legal age. There are two additional important gifting opportunities commonly overlooked. Gifts for medical care or school tuition are also exempt from gift taxes. Why not share the financial costs of education? Let grand-

---

[1] Greenwood, Daphne T. and Edward N. Wolff, "Changes in Wealth in the United States, 1962–1983: Savings, Capital Gains, Inheritance, and Lifetime Transfers," *Journal of Population Economics,* New York: Russell Sage Foundation; paper by Daphne Greenwood, January 5, 1992.

[2] *US News and World Report,* May 7, 1990, pp. 27–36.

parents pay college tuition, parents pay college room and board, and the student earn money for books, fees, and other expenses—a perfect three-generation pipeline and communication network to educate grandchildren.

DIRECTION: THE KEY TO ACHIEVING YOUR PLANNING GOALS

◆ ◆ ◆

Are you rushing from day to day accumulating assets, never taking time to consider their preservation or transfer? You may be in the flood waters of the inheritance boom and not even know it. Inheritance is a creative opportunity. Embrace it with enthusiasm. Your estate plan is your chance to have the last word. Take control of the transfer of your life's work. Don't leave it to luck. If you gamble instead of plan, your family and friends will be the losers.

Direction is the key to achieving your goals. Remember the lost traveler on a country road who asked a farmer how far it was to a certain town? The farmer answered, "If you continue the way you are headed, it will be about twenty-five thousand miles. If you turn around and go in the other direction, it will be three." Are you on the right road, going in the right direction? With accurate and predetermined objectives, giving to those you love should be a pleasant experience. It can also be a long and expensive journey in the wrong direction.

Accumulating wealth is like accumulating knowledge. It's nice to have and helpful to share. But federal and state taxes and estate administration expenses may siphon off a good deal of your assets before they reach your beneficiaries. You can make a difference in how, and how much, your beneficiaries inherit.

What do people consider when they leave their wealth to others? How do they feel when they become the recipients of wealth transfers?

"Whoever's in the house when I die gets it!"[3]

Bill Cosby has been America's most admired and highest-paid entertainer, the creator and star of the number one-rated television series *The Cosby Show,* and a dedicated family man with five children.

Cosby's two main interests in life have proved to be a desire to entertain his fellow human beings and a desire to teach them how to live. Most of the material in *The Cosby Show* expresses thoughts about family caring and giving. While some of Cosby's comments about family giving provide a humorous perspective, they also contain simple truths. Consider the following comments:

---

[3] Bill Cosby, *Fatherhood* (Garden City, NY: Doubleday, a Dolphin Book, 1986), pp. 85, 145, and 142. Reprinted with permission.

"Here's the whole challenge of being a parent. Even though your kids will consistently do the exact opposite of what you tell them to do, you have to keep loving them just as much. So to any question about your response to a child's strange behavior, there is really just one answer: give them love. I make a lot of money and I've given a lot of it to charities, but I've given all of myself to my wife and the kids, and that's the best donation I'll ever make.

"The flow of money between generations always seems to be a problem in American families. Now that my father is a grandfather, he just can't wait to give money to my kids. But when I was his kid and I asked him for fifty cents, he would tell me the story of his life: how he got up at four o'clock in the morning when he was 7 years old and walked 23 miles to milk 90 cows. And the farmer for whom he worked had no bucket, so my father had to squirt the milk into his little hand and then walk 8 miles to the nearest can. For five cents a month. And I never got the fifty cents. But now he tells my children every time he comes into the house, 'Well, let's just see if Granddad has some money for these wonderful kids.' And the moment they take the money out of his hand, I call them over and take it from them, because that's my money.

"I have told my family, whoever's in the house when I die, gets it!"

"Give your children enough money so that they feel they could do anything, but not so much that they could do nothing."[4]

The two sons and the daughter of Omaha investor Warren Buffett were raised with great wealth. Buffett, the chairman of Berkshire Hathaway, is worth at least $1.5 billion. But the Buffett children know they can expect to receive only a few hundred thousand dollars from their father's estate. Most of Buffett's fortune will go to his charitable foundation.

Buffett is withholding larger bequests to his children because he thinks setting children up "with a lifetime supply of food stamps just because they came out of the right womb" is a harmful and "an antisocial act." "My kids are going to carve out their own place in the world, and they know I'm for them whatever they want to do," but he wants them to achieve what they want on their own, not because of his money. So he's leaving them "enough so that they would feel they could do anything, but not so much that they could do nothing."

Buffett is following the same practice of giving limited amounts to his children while he is alive. He put them through college, and each child receives a gift of several thousand dollars at Christmas. "Love is the greatest advantage a parent can give," says Buffett.

Buffett expresses a philosophy about giving, and lives by it. He encourages the classic American value of self-reliance and the work ethic. His children have heard the message, and seem to have adopted these values in their own lives. His giving plan provokes thought.

---

[4] Kirkland, "Should You Leave It All to the Children?", *Fortune*, September 29, 1986, pp. 78–86.

Others, less wealthy, still have much to leave their families. Becky Montoya contributes $39,000 to her family's yearly income of $80,000. Growing up with Hispanic parents that she knows will leave her no inheritance, she is pleased that her hard work will enable her to pass on a modest inheritance to her four grown children. Her idea of inheritance is to give something meaningful and valuable to someone who is valued to her, specifically money or property.

"The love of our mothers and fathers is what we are passing on to our children," says Joanie Morgan, an Irish Catholic whose strong sense of family ties is most valued to her. "I long for my brothers and sisters...knowing I belong and I am cared for and matter to a lot of people...my family...is my inheritance." She also believes her own well-being can be attributed to a genetic inheritance. "It determines a lot of the good and bad characteristics we have."

WHAT DO YOU THINK ABOUT INHERITANCE?
◆ ◆ ◆

In a survey of American experiences, attitudes, and values regarding inheritance, questions were asked of a broad variety of people in the United States.[5] Although many economic and age groups were represented, the survey was directed toward those who would be most inclined to be interested in the matters of inheritance. These are affluent, educated, hard-working men and women. Most are "movers and shakers" who are financially mature, fluent with financial matters, and have money to leave their descendants. These people have thought about inheritance issues, and have a wide range of opinions. Portions of the survey follow.

---

[5] "A Survey of Americans' Experience, Attitudes and Values Regarding Inheritance," report prepared for Neuberger & Berman, July 1991, by The Gediman Research Group, Inc. Neuberger & Berman commissioned this research survey to examine individuals' views on inheritance and estate planning. Special emphasis was placed on covering information about peoples' attitudes, emotions, and values regarding this aspect of life experience. Two hundred four individual telephone interviews of approximately 45 minutes in length were conducted by the Gediman Research Group among the sample of (prospective) inheritance "givers" and "receivers." The sample for this research encompassed a broad array of demographic and socioeconomic variables and is representative of the United States as a whole in many ways (e.g., age, employment status, number of children, divorce). However, the sample differs significantly from the population in regard to gender, income, education, and (presumably) assets. Reproduced with permission from Neuberger & Berman and The Gediman Research Group, Inc., 626 Sixth Street, Stamford, CT 06905.

Attitudes About Inheritance Issues	Respondents with Estates of $500,000 or Less	Respondents with Estates of Over $500,000
Inheritance in a family invokes varying feelings, opinions and decisions. How would you answer the following questions?		
Regarding family generally...I feel		
I should pay more attention to planning what will become of my money after my death.	60%	42%
If I have taken care of my family while alive, they have no further obligation to me in their wills.	20	20
It is more important to build assets for my retirement than to worry about leaving an estate to my heirs; leaving money after my death is not that important to me.	66	65
People ought to give their money to their immediate families before money to nonrelatives or anyone else.	65	73
If a person leaves money to someone, and that individual is not a minor, there should be no stipulation or conditions attached to the inheritance.	43	58
Regarding spouse...		
Husbands and wives should leave everything to one another, letting the survivor make the final provisions for what happens to the assets on the survivor's death.	50	45

(continued on next page)

Attitudes About Inheritance Issues	*Respondents with Estates of $500,000 or Less*	*Respondents with Estates of Over $500,000*
An estate left to a spouse should be left in trust to protect it if the spouse remarries.	38	42

Regarding children…

Parents should leave money in trust for their children, so the children can use the income but the principal will remain intact.	52	51
Most children understand and accept when a parent leaves a substantial sum of money to charity, even if the inheritance is not as much as they expected.	20	17
Children who inherit money after they are educated but before they go out on their own are deprived of finding out what they can accomplish if they have to.	38	42
Providing an inheritance to my loved ones is important to me, even if it means sacrificing some comforts during my retirement years.	40	32
Inheritances have a tendency to cause conflicts in a family.	82	73
Before death, the heirs to an estate should know what they will inherit to avoid later conflict and controversy.	55	42
Parents should leave their estates in equal shares to their children, regardless of the children's financial circumstances.	57	64

(continued on next page)

Attitudes About Inheritance Issues	Respondents with Estates of $500,000 or Less	Respondents with Estates of Over $500,000
It is advisable to leave more to a daughter than a son because the daughter will probably earn less in her lifetime, or have less money of her own.	10	6
It is not necessary to leave the same amount of money to stepchildren as to your natural children.	34	39
A parent should consider his children's circumstances, leaving more money to those who are not likely to inherit from anyone else and less to those who will inherit from others.	46	29
It is not necessary to leave the same amount of money to your adopted children as to your biological children.	10	20

Regarding grandchildren...

Grandchildren, if any, should be provided for separately in a will, rather than leaving the money to your children and relying on them to provide for your grandchildren.	52	55
If a divorced or widowed son-in-law or daughter-in-law remarries, there is no longer the same obligation to provide for natural grandchildren in will.	13	9

(continued on next page)

Attitudes About Inheritance Issues	Respondents with Estates of $500,000 or Less	Respondents with Estates of Over $500,000
Thinking about wealth a different way now, suppose you (had) inherited enough money so that working would no longer be necessary. Would you continue/have continued to work the same way?		
No, would not continue to work the same way (would work less, travel/volunteer more, pursue interest, etc.)	63%	36%
Yes, would work the same as now.	43	34
No response.	7	3

How would you have responded to the following questions asked in the Survey of Americans' Experience, Attitudes and Values Regarding Inheritance conducted for Neuberger and Berman?

◆ How do you feel about some of the other questions raised in the survey?

◆ It is possible for individuals to pass on some of their assets while they are alive, rather than waiting until after they die. Do you think it is a good idea for people to do this?

◆ Looking at it the other way, have you transferred any assets to your heirs with an eye toward saving taxes on their inheritance? Is this something you might do in the future?

◆ Do you currently have a will? When was the last time it was updated? How comfortable are you with that? Please explain.

◆ People have different feelings about dealing with the subject of how to dispose of their assets after death. Which one of the following best describes your feelings?

"Is unpleasant, to be avoided."

"Must be taken care of even though it bothers me."

(continued on next page)

"Gives me good feelings of certain kinds."

♦ Should an estate left to a spouse would be left in trust to protect it if the spouse remarries?

♦ Should parents leave money in trust for their children, so the children can use the income but the principal will remain intact?

♦ If a person leaves money to someone, and that individual is not a minor, should stipulations or conditions be attached to the inheritance?

♦ Thinking about your children as heirs, do you plan to treat them equally or not?

♦ Should you leave the same amount of money to stepchildren as to your natural children?

♦ Is it advisable to leave more to a daughter than a son because the daughter will probably earn less in her life time, or have less money of her own?

♦ If you did not like the person one of your children married, would that affect your decisions about what you would leave that child as an heir?

♦ How would you compare the way you're planning to dispose of your assets with what your own parents did or are doing? Are you handling it...

"Pretty much the same way they did."

"Rather differently from them."

♦ What were your thoughts and feelings upon actually receiving an inheritance?

♦ One of the factors that may affect people's feelings about using or spending an inheritance is that it's money they didn't work for...also money that wasn't theirs before. How, if at all, did any considerations like these enter into the way you thought and felt about using your inheritance?

♦ Thinking of yourself in the role of the recipient, do you like the idea of getting money while the giver is still alive?

♦ How did it make you feel about the giver to receive assets while they were still alive? Did it influence your feelings about that person at all?

The Neuberger & Berman survey found that inheritance proceeds are used in quite conservative ways, and that creativity is limited. Here's how a sampling of Americans use their inheritance.

	Ways Used
Added to investments	61%
Added to operating funds	30%
Education fund	20%
Keep intact to pass on	20%
Pay off debts	16%
For home/hew home	13%
Charity	7%
Pay off mortgages	5%
Special purchases/pleasure	8%
Other (e.g., sharing with family, business/livelihood pursuits)	7%

Think about it. How do you feel about giving and receiving? Develop a philosophy and goals. Information is valuable only if used.

Chapter

9

COMMUNICATION
The Glue That Bonds

Communication is the glue that bonds your estate-planning pieces together: full disclosure with your estate planner; talking to your heirs; sharing philosophies and experiences; writing letters to your family and friends: funeral, burial, and anatomical gift instruction letters, an inheritance letter containing information your heirs will need after you are gone—any or all of these communications say you care. They will help prevent family feuds, help implement your goals, and bring peace of mind to you and the next generation.

After glancing through these model instruction letters you should be able to complete your own in 60 minutes or less. Use the following forms, or develop your own. You will be communicating with folks you care about. No estate planners or attorneys needed. No cost or time delays. Do it now.

INHERITANCE COMMUNICATION LINKS
Which Pattern Best Fits You?

Explanation of Links: You are the largest communication link because you are a concerned person. In this illustration, the estate planner includes the advisors you select to assist and implement your planning, such as an attorney, accountant, life underwriter, financial planner, and trust officer. Detached links show no communication, attached links show some communication.

INFORMATION FLOW CHART

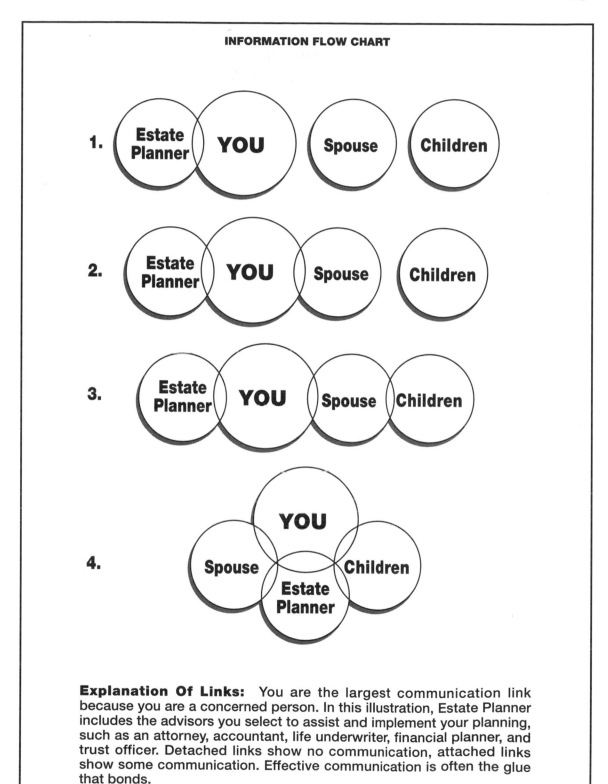

Explanation Of Links: You are the largest communication link because you are a concerned person. In this illustration, Estate Planner includes the advisors you select to assist and implement your planning, such as an attorney, accountant, life underwriter, financial planner, and trust officer. Detached links show no communication, attached links show some communication. Effective communication is often the glue that bonds.

FUNERAL AND BURIAL INSTRUCTION LETTER SAMPLE
❖ ❖ ❖

Dear Family and Friends,

Please follow these instructions as best you can. They are my final wishes concerning my funeral and burial. It is my hope that they will be instructive and save you time and agony in attending to these final arrangements.

Funeral/Burial Preferences

*Write Yes
or No*

_____   1. A postmortem examination may be made if deemed desirable or necessary.

_____   2. My body should be used for medical purposes as follows:

_____   3. I wish cremation with ashes to be disposed of as follows:

_____   4. I wish burial in the following location:

_____   5. I wish a memorial service with no casket present.

_____   6. I wish a funeral with (open casket) (closed casket).

_____   7. I wish a service as follows:

Location:

Clergy:

Music:

Scripture:

Special Messages:

Other

_____   8. Memorial gifts should be directed as follows:

_____   9. I request that the following information be included in notices of my death:

_____   10. Additional requests:

Dated: _____   Signed: _____

(Use additional paper for more instructions and expanded answers.)

ANATOMICAL GIFT LETTER SAMPLE

◆ ◆ ◆

I realize an anatomical gift may be made on forms available from various organizations, in my will, or even in some states on a driver's license. I further realize that any person of sound mind and at least 18 years of age may give all or any part of her or his body to a hospital, accredited medical or dental school, or bank or storage facility for medical or dental education, research, advancement of medical or dental science, therapy or transplantation, or a specified individual for therapy or transplantation.

I hereby give, at the time of death, any of my organs and tissues designated below that may be needed for transplantation, therapy, research or education:

_____ Any needed organ or tissue including my entire body.

_____ The following organs or tissues described _____

_____

I make these anatomical gifts to _____

(Name of hospital, bank, storage facility or physician)

If any anatomical gifts cannot be effectuated because of the inability or unwillingness to accept it, I request that one of the authorized persons make anatomical donations in a manner consistent with my desires expressed in this letter. If there is any conflict between the statements made in this letter and any other instructions regarding my burial, cremation or other disposition of my body, my wishes regarding anatomical gifts shall be given preference over my instructions regarding the disposition of my body. This letter is to be interpreted pursuant to anatomical gift laws of the state which has jurisdiction over my body.

My closest relatives, have been told of this anatomical gift. At my death, agree to immediately notify the appropriate authorities. If transportation does not extend to the locale of my death, I understand it will be up to my survivors to arrange for transporting my body and, if required, arrange for non-cosmetic embalming. I direct that all costs and expenses incurred be paid from my estate.

_____

Signature of Donor

Signed in the presence of the following witnesses who sign in the presence of each other:

1. _____   2. _____
Address _____   Address _____

_____   _____
Phone _____   Phone _____

Warning: Because the law regarding anatomical gifts may vary from state to state, this letter should be considered a sample only. You should check with authorities in your state to determine specific laws and forms required to achieve your anatomical gift goals.

Note: The first and last paragraphs of this letter are intended to show the writer's informed consent.

INHERITANCE INFORMATION FORM
◆ ◆ ◆

To Family and Administrators,

This is my Inheritance information you will need after I am gone. I realize it is not legally enforceable. It is intended as a compilation of information concerning my worldly affairs that may save you many hours of work and emotional agony. I thank you, and my inheritors thank you, for helping take care of these worldly affairs.

Name _____

First Things to Do

1. Call _____to help.
   (relative or friend)

2. Notify my employer: _____
   (phone)

3. Make arrangements with funeral home.

4. Request at least 10 copies of the death certificate. (Usually, the funeral director will get them).

5. Call our lawyers: _____
   (name, phone)

6. Contact local social security office.

7. Get and process my insurance policies.

8. Notify bank that holds our home mortgage.

Benefits You Can Expect

From my employer: _____
(Person to contact, dept. phone)

_____
(life insurance)   *(profit sharing)*

_____
(accident insurance)   *(pension plan)*

_____
(other benefits)

From insurance companies: _____
(total amount)

From Social Security: _____
(lump sum plus monthly benefits)

From the Veterans Administration: _____
(You must inform VA)

From other sources: _____

Social Security

Name: _____ Card Number: _____

Location of card: _____

File a claim immediately to avoid possibility of losing any benefit checks. Call local Social Security office for appointment. They tell you what to bring. _____
(phone)

Expect a lump sum of about $ ____ , plus continuing benefits for children under 18, or until 22 for full-time students.

Safe-Deposit Box

Bank: _____

Address: _____

In whose name: _____ Phone: _____

Location of key: _____

List of contents: _____

Post Office Box

Address: _____

Owners: _____

Number: _____

Location of key/combination: _____

Location of Personal Papers

Last will and testament: _____

Birth certificate: _____

Marriage certificate: _____

Military records: _____

Naturalization papers: _____

Other (adoption, etc.): _____

Checking Accounts

Bank: _____

Address: _____

Name(s) on account: _____

Account number: _____

Type of account: _____

(*Note:* You may need to repeat this information to cover all accounts of husband and wife.)

Canceled checks and statements are in: _____
                                      (location)

Savings Accounts and Certificates

Bank: _____

Address: _____

Name(s) on account: _____

Account number: _____

Type: _____

Location of passbook (or certificate receipt): _____

Any special instructions: _____

(*Note:* Repeat for each account.)

Doctors' Names/Addresses

Doctor(s): _____

(name, address, phone, whose doctor)

Dentist(s): _____

Pediatrician: _____

Children's dentist: _____

Credit Cards

All credit cards in my name should be canceled or converted to your name.

Company: _____ Phone: _____

Address: _____

Name on card: _____

Location of card: _____

(*Note:* Repeat for each card.)

Loans Outstanding (Other than Mortgage on Home)

Bank: _____

Address: _____

Name on loan: _____

Account number: _____

Monthly payment: _____

Location of papers: _____
                (and payment book, if any)

Collateral, if any: _____

Life insurance on loan? ❏ (yes) ❏ (no)

(*Note:* Repeat for all loans.)

Debts Owed to Me

Debtor: _____

Description: _____

Terms: _____

Balance: _____

Location of documents: _____

(*Note:* Repeat for each debt.)

Car

Year, make, and model: _____

Body type: _____

Cylinders: _____

Color: _____

Identification number: _____
               (title, registration)

(*Note:* Repeat for each car.)

Income Tax Returns

Location of all previous returns—federal, state, local: _____

_____

Our tax preparer: _____
             (name, address, phone)

Check: Are estimated quarterly taxes due?

Investments

Stocks

Company: _____

Name on certificate(s): _____

Number of shares: _____

Certificate number(s): _____

Purchase price and date: _____

Location of certificate(s): _____

(*Note:* Repeat for each investment.)

Bonds/Notes/Bills

Issuer: _____

Issued to: _____
                 (owner)

Face amount: _____ Bond number: _____

Purchase price and date: _____

Maturity date: _____

Location of certificate(s) _____

Mutual Funds

Company: _____

Name on account: _____

No. of shares or units: _____

Location of statement(s), certificate(s): _____

Funeral and Burial
(See separate Funeral and Burial Letter for important preferences)

Cemetery Plot

Location: _____

When purchased: _____

Deed number: _____

Location of deed: _____

Other information: _____
                 (perpetual care, etc.)

Facts for Funeral Director (bring this with you, and bring cemetery deed, if possible)

My Full Name: _____

Residence: _____ Phone: _____

Marital status: _____ Spouse: _____

Date of Birth: _____ Birthplace: _____

Father's name and birthplace: _____

Mother's maiden name: _____

Length of residence in state: _____ In U.S.: _____

Military service: ❑ (yes) ❑ (no)　When: _____

(Bring veterans' discharge papers if possible.)

Social Security number: _____ Occupation: _____

Burial Insurance (bring policy if proceeds will be used for funeral expenses):

_____

(company names and policy numbers)

Life Insurance

Location of all policies: _____

Policy: _____
　　　　(amount)

Whose life is insured: _____

Insurance company: _____

Company address: _____

Type of policy: _____ Policy number: _____

Beneficiaries: _____

Issue date: _____ Maturity date: _____

How paid out: _____

Your other options on payout: _____

Other special facts: _____

(Note: Repeat information above for each policy.)

For _____ in veterans' insurance call local
　　　(amount)

Veterans' Administration office: _____
　　　　　　　　　　　　　　　　(phone)

Other Insurance

Accident

Company: _____

Address: _____

Policy number: _____

Beneficiaries: _____

Coverage: _____

Location of Policy: _____

Agent, if any: _____

Car, Home, and Household

Coverage: _____

Company: _____

Address: _____

Policy number: _____

Location of policy: _____

Term (when to renew): _____

Agent, if any: _____

(*Note*: Repeat for each policy.)

Medical

Coverage: _____

Company: _____

Address: _____

Policy number: _____

Location of Policy: _____

Through employer or other group): _____

Agent, if any: _____

(*Note:* Repeat for all medical insurance policies.)

House, Condo, or Co-op

In whose name: _____

Address: _____

Lot: _____ Block: _____ On map called: _____

Other descriptions needed: _____

Location of statement of closing, policy of title insurance, deed, land survey, etc.:

_____

Mortgage

Held by: _____
        (bank)

Amount owed now: _____

Method of payment: _____

Location of payment book, if any (or payment statements): _____

_____

Life insurance on mortgage: ❏ (yes) ❏ (no)

If yes, policy number: _____

Location of policy: _____

Notify bank of my death. The unpaid amount will be paid automatically by the insurance, and the house is owned free and clear.

House Taxes

Amount: _____

Cost of house:

Initial buying price: _____

Itemized house improvements

Improvement: _____ Cost: _____ Date: _____

Location of bills: _____

If Renting: ❏ (yes) ❏ (no)

Lease location: _____ Expires: _____
                                               (date)

Household Contents

Names of owners: _____

Form of ownership: _____

Location of documents: _____

Location of inventory: _____

Important Warranties, Receipts

Item: _____

_____

(warranty location) (receipt location)

Additional Information and Wishes

_____

_____

_____

Dated: _____ Signed: _____

(You may attach additional papers or refer the recipients to other sources of information. If so, you should clearly note that you have done so in the letter.)

FAMILY AND FRIENDS LETTER SAMPLE
❖ ❖ ❖

The following letter was written by J. W. McMullen, M.D., to his family in 1952 when his children were very young. Dr. McMullen died in 1992. This letter exemplifies that a person's philosophy of life and values are timeless. His children and grandchildren included medical doctors and many other high achievers. It has been read and re-read by generations of the McMullen family who now desire to share it as an inspiration to others to write family letters. Last letters to family and friends become treasures to the next generation. Do it now.

My Dearest Family,

I am writing this letter to you now so that in case that I precede you in death it will serve as something of a guide—first as to what I wish done with my remains and second as advice concerning any estate that has been left you.

When my life on this earth ends I wish the processes of nature to take place with as little trouble as possible. I wish my going to be as painless and economical as possible to my family. I have long felt the pagan-like custom of embalming and keeping the remains on public display longer than necessary to be an unkind trial for a sorrowing family. I realize that state laws being what they are that embalming is a must. That isn't so bad. I object more to the unnecessary expense of a casket and all the trimmings that go with it. Money spent for a lavish funeral, and all funerals these days seem excessively lavish, is money spent wastefully. It serves no useful purpose except lining the pocket of the "funeral director." Better that it be spent for the education of children. If not the deceased's then someone elses. Generally the widow or the family of the widow needs the extra money. The idea of burying several hundred dollars worth of casket to me seems utterly ridiculous. I believe it would be best for all concerned if my remains were to be cremated. At least if it can be done more reasonably than the conventional burying ceremony. I regret that in this country that it is practically unheard of to bury an unembalmed body so that it may really return to dust with the least possible trouble. So if it does not prove embarrassing to my family, I would prefer to be cremated, then to have the ashes disposed of in the easiest way possible. The idea always appealed to me to have my ashes dropped into the Missouri River from the Brownville Bridge or to have them scattered from an airplane over the home farm. Since such a thing might seem like a queer request, I do not want this desire to be an ironclad demand. In lieu of the above it would probably be best to dispose of the remains in the smallest cheapest available plot or crypt in a VA cemetery. Would that one could simply take a post hole auger, bore a 6 foot hole and drop the small urn of ashes to the bottom.

Another unfortunate custom that exists is that of having a large ornate and expensive tombstone marking a grave. There are so many better ways of remembering loved ones. My parents wanted to live in the memory of their children, I am sure, for the work they had done and the sacrifices they made. They did not want this remembrance in the form of an expensive casket and tombstone. Revere the memory but do not worship a fancy marker or the plot of ground. Better for mankind to destroy all cemeteries and plant corn or something that is productive. I have had as great a reverence for my mother as anyone but I have had little or no desire to visit her grave. I don't believe that it has even been marked—I couldn't find it the last time I looked for it some years ago. She wanted her monument to be a live one—her children.

I have always loved flowers and the things that grow on this earth but here again I feel that money spent for funeral flowers is money that could be spent for a better purpose. I know that the money spent for camp time for underprivileged children would bring more happiness to this world. Or give it to a hospital—they always can use money.

A funeral service is almost a must these days. There is nothing particularly objectionable about this but I do want it to be simple. If there has to be a sermon, let it be on the wonders and beauty of nature, not a eulogy on traits that I didn't possess.

To summarize: I wish the least expensive method of burial; the most sensible type of crypt or plot that is available and no flowers.

It was always my hope that you, Charlotte, would never have a financial worry after my death. With the degree of inflation that has gone on during the past ten years I cannot be sure that any plans that I have made in recent years may not have gone awry before they could be put into effect. Since you had to be without a father during much of your adolescent and adult life, you had an ample opportunity to learn the value of money. Your financial judgment has always been good—this has been proven in the way you handled the purchase of two houses, the buying of furniture—any major expenditure that you have made has always turned out to be a wise one. You have had the courage to take steps that I was fearful to take and always your judgment proved excellent. To be sure, your investment tendencies have tended to be ultraconservative mostly because of some speculations made by Aunts and Uncle that turned out sour. Your conservativeness would not have paid off the past ten years, tho that is no sign that it may not during the next ten years. Common stock has been one of the best things that a person can own the last decade. Perhaps the next decade this will not hold true, but in view of the great degree of inflation that occurred and cannot help but continue to occur, stock still seems to be a good investment. I hope that in time you will be convinced that owning common stock is a sound investment program as long as the U.S. Gov't continues to permit private ownership. Mutual funds are probably the best device whereby a widow can keep her money invested and supervised at a not too excessive price. I feel sure that your brothers can advise you on investment matters tho I suspect that your judgment is equally good. Remember that it is a simple matter to sell shares of common stock or shares of a mutual fund thru a broker.

At whatever time my death occurs, it will probably greatly curtail your income and thus your standard of living. I feel that a considerable sacrifice in the standard of living is indicated if money is needed for the education of children. We did not live lavishly and it was by your cooperation in large part that this was so. You did without maids, fur coats, expensive entertainment, expensive vacations that most other women in similar conditions learned to expect. We generally lived below the standards of people making similar amounts of money. I appreciated this. None-the-less, we spent a good deal more than was really necessary and corners could have been cut had we seen a real need for it. I believe that you have the facility to be happy whether rich or poor.

Cars are one of the world's greatest luxuries and as you have heard me remark—anything more than a Ford, Chev. or Plymouth is salving the ego. There is no good reason except pride that the modern car cannot be used for ten yrs. or more. A car costs, according to present day estimates, about $40 per mo. counting depreciation, taxes, upkeep and so on. Unless you have a fairly generous income, a car is a luxury. Taxis are cheaper and so are buses.

Another luxury for a family of five is the house that was our home for some years at 1528 Wood Ave. unless income stays high. Present taxes amount to $43 per mo. Utilities amount to $25 per mo. Repairs on a house of this size and age amount to 1-2% for an average of some $350 a year or $30 per month. Fire insurance costs $10 per mo. Phone bills run $5.50 per mo. These items alone run about $115 per mo. and take a big chunk out of a reduced income. Unless you feel that you can happily convert to apartments or rent rooms—both ideas would cause a lot of grief—I believe that it would be wiser to sell the big house and buy a smaller 3 bedroom home in a lower tax area.

A reduction in income may be a blessing in disguise. Of course, it means harder work, fewer pleasures bought with money and more cooperation in the family group. The most good that could be expected would be to the children's advantage. Too often too much money means selfishness and idleness. I feel that much of your kindness, thoughtfulness and sensible ways were the result of having to sacrifice and share with a family that had suffered a great loss of income. To be sure, a lot of these traits came from your father and mother and some you were born with. But a lot of them came as a result of the struggle that you all had after your father's death. If it becomes necessary, I hope you will be able to transmit the same desirable characteristics to our children. At times I feel sure that they have had more than has been good for them—too much given to them without realizing where it came from. In other words, they have been spoiled some. I feel certain that I depended too much on my mother, and that after her death I became more self reliant.

My greatest hope is that you will be able to pass on to our children your greatest asset— the ability to get along with people and to be liked by them. This I believe has been the strongest asset that the Capp family has had and has done them more good than all the formal education they have been given. Children, observe your Uncle Jack to see what I mean. The ability to talk to people, to be pleasant to them, to have them like you, will do more to make you happy in this world than any other thing. It is worth dollars and cents to you in any business or profession. This endowment passed on to the Capp children has made them stand above the rest of their fellowmen.

Children, remember that the average individual, to be happiest and to get the farthest in this world, must have a good education. Some persons endowed with exceptional traits can overcome this lack of formal education, but such people are unusual unless they have the ability to be supersalesmen or have uncanny business ability. Skimping on nonessentials will pay off in the long run if money is needed for education.

My parents made great sacrifices to give my brothers and me an education. They denied themselves many of the niceties of life that most people thought were essentials. The money saved was for one major purpose—that of higher education. I would probably never have had the chance to go to medical school had not my father made big sacrifices for us. Their great objective was to give all their children all the education that they desired. Educational degrees are becoming more and more important these days in getting jobs. Without them, unless one has unusual ability as a seller or business man, it is difficult for anyone to earn a satisfactory income. I don't mean by this that a large income is necessary for happiness; however, I believe that the people that earn at least the national average are happier than those earning below the national average.

My father and mother never made any attempt to push us into any particular field of work. It was our life to live so we should be the ones to make the decision. They did want however to be able to help as much as possible after that field was picked. It is better to be a happy and good carpenter than an unhappy millionaire. It has been my hope to also be able to leave the means for anyone of you to be able to pursue any field of endeavor that you desire. I cannot leave you enough to purchase a large business which you might run, but I may be able to leave enough for you to get a professional education whereby you will be able to gain a good living. You should pick a life work that you really like and not on what you have been pushed into. You children have inherited mentalities that are not much, if any, above average nor, on the other hand, are they below average. By working hard I am sure that any one of you can master law, engineering or medicine or any one of several professions. If you don't like meeting people and the public as I did not, there are fields where these things can be minimized. In medicine, pathology and radiology are good examples. Owning and running a business of your own is admirable but usually means extremely hard work and generally means raising a good deal of capital initially.

We have tried to live considerably below the standard of living that we could have probably afforded because it is unlikely that any of you will have the good luck to have as much money—and believe me luck has a good bit to say in this regard. Too many persons become accustomed to living high then are unhappy later on when they cannot maintain that level after they are married and starting out on their own. Learn to be content with spending only a part of what you make and always save something. Your grandparents have all been economy minded in spite of recent trends federally and in the people as a whole to not save for a rainy day and to expect the government to take care of them. They have not skimped for books, healthful entertainment and gracious living, but they, as I and your mother have, greatly object to wasting money on movies, tobacco and liquor. I cannot emphasize too strongly how wasteful the habit of smoking is or how disastrously the habit of drinking may turn out. I sincerely hope that you will develop neither habit. For your sake, and your mother's sake.

Be kind to your mother and to each other. Stand up for each other always.

> Your loving husband and father,
> J. W. McMullen, M.D.

Personalized Will

◆ ◆ ◆

"In this document I can only give you things, but if I had the choice to give you worldly goods or character, I would give you character."[1]

Jack Kelly enjoyed success as an Olympic champion and businessman, but never lost his sense of values or humor. His daughter, Grace Kelly, became a famous movie actress and later princess of the country of Monaco. His son also participated in the Olympics. His will became his last opportunity to communicate with his family. In part of his will, he wrote:

---

[1] Menchin, Roberts, *The Last Caprice,* Simon & Schuster, 1963, pp. 112–116; Encyclopedia Britannica, 1986, vol. 6, pp. 790–791.

I can think of nothing more ghastly than the heirs sitting around listening to some representative reading a Will. They always remind me of buzzards and vultures awaiting the last breath of the stricken. Therefore, I will try to spare that ordeal and let you read the Will before I go to my reward—whatever it will be. I do hope that it will never be necessary to go into Court over spoils, for to me the all-time low in family affairs is a court fight, in which I have seen families engage. If you cannot agree, I will direct that the executor or trustees, as the case may be, shall decide all questions of administration or distribution, as the executor and trustees will be of my choosing or yours....

I will try to give each of you all I can during my life so that you will have money in your own right—in that way—you will not be wholly dependent on my bequest. I want you all to understand that U.S. Government Bonds are the best investment even if the return is small, and then come Commonwealths and Municipals, that have never failed to meet their interest charges. As the years gather you will meet some pretty good salesmen who will try to sell you everything from stock in a copper or gold mine to some patent that they will tell you will bring you millions, but remember, that for every dollar made that way, millions have been lost. I have been taken by this same gentry but that was perhaps because I had to learn from experience—when my father died, my hopes were high, but the exchequer low, and the stock market was on the other side of the railroad tracks, as far as I was concerned.

I have written this Will in a lighter vein because I have always felt that Wills were so dreary that they might have been written by the author of "Inner Sanctum" and I can see no reason for it, particularly in my case. My family is raised and I am leaving enough so they can face life with a better than average start, financially.

As for me, just shed a respectful tear if you think I merit it, but I am sure that you are all intelligent enough not to weep all over the place. I have watched a few emotional acts at graves, such as trying to jump into it, fainting, etc. but the thoroughbred grieves in the heart.

Not that my passing should occasion any scenes for the simple reason that life owes me nothing. I have ranged far and wide, have really run the gamut of life. I have known great sorrow and great joy. I had more than my share of success. Up to this writing my wife and children have not given me any heartaches, but on the contrary, have given me much happiness and a pardonable pride, and I want them to know I appreciate that. I worked hard in my early life, but I was well paid for that effort.

In this document I can only give you things, but if I had the choice to give you worldly goods or character, I would give you character. The reason I say that, is with character you will get worldly goods because character is loyalty, honesty, ability, sportsmanship and, I hope, a sense of humor.

If I don't stop soon, this will be as long as *Gone With the Wind,* so just remember, when I shove off for greener pastures or whatever it is on the other side of the curtain, that I do it unafraid and, if you must know, a little curious.

Jack Kelly signed his will on April 14, 1960, with his standard flourish of green ink. He died two months later at the age of 70.

Jack Kelly was right. Wills are cluttered with legal terms and what the trade calls "boilerplate" (verbose, and often unnecessary, language). High-technology word processors have compounded the problem, because now long-winded documents are usually stored on hard or floppy disks for rapid-fire modification and repetitious use. Why not include philosophy and affection in estate planning documents? Children need to hear more expressions of values. You should not be embarrassed or intimidated when a lawyer discourages personalizing a will. Write your thoughts on paper and ask they be included. Or write a separate letter to your heirs, to be opened only after you are pushing up daisies.

TRANSFER PERSONAL VALUES

Every estate plan reflects transfers of personal values, good or bad, to future generations. Values are not permanent. They must continuously be strengthened, changed, or redefined. Consider leaving a lasting written reminder of the personal values you believe to be most important. Transfer these same values during your lifetime. Although a Personal Values Will is not a legal document, it does offer an interesting communication link. Consider the following form as a starter.

PERSONAL VALUES WILL[2]

If I had the choice to give personal values or worldly goods, I would give personal values. With personal values you will get worldly goods and much more. Personal values include loyalty, honesty, ability, compassion, sportsmanship and, I hope, a sense of humor.

I have run the gamut of life, fortunately with exceptional family and friends. During my lifetime I tried to make a difference. Hopefully, I have had some success in giving to future generations the personal values I believe to be important. While actions are always better than words, by the time you read this, I will be in greener pastures on the other side of the hill. Perhaps these words will remind you of choices.

I give the following personal values to those who accept them:

- ◆ Religious Faith   (explain if desired)

- ◆ Loyalty   (explain if desired)

- ◆ Honesty   (explain if desired)

---

[2] Permission granted to the reader to copy and adapt this Personal Values Will to express the personal values you wish to transfer. Developed from personal value transfer studies by Fountain Institute, Colorado Springs, Colorado, and some wording borrowed from or inspired by the Last Will of John B. Kelly, Sr.

- ◆ Work Ethic   (explain if desired)

- ◆ Curiosity   (explain if desired)

- ◆ Compassion   (explain if desired)

- ◆ Sportsmanship   (explain if desired)

- ◆ Sense of Humor   (explain if desired)

- ◆ Creativity   (explain if desired)

- ◆ Other   (explain if desired)

If I don't stop soon, this will be as long as my worldly goods Will, heaven forbid. See you on the other side of the hill.

_____   _____

Date   Signature

_____

Place

KEY POINTS TO REMEMBER: COMMUNICATION

1. Fully disclose your goals, family information, and financial situation to your qualified estate planner.

2. Complete a funeral and burial instructions letter now.

3. Write final letters to family and friends now.

4. Complete an Inheritance Information Form to provide instructions and information to your estate administrators and loved ones.

5. Prepare your own Personal Values Will now. Review and change it regularly. Transfer the same values while you are alive. Make sure selected loved ones and friends read it now or later.

Chapter 10

MEDICAL TREATMENT, THE RIGHT TO DIE, AND ANATOMICAL GIFTS

A few months before his heart attack, Edward H. Winter watched the slow, agonizing death of his wife of 55 years, who had suffered brain damage after shock resuscitation from a heart attack of her own, and he resolved that nothing like that would happen to him. When his time came, he told his children, they should simply let him die. He told his doctor the same thing.

Winter was visiting friends at a Cincinnati center for the elderly when he felt chest pains and collapsed. In the hospital's coronary care unit, he told his doctor that should his condition worsen, he did not want to be resuscitated. Winter gave the same instructions to his three daughters. His doctor entered those instructions on Winter's chart, but the instructions were not recorded on the monitor by Winter's bed. Thus, three days later, when he began experiencing ventricular fibrillations that signal sudden death, a nurse applied electrodes to his chest and revived him.

Winter would probably have died of the heart attack, when he was 82, if the nurse at St. Francis–St. George Hospital in Cincinnati had not revived him. In some ways, the case of Edward H. Winter is a miracle of modern medicine. He marked his 84th birthday with his daughters and grandchildren. It was not the fate Winter wanted, since two days after he was revived, he suffered a debilitating stroke. Winter was angry over what happened. His daughter stated: "He said he could have died in peace if they had left him alone and that now he was completely dependent. He was upset being the way he was. My father is a pretty staunch Catholic, and would never have taken his own life, but he didn't believe in dragging people back to life."

For Winter, things turned out to be even more nightmarish than he imagined, and Winter filed a lawsuit accusing the hospital of wrongfully saving his life, perhaps the first "wrongful life" case filed by a patient. The suit, brought in the Hamilton County Court of Common Pleas, accused the hospital of negligence for failing to follow Winter's instruction and with battery for giving him a jolt of electricity without his authorization. If it hadn't been for the hospital's intervention, he charged, he could have died, and with dignity.

Winter's medical bills spiraled over $100,000 by his 84th birthday. His life savings were depleted. His doctors gave him little chance for physical improvement, but said he could live for years. The hospital took the position that saving a life can never be considered, in legal terms, an injury that can be compensated. The case was settled out of court after Mr. Winter's death.[1]

The bad news is that, in the case of Mr. Winters, his last illness medical directives did not work. The good news is that health care providers are becoming more educated in life and death situations.

THE "RIGHT TO DIE": COMMUNICATION IS KEY

◆ ◆ ◆

You have a "right to die," but your desire to exercise your right should be clearly expressed while you are competent.

Communications to hospitals, doctors, and nurses are all important. You must clearly express your wishes to control and direct your medical treatment under last illness conditions. Do it through living wills, health care powers of attorney, other written documents, letters, and verbal statements. Tell your family, hospitals, doctors, and nurses, and then tell them again.

The intertwining of legal, medical, religious, ethical, and personal values will always make the right to die a topic of discussion and controversy. As medical science extends life, and the associated financial and family requirements, life and death will increasingly affect inheritance.

---

[1] *The New York Times*, March 18, 1990; *Colorado Springs Gazette Telegraph*, March 18, 1990, p. A4.

WHAT YOU NEED TO KNOW ABOUT THE PATIENT SELF-DETERMINATION ACT

❖ ❖ ❖

Recognizing that most states have statutes that define an individual's right to accept or refuse medical or surgical treatment and right to formulate advance directives, such as through the appointment of an agent or surrogate to make decisions on his or her behalf ("durable power of attorney") and written instructions about health care ("living wills"), Congress enacted the Patient Self-determination Act of 1990 as part of the Budget Reconciliation Act of 1990.[2] The Act provides that hospitals, skilled nursing facilities, home health agencies, hospice programs, HMOs/CMPs, other prepaid organizations, and comprehensive outpatient rehabilitation facilities receiving Medicare and Medicaid funds must provide adult individuals with written information concerning an individual's rights under state law to make decisions concerning medical care, including the right to accept or refuse medical or surgical treatment and the right to formulate advance directives. The provider or organization is required to document in the individual's medical record whether or not the individual has executed an advance directive. The provider organization is required to ensure compliance with requirements of state law, respecting advance directives at facilities of the provider or organization. The act provides, however, that it shall not be construed to prohibit the application of a state law that allows for an objection on the basis of conscience for any health care provider, or any agent of such provider, which as a matter of conscience cannot implement an advance directive.

Because an advance directive or living will states your wishes concerning life-sustaining treatment, it is the best evidence as to when you want life-sustaining procedures withdrawn and withheld. In fact, in light of the Patient Self-determination Act and the numerous state statutes governing the right to die, if you don't state in writing that you do not want life-sustaining treatment, the presumption may be that you do. Act now.

PUT YOUR WISHES IN WRITING

❖ ❖ ❖

Cardiopulmonary Resuscitation Directives

States are passing new laws relating to cardiopulmonary resuscitation (CPR). By signing the necessary paperwork initiating a CPR directive, patients can document their wishes to refuse CPR and can be sure that emergency medical service personnel and first responders are aware of those wishes.

---

[2] P.L. 101-508, 104 Stat. 1388 (1990).

This is important to physicians. Unlike the living will or a medical durable power of attorney for health care decisions, which can be completed in full by the patient and require no physician signature, the CPR advance directive is typically valid only when signed by a physician. This emerging new law recognizes the attending physician's role in the process of initiating CPR.

CPR directives may not be appropriate for everyone. While legislation in some states provides this option only to the frail elderly or to the terminally ill, other states allow persons over the age of 18 to execute a CPR directive. Still there are many for whom a CPR directive would be premature. The physician must provide clear explanations of the procedures which constitute CPR and discuss the risks and benefits of withholding or providing CPR. These laws are becoming increasingly complex, and involving more physician and medical staff time. CPR directives will probably be useful in very limited special medical circumstances.

Health Care Power of Attorney (Proxy)

A health care power of attorney (also called a medical power of attorney or health care proxy) is a written document authorizing someone you name (your "agent" or "attorney in fact") to make health care decisions for you in the event you are unable to speak for yourself. The document can also contain instructions or guidelines you want your agent to follow.

Should you ever lose your capacity to make or communicate decisions because of a temporary or permanent illness or injury, the health care power of attorney lets you retain some control over important health care decisions by choosing a person to make and communicate these decisions for you. Without a formally appointed person, many health care providers and institutions will make critical decisions for you, not necessarily based on what you would want. In some situations, a court-appointed guardian may become necessary unless you have a health care power of attorney, especially where the health care decision requires that money be spent for your care.

Your health care power of attorney can also include a statement of your wishes and preferences regarding specific medical decisions. The existence of the document can relieve some of the stress or conflict that otherwise might arise if family or friends have to decide on their own what you would want done when you cannot speak for yourself.

What Is the Difference Between a Health Care Power of Attorney and a "Living Will"?[3]

A living will is a written statement of your wishes regarding the use of any medical treatments you specify. The statement is to be followed if you are unable to provide instruc-

---

[3] *Health Care Powers of Attorney,* Commission on Legal Problems of the Elderly, American Bar Association, Public Services Division (1990).

tions at the time the medical decision needs to be made. Living wills have been recognized by law in most states, but they are commonly limited to decisions about "life-sustaining procedures" in the event of "terminal illness."

The health care power of attorney is different from and more flexible than the living will in three important ways:

1. A health care power of attorney establishes a person to act as your agent if you cannot act, but a living will does not. The advantage of appointing an agent is that, at the time a decision needs to be made, your agent can participate in discussions and weigh the pros and cons of treatment decisions in accordance with your wishes.

2. The health care power of attorney applies to all medical decisions, unless you decide to include limitations. The living will normally applies only to particular decisions near the end of your life.

3. The health care power of attorney can include specific instructions to your agent about any treatment you want done or want to avoid or about whatever issues you care most about.

Logic would encourage combining the living trust and health care power of attorney in one document. However, law often develops more historically than logically. The living will was developed first. Therefore, the documents are often prepared separately and require different formalities for signing.

Health care powers of attorney are a variation of the ordinary "power of attorney". Ordinary powers of attorney allow an individual to give legal authority to another to handle business or property transactions for the principal. During the last 20 years or so, every state and the District of Columbia have enacted durable power of attorney statutes that allow power of attorney for property to remain in effect even if the person later becomes mentally incapacitated. This "durability" element is very helpful in health care decision making for incapacitated persons. Many legal scholars believe that existing durable power of attorney statutes are broad enough in principle to include health care decision-making powers within their scope. But, to eliminate uncertainty and to build in protection for patients, an increasing number of states are enacting statutes that clearly recognize health care powers of attorney, and many of these states provide special forms and procedures for creating the document. Separate health care powers of attorney also carry important "moral weight and judgment." You are best advised to execute a separate health care power of attorney.

Up-to-date information about health care powers of attorney (and living wills) in your state, along with statutory forms, if they exist in your state, can be obtained from Concern for Dying/Society for the Right to Die, 250 West 57th Street, New York, NY 10107.

Following is a simple statutory form power of attorney for health care. This particular form may not satisfy the legal requirements in your state or meet all of your individual needs. Take the time to consider all possibilities and seek competent advice. Locate the form used in your state and use it. Do not use the following form without first seeking legal advice.

DURABLE POWER OF ATTORNEY FOR HEALTH CARE SAMPLE

❖ ❖ ❖

I, _____, hereby appoint:

as my agent to make health care decisions for me if and when I am unable to make my own health care decisions. This gives my agent the power to consent to giving, withholding or stopping any health care, treatment, service, or diagnostic procedure. My agent also has the authority to talk with health care personnel, get information, and sign forms necessary to carry out those decisions.

If the person named as my agent is not available or is unable to act as my agent, then I appoint the following person to serve:

By this document I intend to create a power of attorney for health care which shall take effect upon my incapacity to make my own health care decisions and shall continue during that incapacity.

My agent shall make health care decisions as I direct herein or as I make known to her or him in some other way.

Special provisions and limitations: _____

_____

_____

_____

_____

BY SIGNING HERE, I INDICATE THAT I UNDERSTAND THE PURPOSE AND EFFECT OF THIS DOCUMENT.

Dated _____, 199

_____

Witnesses

The foregoing instrument was signed or and declared by _____, to be his/her declaration, in the presence of us, who in his/her presence, in the presence of each other, and at his/her request, have signed our names below as witnesses, and we declare that, at the time of the execution of this instrument, the declarant, according to our best knowledge and belief, was of sound mind and under no constraint or undue influence.

I further declare that I am not related to the patient by blood, marriage, or adoption, and, to the best of my knowledge, I am not entitled to any part of his estate under a will now existing or by operation of law.

Dated at _____, _____, this _____ day of _____, 199 .

_____   _____

_____   _____

_____   _____
                Address   Address

STATE OF _____)

                                : ss.

COUNTY OF _____)

SUBSCRIBED and sworn to before me by _____ and _____ and _____, witnesses, as the voluntary act and deed of the declarant, this _____ day of _____, 199___.

My commission expires:

_____
                Notary Public

Warning: Because the law regarding medical treatment may vary in each state, this form should be considered a sample only. You should check with authorities in your state to determine specific laws and forms required to achieve your medical treatment goals.

Gifts of the Body Are Legacies of Life
❖ ❖ ❖

When Margo Molthan insisted on marrying Mike, her high school sweetheart, her parents were understandably upset. The groom was a mere 20-year-old and Margo was still a teenager.

Fortunately for Margo her parents were wrong. Not only has the marriage survived happily for two decades, but Margo proved that when she promised to love Mike in "sickness and in health, for better or for worse," she wasn't kidding, even when it meant donating one of her own kidneys to her ailing husband.

Mike's health problems began in his early twenties, when he passed some excruciatingly painful kidney stones. A nephrologist diagnosed glomerulonephritis, a progressive kidney disease with no known cure.

Despite the grim prognosis, Mike felt fine for several years. In his thirties, however, his kidneys began deteriorating rapidly and Mike faced the grim prospect of a lifetime wedded to a dialysis machine, unless a suitable donor for transplant was located.

Since there is a long waiting list for kidneys and the chance of rejection is high, the ideal donor would have been one of Mike's two sisters. Both offered Mike a kidney, but Mike's older sister was the wrong blood type and his younger sister showed some signs that she, too, might be a candidate for renal disease.

Margo, who had the same blood type as Mike, volunteered her kidney.

At first, Mike resisted the idea. But after lengthy discussions with Margo and their two sons, he began to accept the idea.

The surgery was successful and, today, Mike no longer suffers from terrible headaches, muscle spasms, and bouts of diarrhea and vomiting. He is full of energy and zest for work and home life. Margo's gift to her husband has been one of health, and now Margo and Mike are again enjoying "for better" days in their marriage. As Margo explains; "We joke that we can't get divorced because we'd never be able to agree to who'd get custody of our kidney."

Shocking Footnote: Lois Duncan, who wrote about the Molthans' story, added a shocking additional chapter from her own family when she reported the following: "When I returned from a trip to Texas where I had interviewed the Molthans I told my family about the great need for organ donors. My 18-year-old daughter, Kaitlyn Arquette, immediately completed a donor card. The following month Kait was chased down in her car and shot twice in the head. She died twenty hours later; five of her organs were transplanted. I received a wonderful letter from the mother of the young man who received her heart and lungs. It's a comfort to us to know Kait did not die an empty death. I hope your book will inspire other healthy young people to sign donor cards."[4]

POSTHUMOUS GIFTS OF THE BODY

❖ ❖ ❖

Margo Molthan made her organ gift during her lifetime. An anatomical gift at death asks less of the donor, but equally serves the recipient. There are rapidly increasing unmet needs for anatomical gifts of human organs, such as eyes, kidneys, hearts, other organs, tissue, bone marrow, or entire bodies.

An anatomical gift of all or part of the human body may also be made for the purpose of research or education, in addition to transplantation.

Any person of sound mind and at least 18 years of age may give all or any part of his or her body upon death to (1) a hospital, surgeon or physician for medical or den-

---

[4] Lois Duncan, "The Ultimate Gift," *Woman's Day,* October 3, 1989, p. 74.

tal education, research, advancement of medical or dental science, therapy, or transplantation; (2) an accredited medical or dental school, college, or university for education, research, advancement of medical or dental science, or therapy; (3) a bank or storage facility for medical or dental education, research, advancement of medical or dental science, therapy, or transplantation; or (4) a specified individual for therapy or transplantation needed by him or her.

An anatomical gift may be made by will. The gift becomes effective upon death without waiting for probate of the will. If your anatomical gift is made by will, make sure you let your family know of your bequest so that the donation can be made immediately after your death. Otherwise, by the time your will is located and read, the opportune time for the donation may have passed.

In most states, there is a form for an anatomical gift on the back of each driver's license, provisional license, and identification card issued by the state as follows:

DRIVER'S LICENSE ANATOMICAL GIFT SAMPLE
◆ ◆ ◆

I hereby give, at the time of my death, any of my organs and tissues designated below that may be needed for transplantation, therapy, research, or education.

I give:

    A. Any needed organ or tissues   Dated: _____

    B. Organs or tissue listed: _____

Signature of Donor: _____ HLA typing (if known): _____

Witness: _____ Witness: _____

One drawback to the use of this form is that the gift is deemed revoked on the expiration date of the driver's license to which it is attached or at any time the license is revoked or suspended.

An anatomical gift can also be made by a document other than a will or license. The document may be a card designed to be carried on the person. Forms are available from hospitals, medical schools, anatomical gift organizations, and some doctors' offices.

KEY POINTS TO REMEMBER:
MEDICAL TREATMENT, THE RIGHT TO DIE,
AND ANATOMICAL GIFTS
◆ ◆ ◆

1. A health care power of attorney is the most important written document authorizing someone you name to make health care decisions for you in the event you are unable to speak for yourself.

2. Your health care power of attorney can also include a statement of your wishes and preferences regarding specific medical decisions.

3. The existence of the document can relieve some of the stress or conflict that otherwise might arise if family or friends have to decide on their own what you want done when you cannot speak for yourself.

4. A living will is also a helpful written document recognized by law in most states, but is commonly limited to decisions about "life-sustaining procedures" in the event of "terminal illness."

5. Health care powers of attorney and living wills should be short, simple documents, usually available in preprinted form by health care and elder care organizations.

6. Any person of sound mind and at least 18 years of age may give all or any part of his or her body upon death. This is a legacy unrelated to economics.

7. Demand far exceeds supply for organs such as eyes, kidneys, hearts, tissue, and bone marrow.

8. There are many designated organizations who accept anatomical gifts without cost to you. There they may be stored before transplantation.

9. Each state has its own anatomical gift laws. Make sure you check in your state and sign a proper form to make the ultimate gift of a part of yourself to save or improve the life of the recipient.

Chapter

11

ESTATE ADMINISTRATION

In every legal jurisdiction in America there exists a special court that concerns itself with the administration of estates. Sometimes called the "surrogate" or "chancery" court, its most common name is "probate" court.

A properly drawn will should state your wishes as to the disposition of your property and name an "executor" whose duty it is to see that the will terms are carried out. The executor presents the will to the probate court and later an inventory of the assets and the liabilities of your estate. The court will determine if the document is acceptable for probate. The court will order a legal notice published in a local newspaper notifying your creditors of your death and giving them an opportunity to present claims. The notice is also intended to alert interested parties who may wish to contest your will. The court will hear any claims or disputes, and interpret any ambiguous provisions in your will.

If you die intestate, that is, without leaving a valid will, the state will write your will for you. This means that, in the absence of a valid will, your estate will be distributed in accordance with the laws of the state in which you lived. That distribution may bear no resemblance to the one you would have specified had you timely elected to spell out your wishes in a will. The probate court will appoint an "administrator," whose duties will approximate those of an executor and who will tend to the details of probate in your estate.

The probate administration will proceed forward with accountings of all receipts and disbursements. Asset management and appraisals may require consultants and experts. Income, gift, state, and generation-skipping tax issues will be analyzed and the necessary tax returns prepared. Proper allowances and claims will be paid. Compensation and fees due executors, attorneys, and accountants will be disbursed. Probating an estate to closing generally takes six months to two years.

WHAT AN EXECUTOR NEEDS TO KNOW
◆ ◆ ◆

Being an Executor Takes Time

The job of an executor may take more time than some people are willing to give:[1]

The most frustrating thing for John Sullivan of Concordia, Kansas, about being the executor of his sister Genevieve's estate was the slowness of the procedure. "Everything should have been cleared up in a year," John says. But the process dragged on for three years.

Genevieve knew that she was dying of cancer, and she told John that she had named him executor in her will. The fact that there was a will made things much easier for John. "It was clear what she wanted done with her possessions," John says.

Genevieve's estate included 640 acres of farmland, stock, life insurance, savings, and a car. Genevieve was childless. "The heirs were my other sisters or their offspring, my brother's widow and myself."

"An executor must keep some money aside to meet various expenses," John says, "but you don't have to wait until everything's paid to begin distributing assets. For instance, I distributed most of my sister's stock three months after her death."

Just before the estate was to be settled, one of John's brothers died. "This meant going back to court and explaining that because of his death, the estate had to be divided differently. Worse, the lawyer working on the estate with me really dragged his feet."

Being an Executor Requires Finding Competent Professionals

John feels it's important to have a competent attorney in a complicated estate unless the executor "is abreast of all the latest estate tax changes and obligations." He hired an attorney to help him prepare federal and state tax returns for the first estate he handled—that of his wife's uncle, Stephen Murray. Technically, because Stephen left no will, John was the estate's administrator, appointed by the probate court, rather than its executor. Some 19 relatives were Stephen's heirs. Stephen's estate consisted of two farms, an office building, bank accounts, stocks, bonds, and farm inventory.

---

[1] John Sullivan, "My Experience: An Executor Summons His Will Power," *Money,* Vol. 13, December 1984, pp. 233–234. Portions reprinted with permission.

Being an Executor Requires People and Management Skills

John learned that an executor is responsible for seeing that the estate's assets are sold for the highest possible price and distributing the proceeds to the heirs. Debts and taxes must also be paid out of the proceeds. "Frequently, an executor has to be almost a Solomon," John says. "I've found myself taking late-night calls from an heir who'd had a few drinks and was anxious to get his hands on his inheritance. And I've gone through complicated contortions in disposing of property just to accommodate the whim of another heir."

John planned to auction Stephen's farmland. "That's the custom here because land tends to bring more at an auction, and in less time, than if it were sold through a real estate agent."

The farms had been appraised to establish their value for tax purposes, but John hired a surveyor to evaluate the worth of an abandoned stone house on one of the farms. He did this because one of the heirs, Stephen's niece, decided she might like to move into the house and open an antique store. "She wasn't interested in the rest of the farm," says John. "The easiest way to handle the situation was to give her the opportunity to buy the building at auction." The survey cost the estate $200, but John thought that was preferable to having a disgruntled heir.

"My feeling was that she would have been foolish to buy this property, because the house needed thousands of dollars of repairs, and it didn't seem as if you'd sell a lot of antiques way out in the country, either. She must have had second thoughts herself, because when this parcel was offered there were no bids." The two farms eventually sold.

John was able to sell the two-story brick office building, "but only after I negotiated a new lease with the post office that was renting part of the building. It would have sold for next to nothing without the rent the post office had been paying."

After the assets were distributed and expenses paid, a process which took about two years, the court released John as administrator. The estate was distributed according to state law because there was no will. "There was no discretion required on my part," John says. "I feel [the heirs] trusted me. I can see where a lot of bitterness and jealousy might arise in settling an estate. I was lucky. I had none of that."

WHAT AN EXECUTOR NEEDS TO DO

❖ ❖ ❖

Even with an attorney, the job of an executor is a big one. It begins with finding and reading the will, hiring an attorney (it's a good idea to hire an experienced estate lawyer, particularly in states that have not adopted modern probate codes), and filing the will with the court for probate. After the court issues letters testamentary, which empowers the executor to act, the executor must notify all named and potential heirs.

The executor then has to find all the deceased person's property that makes up the estate. This may involve extensive searching, and there are unforeseen pitfalls. For instance, if property isn't insured, the executor may be responsible for any losses.

Certificates of deposit may have early withdrawal penalties and should be left to mature unless immediate cash is needed.

The executor has to keep track of assets received and sold, expenses paid, and amounts due to the heirs. Record keeping is the most important part of the executor's job.

Most of the risks involved in being an executor stem from his or her obligations as a fiduciary. As John found out, an executor or administrator is required to act in the best interests of the heirs and must preserve the value of the estate during the probate process. If securities are part of the estate, the executor will need investment advice. Neglecting this responsibility can entail substantial legal risks for the executor.

The federal and state estate taxes in Stephen's estate came to less than $10,000. The attorney's fees were $4,500 and John received $2,500 for his services as administrator. In his sister Genevieve's estate, John declined the executor's fee.

The Pros and Cons of a Professional Versus a Nonprofessional Executor

As John learned, administering an estate can be time consuming and may be a difficult and risky business. According to *Money* magazine,[2] some estate lawyers tell their clients that the first rule of being an executor (or personal representative as executors are called in some states) is not to be appointed one in the first place. It may be better to hire a professional executor rather than a relative. But professional executors charge for services, and they can be insensitive to the needs of the family.

For the nonprofessional, the job of executor may be interesting and educational, but it requires lots of dedication, attention to detail, and more time than some people may be willing to give.

Postmortem Estate Planning Can Increase an Estate's Value

Most postmortem estate planning can be completed with full cooperation and support by all trustees, executors, administrators, and heirs. Postmortem estate planning also includes the right to disclaim property. Any heir may disclaim his or her rights within nine months of the benefactor's death. The law provides that a legally sufficient disclaimer is the same as the heir predeceasing the benefactor. (See pages 126 & 128 for details.) Research legal and tax-planning options and elections in every estate administration.

Tax Elections Are Complex and Important and Mistakes Can Be Costly

The Internal Revenue Code grants to the executor of an estate after death a number of elective opportunities that not only affect the amount of tax to be paid but also who

---

[2] Evan Thomas, "How to Be an Executor Without Coming to Grief," *Money,* Vol. 11, September 1982, pp. 104–106.

receives the inheritance. These elections involve the valuation of the estate, the time for payment of the tax, and availability of deductions, exemptions, and exclusions. The provisions relating to these elections are extremely complex and technical. In many cases, the use of the election will benefit one or more beneficiaries to the disadvantage of the others. Often, the desirability of the use of the election will be affected by future events beyond the executor's control. The executor and the attorney or accountant for the estate have very important duties in making decisions and completing the necessary forms. Tax elections always include trade-offs.

Combination of Revocable Trusts and Probate Estates

At the election of the trustee and executor, a decedent's estate and revocable trust may be combined for income tax reporting purposes.

Alternate Valuation Election

Instead of valuing assets as of the date of death, the executor may elect to value the estate as of an alternate valuation date. Property not disposed of may be valued as of the date six months after the date of death. If the alternate valuation date is elected, property distributed, sold, exchanged, or otherwise disposed of within the six-month period must be valued as of the distribution, sale, exchange, or other disposition date. Many rules apply to special situations.

Special Use Valuation

For estate tax purposes, an executor may elect to value certain real property used in farming or other closely held business operations at its current use value rather than its highest and best use value. The decrease in the value of the gross estate as a result of this election is limited to an aggregate of $750,000 plus cost of living adjustments. The prerequisites to the availability of this election and the mechanics of making the election are extremely complex and the Internal Revenue Service has been rigid and literal in its interpretation of the statutes. Particularly in family farm situations, if the next generation of heirs intends to continue the family farm, large estate tax savings opportunities exist. More information appears on page 163.

Exclusion for Qualified Family-Owned Business

Qualifying and recapture conditions are worms in this tax savings apple. Coincidence, rather than planning, will produce the most tax savings from this election. More information appears on page 163.

Election to Defer Payment

The executor may elect to have the estate pay the portion of the federal estate tax attributable to the value of the closely held business in two to ten equal annual installments commencing five years after the due date of the federal estate tax return. Interest is payable only for the first four years. A very low rate of interest is payable on the amount of the estate tax due but unpaid. An interest in a closely held business may consist of an interest in a proprietorship, an interest in a partnership, or stock in a corporation if other special requirements are satisfied. The executor remains personally liable for payment of the deferred portion of the tax unless a written application for discharge is made and the required bond is furnished or a special lien is elected. The estate may remain open until all estate taxes are paid. This election is particularly helpful when a family business has no liquidity.

Administration Expenses and Casualty Losses

Administration expenses, including executor, trustee, attorney, accountant, and appraisal fees and commissions, as well as court costs and casualty losses may be claimed as tax deductions from the gross estate for estate tax purposes. However, the executor may elect to take such items as deductions for income tax purposes provided an appropriate waiver of the right to claim them as estate tax deductions is timely filed. Such waiver is binding and irrevocable, even if it subsequently turns out that the income tax deduction is wasted. If no estate taxes are due, these expenses and losses should be deducted for income tax purposes by the beneficiaries.

Final Medical Expenses

Unpaid medical bills after death may also be deducted for either estate tax or income tax purposes, but not both, at the election of the executor. Medical expenses paid out of the estate within the year after death may be deducted on the decedent's income tax return for the year when the expenses were incurred (normally, but necessarily, the final return), but the right to deduct such expenses for federal estate tax purposes must be waived. Medical expenses paid by insurance or government programs may not be deducted. For income tax, medical expenses must satisfy the nondeductible threshold.

Savings Bond Income Tax Election

Another income tax election that may affect an estate tax liability is the election to treat accrued savings bond interest of a cash basis decedent as taxable on the decedent's final income tax return. If this election is made, it will increase the liability for income tax thus reducing the gross estate.

Qualified Terminal Interest Property Election

Perhaps the most significant and sometimes the most difficult decision by the executor is whether to make the election to qualify a qualified terminal interest property (QTIP) trust for the marital deduction. Once the decision has been made to make the election, many executors have had difficulty in executing the mechanics. The election must be made on the estate tax return and once made is irrevocable. A fractional or percentile election is permitted.

Generation-Skipping Elections

Since the generation-skipping tax (GST) exemption of $1,000,000 plus cost of living adjustments exceeds the estate tax unified credit producted maximum exclusion, it would appear that the use of the unlimited marital deduction to defer all federal estate tax until the second death would waste at least some of the GST exemption. However, Congress provided a method for executors to use a GST exemption by providing a special election for GST purposes to treat a QTIP trust for which an election has been made for estate tax purposes as though the election had not been made. Because no partial reverse QTIP election is permitted, it is necessary to plan so that there will be a QTIP trust containing the exact amount needed to use any remaining balance of the GST exemption. A postmortem reverse trust may be created and then a reverse QTIP election must be made by the due date of the estate tax return. The other major election to the executor is the apportionment of the $1,000,000 plust cost of living adjustments exemption for GST purposes. If the testator has planned properly, the optimum apportionment will be obvious.

In conclusion, the task of the executor, attorney, or accountant in dealing with estate and gift tax issues for an estate is difficult. Rules and regulations continue to change. There is need for simplification and elimination of the draconian consequences of making wrong decisions.

HOW TO AVOID ESTATE LITIGATION
◆ ◆ ◆

It is difficult to break wills or trusts or reverse gifts that appear to comply in form with the state law where they were executed. Arguments of undue influence and incompetence are difficult to prove in court. The evidentiary burden of proof falls on the heirs trying to break the will. Judges and juries have limited sympathy for the disinherited contestants.

An individual often writes several wills during his or her lifetime. Each will should state that all prior wills are revoked. Old wills should be destroyed. Make sure your estate planning documents are complete and signed. Retain your original will under your control and personal possession. Don't leave your original will with an attorney if alternatives are available, since that attorney may retire, die, or move away. Help your estate administrators by making your estate plan complete, understandable, and free from controversy.

Many lawyers include a noncontestability clause in their wills and trusts. Courts do not uniformly enforce such clauses. However, it often discourages dissatisfied heirs from filing nuisance lawsuits. Consider the following sample language:

NO CONTEST: Should any person, whether or not a beneficiary hereunder, contest the provisions of this document or object to any provisions contained herein or institute any proceedings relating to the estate, then if no probable cause exists for instituting such proceeding in accord with the Colorado Revised Statutes 15-11-517, then such person shall receive the sum of $5.00 and no more from this trust, hereby rendering null and void any other bequest or devise that may have been made herein to such person contesting or objecting to the provisions hereof.

KEY POINTS TO REMEMBER:
ESTATE ADMINISTRATION

◆ ◆ ◆

1. Select an executor (personal representative) to administer your estate who has the interest, time, and dedication to complete the paperwork in a competent and efficient manner. Ask the person if he or she is willing to perform the responsibilities before naming the person in your will. Offer to pay reasonable compensation.

2. In selecting a trustee to manage the assets of a trust, choose someone who is competent and comfortable managing assets and is willing to do the necessary periodic accounting and tax reporting. Offer to pay reasonable compensation.

3. Consider selecting a qualified corporate trustee to be executor (personal representative) or trustee if your estate is large or complex. Also consider a qualified corporation to act in concert with an individual as co-executor or co-trustee. Trust departments are in the business of performing these functions and generating timely accurate reports and tax returns. Often they more than earn their management fees by generating a higher return on invested assets. Most important, they can relieve the heirs from the time-consuming agony of estate and trust administration.

4. Seek professional investment advice when managing assets of an estate or trust. Consider delegating investment responsibilities to life insurance companies, brokerage services, or trust departments that are in the business of assets management. Always ask about performance before making final decisions.

5. Compensation agreements and engagement letters should be a part of every relationship. You should know in advance how the estate or trust will be charged for attorney and accounting services, trust management, and commissions. Insist on a written agreement, and do not sign it until you are completely satisfied.

6. Work with individuals and organizations who enjoy superior reputations for integrity and competence.

7. Insist on timely completion of all estate administration and trust work. Use the simplest procedures available that would achieve effective completion of all tasks.

8. Postmortem estate planning may save taxes and simplify estate administration. The use of such tax elections as alternate valuation, tax payment deferral, administration expense, casualty loss, and final medical expenses deductions, qualified terminable interest property, and generation skipping can save taxes. Wrong decisions can have draconian results and liability.

9. Add a noncontestability clause to your will and trust to reduce litigation.

Chapter 12

THE ART OF INHERITANCE PLANNING

Your estate plan will either enable or disable future generations. I have noted consistent factors that contribute to a successful estate plan and assure responsible and productive children.

1. Limit the availability and control of property prior to adult age.

2. Do not tell children the value of future inheritance.

3. Teach children discipline and frugality.

4. Emphasize individual achievements.

5. Make gifts with statements of expectations.

6. Don't compare your child to anyone else.

7. Remember values always transfer with property. Make them good ones.

Remember the inheritance planning acronym "KISS"--Keep It Smart and Simple. Strong decisions give you the power to create a smart and simple plan with the emphasis on smart.

Building an estate is like developing a new miracle drug. No matter if it took scientists a lifetime of education, research, and development, it helps no one until it is available when needed. You may not have patented a life-saving drug, but you have devoted your life to accumulating an estate. This estate may be just the medicine to make your children's life meaningful. But until a plan is devised for making it available to them, it will remain only a hope for the future.

Inheritance is the act of receiving property. But inheritance is more. It is the reception of genetic qualities, such as blond hair, dark skin, brown eyes, big feet, athletic ability; spiritual and religious values; cultural and family traditions; political power; and even a good sense of humor.

Inheritance planning is more than just estate planning. It includes not only planning on how to protect and increase your reservoir of assets, but how best to distribute them to your heirs, friends, and society.

A Recipe for Trouble:
Lots of Income, Limited Control over the Principal
◆ ◆ ◆

For Delphine Dodge and Horace Dodge, Jr., there was no connection between the money they inherited as a result of the successful Detroit auto company and its source.[1] Instead, they were connected by an umbilical cord of money to their mother, Ann Dodge, who received all the income from two $40 million trusts set up by her husband, Horace Dodge, one of two brothers who founded the company. Ultimately, Ann Dodge became the richest woman in America, with, at one time, a daily income of $40,000.

The children were left no capital or income of their own and had to ask their mother for every penny. In his midfifties, a dependent, and ill, Horace, Jr., still had to beg his mother for money. "Without your help, Mother, I don't know what I will do," he wrote. As always, Ann Dodge sent a check. Horace, Jr.'s last words before his death were "Where's Mommy?"

Horace, Jr.'s sister, Delphine Ione Dodge, died after a disastrous succession of personal relationships. Her last romantic liaison was with boxer Jack Doyle, whose wife sued Delphine for $2 million, claiming that Delphine destroyed the couple's marriage. Mother stepped in and bought Delphine out of this highly publicized lawsuit. In return, she demanded that her daughter stop her own divorce action. Delphine lived out the rest of her days in seclusion at her estate in Rye, New York, drinking until alcohol killed her at age 43.

The grandchildren from the many marriages of Horace, Jr., and Delphine were alternately indulged and ignored. They became victims of the Dodge legacy as well.

---

[1] Caroline Latham, "Where's Mommy," *Forbes 400,* October 13, 1989, p. 86.

Ann Dodge died in 1970 at the age of 98. Finally, after 50 years, Horace Dodge's trust could be distributed.

Ann, herself a victim of her husband's estate plan, described the estate transfer as an ordeal of unbelievable horror: "The money, the power, the corruption, the conniving, the scheming, and intrigue."

MAXIMIZE BENEFITS, MINIMIZE LOSS WITH AN UP-TO-DATE ESTATE PLAN

◆ ◆ ◆

President John F. Kennedy lay on his deathbed four times before November 22, 1963.[2] As a child, he had a severe case of scarlet fever and nearly died of diphtheria. He almost lost his life during his service in the Navy during World War II when his PT boat was sunk in the Pacific. He contracted malaria during the war. He also had an adrenal gland disorder known as Addison's disease. In 1954, when his chronic back problems threatened to cripple him, Kennedy decided to undergo spinal fusion surgery. His adrenal insufficiency caused near-fatal complications following the operation. Twice he was placed on the critical list, and his family was summoned and told to prepare for the worst.

Because of his close brushes with death, and perhaps also because his back pain was a constant reminder of his mortality, Kennedy "accepted death as an inevitable fact of life." According to Theodore Sorensen, his friend and special advisor, Kennedy recognized assassination "as an unavoidable hazard of any Presidency....He mentioned more than once...that no absolute protection was possible, that a determined assassin could always find a way, and that a sniper from a high window or rooftop seemed to him the least preventable." Kennedy wrote his last will and testament when he was in the Senate. The document was witnessed by Sorensen and another friend, Ted Reardon, on June 18, 1954. "It's legal for you to do this," he joked on that occasion, "because I can assure you there's nothing in here for either of you."

The will begins: "I, John F. Kennedy, married and residing in the City of Boston...and mindful of the uncertainty of life...give and bequeath unto my wife Jacqueline B. Kennedy, if she survives me, the sum of twenty-five thousand dollars." Jacqueline didn't receive much money from the estate, although she was to receive all of Kennedy's personal effects, "furniture, furnishings, silverware, dishes, china, glassware, and linens, which I may own at the time of my death." The president's two children, Carolyn and John, were referred to in this will only in a general way as children they might have in the future.

The estate plan was designed in tax lawyer legalese to minimize federal income and estate tax payments. Kennedy used the well-established standard marital estate tax deduction formula in his will, creating a trust that bypasses Jacqueline's estate, but pro-

---

[2] Theodore C. Sorenson, *Kennedy* (New York: Harper & Row, 1965), and Ralph G. Martin, *A Hero for Our Time: An Intimate Story of the Kennedy Years* (New York: Macmillan, 1983).

vides her benefits. This method prevents stacking all property of the first spouse to die in the second spouse's estate and reduces estate taxes.

Proceeds from the trust fund were to be administered to Jacqueline in annual amounts as "necessary to ensure her health, welfare, or comfort or to enable her to maintain the standard of living to which she is accustomed." Kennedy's executors were his wife and his brothers, Edward and Robert.

Kennedy's sudden death prevented him from updating his will, which makes no mention of presidential papers and other historical documents. His family eventually turned the papers over to the Kennedy Library and Museum.

Kennedy's failure to revise his will after the birth of his two children and becoming president of the United States is a classic case of the tragedies that often result from deferred family and estate planning. By language in the testamentary documents and selection of fiduciaries, the president denied Jackie meaningful management or control over his estate or trust. She was left to rely on the discretion of the administrators to determine what was good for her health, welfare, and comfort. President Kennedy's controlling estate plan undoubtedly caused Jackie's early remarriage to billionaire Aristotle Onassis which gave Jackie financial independence.

PAPERS, PHOTOGRAPHS, AND MEMORABILIA: ELIMINATE EVERYTHING THAT HAS LOST ITS VALUE

◆ ◆ ◆

You may remember Ernest Hemingway as the Nobel Prize–winning American author of such fiction classics as *The Sun Also Rises, For Whom the Bell Tolls,* and *The Old Man and the Sea.* His many books, short stories, and poems often re-created the physical sensations he experienced in his own life. Hard drinking, witty, uninhibited, generous, egocentric, in love with life, yet by his own admission, obsessed with death.

He was a collector, saving old newspapers, magazines, letters, manuscripts, photographs, and even gum wrappers. He seemed never to discard anything, believing that it might someday become a resource or an inspiration.

His will was a holographic document, written in his own hand, bequeathing his entire estate to his wife, Mary Welsh Hemingway, and excluding his children by previous marriages. He rejected his own children while saving meaningless memories.

After his death, the most agonizing family task was the sorting of Ernest's thousands of papers, magazines, correspondence, photographs, and trash. Wheelbarrows were used for days to cart away boxes, bags, and drawers full of worthless papers. Regardless of family relationships, sorting should not be delegated to the next generation. Save what is important—throw out the rest.

Inheritance Planning Is Like Designing an Irrigation System

Picture your estate as water in an irrigation reservoir. If this water is timely and effectively directed to moisten the roots of new seedlings, a thousand plants will germinate and blossom. A bountiful harvest will follow the next growing season. If, however, the drainage valve is opened allowing the collected water to surge out from the dam and race down a channel, it will quickly flow by the crop land that needs moisture, water unknown distant fields, or erode and wash away the next crop generation.

A successful irrigation project requires both an effective collection and distribution system. Similarly, your inheritance plan requires a well-thought-out collection and distribution system. If your reservoir of assets has no planned irrigation system, it will either dry up or become an uncontrolled downstream flash flood. Benefits will be minimal. On the other hand, if a well-engineered irrigation system delivers water to growing plants as it is needed, the water value will be doubled many times as new growth is harvested.

Similarly, inheritance plans require educated calculations to maximize benefits to the next generation and minimize loss from taxes and probate. Your inheritors are the seedlings. Does your plan nurture their growth into healthy, mature members of the next generation?

WHY A WILL IS ESSENTIAL

❖ ❖ ❖

John died suddenly of a heart attack at age 37, leaving a wife, Debbie, and two children, who were ages 7 and 10, and no will. The estate amounted to about $250,000, including a house, life insurance, and some savings. This would have been enough for Debbie if she had received the whole estate, but without a will, under state law, she got only half. To manage the children's half, she had to set up a conservatorship by court order and supervision, which required the posting of a costly bond. The children will receive their shares as they reach age 18.

Dying Without a Will Can Be Expensive

Debbie had to pay filing, court, and attorney fees. Much money and time could have been saved if John had left a will containing the single sentence, "I leave my entire estate to my wife, Debbie, and I make her personal representative, to serve without bond."

John was far from unique. Seven out of ten Americans die without a will. Most don't realize that if you die intestate, that is, without a will, each state has already decided exactly how your property will be distributed. Although state laws vary, many divide separate property between spouse (one-third to one-half) and children. Without a will, your family may pay more than is necessary in federal and state transfer taxes.

Even if you have a living trust, a will is desirable to provide for the guardian of minor children in the event that there is no surviving parent and to "pour over" nontrust assets into the trust.

Although most attorneys charge a nominal fee for a simple will, many people feel they don't have enough money to justify estate planning. Actually, the poorer you are, the more you need a will. Heirs of poorer people often get bogged down in bonds, accountings, and legal fees that rich people can more easily afford.

What You Should Know About Wills

"Law is complications and complications are law.
If everything was just plain, there wouldn't be any lawyers."[3]

Will Rogers could have been commenting about today's high-tech word-processed wills. Don't let your estate planning become evidence of Will's allegation that "Modern history has proven that there has never yet been a will left that was carried out exactly as the maker of the money intended." The best way to assure that your goals will be fulfilled is by timely planning and engaging competent professional help.

Do-It-Yourself Wills

Statutory wills are available in some states, such as California, Maine, Michigan, and Wisconsin. These are forms on which you fill in the blanks. They are intended for those who need simple wills.

California was the first state to adopt the concept of statutory wills. An estimated 500,000 statutory will forms have been distributed there. But so far, other states have been slow to follow suit.

Even without the convenience of statutory wills, plenty of self-help books now on the market give rules state by state. And, if you are into computers, valid wills may be prepared by using software that comes with a comprehensive guide to estate planning.

If you decide to write your own will, beware of the risks. Consider the man who specified that "If my wife becomes completely disabled, I give everything to my children." He didn't realize with that sentence, he would have effectively disinherited his wife had she become disabled, instead of providing for her, as he intended. His wife would have been forced to initiate proceedings to elect to take her statutory share against the will or to rely on her children to provide for her needs. And her children would have faced several legal hurdles and tax consequences, complicating their ability to care for her adequately. If you use a do-it-yourself will, have an attorney check it before signing.

Can You Disinherit Your Spouse and Children?

Even with a will, most states will not allow a spouse to be wholly disinherited, and in Louisiana there is a law against disinheriting children. Apart from this, you can leave the bulk of your estate to whomever or whatever you like.

Intestate Succession Is Controlled by State Law

What happens if you have not designed your own estate plan to dispose of your assets? This means you die intestate. All states have statutes governing "intestate succession." Any part of your estate not effectively disposed of by your will, trust, joint ownership, beneficiary designation, or otherwise will be distributed as the state law has prescribed in the intestacy statutes. Although each state's statutes vary, one thing is uniform: only the surviving spouse and the decedent's blood relatives or legally adopted relatives may inherit under the intestacy laws.

---

3 Paula McSpadden Love, *The Will Rogers Book* (Waco, TX: Texian Press, 1971), p. 64.

WHO ARE YOUR LEGAL HEIRS?
Table of Consanguinity

This table shows your potential inheritors should you die without a plan. It also allows you to identify distant relatives.

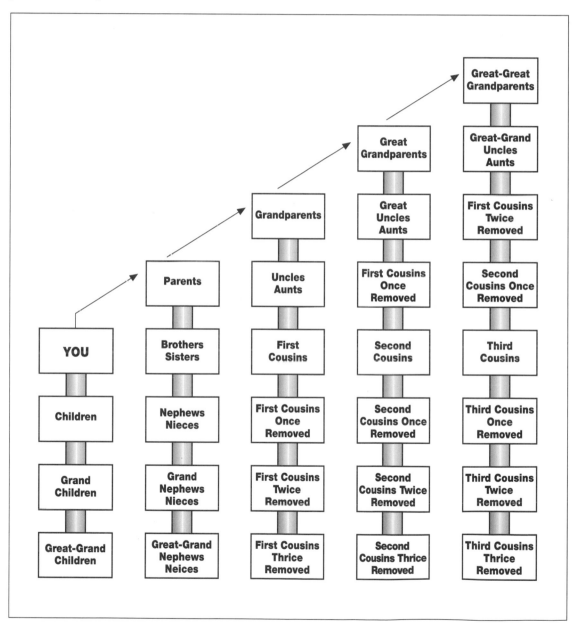

DISTRIBUTION PER CAPITA
Intergenerational Pipelines

Distribution per capita (or pro rata or share and share alike) means that the surviving descendants will receive equal shares of the inheritance, regardless of generation. Let's say Ruth, a widow, has two children, Jill and John. John has two children, Wilma and Wayne. Wayne has two children, Larry, and Lori. John and Wayne predecease Ruth. Jill, Wilma, Larry, and Lori each receive an equal share of Ruth's estate under the per capita distribution system.

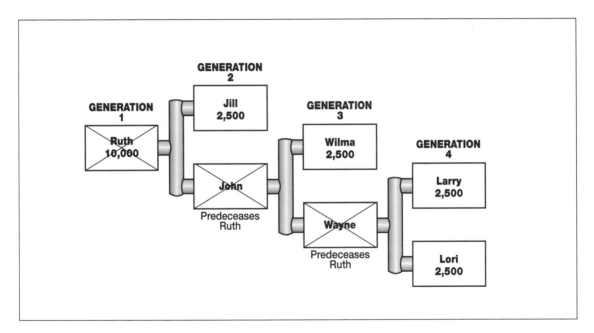

DISTRIBUTION PER STIRPES OR BY REPRESENTATION
Intergenerational Pipelines

Distribution per stirpes (or by representation) means that the surviving descendants will receive only what their immediate ancestor would receive. Let's say Ruth, a widow, has two children, Jill and John. John has two children, Wilma and Wayne. Wayne has two children, Larry and Lori. John and Wayne predecease Ruth. John would have received the same amount as Jill. Larry and Lori each receive 50 percent of what Wayne would have received.

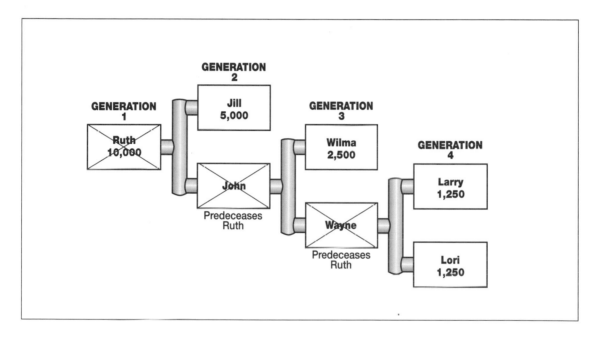

AVOID THIS MAZE OF POTENTIAL INTESTATE HEIRS IN A SECOND MARRIAGE SITUATION BY GOOD PLANNING

This maze of pipelines illustrates the many potential inheritors in a second marriage situation. If you die intestate (without a will, a living trust, or other property disposition options in place), your property will be distributed pursuant to state law. Your inaction may cause your property to go to unintended inheritors with unintended results. Only a good estate plan will save your family from this grief, conflict, and unnecessary risks.

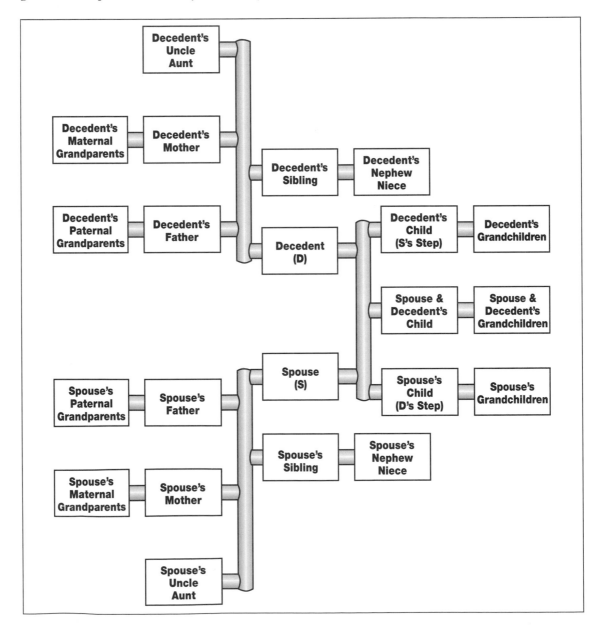

KEY POINTS TO REMEMBER: THE ART OF INHERITANCE PLANNING
❖ ❖ ❖

1. Remember, values always transfer with property. Make them good ones.

2. Do not try to substitute money for love.

3. Create a "KISS" plan using the estate planning acronym for Keep It Smart and Simple, with the emphasis on smart.

4. Do not make your heirs dependent upon an income stream over which they have no control. You risk destroying their self-confidence, judgment, and productivity.

5. Give your heirs control of some principal.

6. Do not tie your surviving spouse to your estate plan forever. Give her or him some control and discretion over financial matters after you are gone.

7. Do not create an estate plan designed to forever pull strings from your grave to manipulate the living. Let them remember you as loving and generous instead of manipulative.

8. Leave your affairs in order. Sort through collections of papers and memories, and throw out everything that has lost its value, sentiment, or significance.

9. Children may be completely disinherited in most states. Under all state laws, surviving spouses have a statutory right to a percentage of the decedent's estate. Plan accordingly to your state law.

10. Wills and living trusts may be changed at any time, as long as the person signing the document is legally competent. Make changes timely.

11. It is difficult to break a will or a trust if it appears to comply in form with the state law where it was made and executed, because the burden of proof falls on the petitioner seeking to challenge the document.

12. If you die without a will or funded living trust, state law will determine who will receive what portion of your property, a court will select your estate administrator, your estate may be subject to large fees and costs, and tax planning opportunities may be lost.

Chapter 13

SPECIAL NEEDS OF THE OLD AND THE YOUNG

There will always be a sandwich generation in every family. One or more individuals will be squeezed and need special help. Finances may be a problem. A minor child may lose both parents by death or desertion. A broken marriage may deny children a fair opportunity for education or training. Elderly parents may require constant care in an expensive nursing home. As employment opportunities become limited and salaries stagnate, intergenerational help in buying a car or home is becoming a pipeline of support for some, a means of survival for others.

ELDER CARE:
A COSTLY CHALLENGE
◆ ◆ ◆

"I'll never send you to a nursing home," Judy Jones promised her 83-year-old mother. Although the elderly woman was suffering from hardening of the arteries and was increasingly confused, she seemed to be able to take care of herself most of the time.

But then Judy's mother was hospitalized for a bladder infection. When she came home, it soon became obvious that she could no longer live alone. Judy's job and her two children who still lived at home precluded having Mom move in with the Joneses.

Judy and her mother had always been close. After Judy married John, an auto mechanic, the couple worked together in establishing their own business. John did the repair work, and Judy kept the books. Judy's mom helped by frequently babysitting for the four daughters and a son.

It soon was obvious that the elderly woman could not stay at home, even with visiting nurses and family members calling on her several times each day and a local college student staying with her at night. She did not eat. Once her college student caregiver discovered all the burners on the gas stove turned on high.

Sadly, Judy and John admitted that Mom needed round-the-clock care. They came to the inevitable conclusion that a nursing home was the only solution—if they could find a way to pay for one. The average cost of resident care in their area was nearly $1,500 a month—far more than they could afford. Medicaid was unavailable because Mom owned too many countable assets.

Finally, they worked out a plan that involved several other family members. Mom was able to claim benefits because her husband had been a veteran; Judy's oldest daughter, who had just graduated from college, and her roommate agreed to rent Mom's house; the Joneses were able to contribute the rest.

Making the best of the situation is what an increasing number of families are having to do. Like Judy and John, they are members of the "sandwich generation"—middle-aged, working people who are supporting and caring for both dependent children and aging parents. There are currently some 680,000 such families in the United States,[1] and their numbers are growing. As the baby-boom generation itself grows old, the problem will worsen rapidly, placing great demands on families, government, and other social institutions.

PLANNING AHEAD FOR LONG-TERM CARE

◆ ◆ ◆

There are serious if not devastating financial and emotional perils for the elderly when in need of long-term care. Many folks are under the mistaken impression that a government program or their private health insurance will cover long-term care.
The facts are these:[2]

---

[1] See Andres Gross, "The Good Daughter," *Ladies Home Journal,* November 1989, pp. 216–309; "My Mother Could No Longer Care for Herself," *Good Housekeeping,* July 1989, pp. 40–45; Eric Schurenberg, "The Crunch of Caring for Both Parents and Kids," *Money,* March 1989, pp. 93–94.

[2] Research study and private report by Terry J. Hjelkrem prepared for Sandy F. Kraemer on long-term care insurance, August 1997.

♦ One of every 2.5 persons 65 years of age and over will need long-term care, and it is growing worse.

♦ Seven out of 10 couples now 65 can expect that at least one spouse will enter a nursing home.

♦ Almost one-third of persons 65 years of age or older have a disability that limits their mobility.

♦ The probability of contracting Alzheimer's disease at age 65 is 8%; at age 75 is 20%; and at age 85 is 47%.

♦ Life expectancy is increasing: from age 38 in the year 1850, to age 75 in 1985, to age 82 in 1993.

♦ Medical insurance and Medicare are limited in what may be paid for nursing home care.

♦ The use of Medicaid has a dismal reputation for access, quality, reimbursement, discrimination, and institutional bias.

♦ No one wants to put a parent or spouse in a nursing home, but sometimes there is no choice.

♦ The average long-term stay is 2½ years.

♦ Over one-half of all people entering nursing homes will spend their entire net worth before they die.

♦ Even though financial planning for long-term care ranks second in importance to saving for retirement, 69% haven't planned for nursing home or other long-term care, and 43% never heard of long-term care insurance.

Currently there are several types of care facilities for older Americans. Which one is appropriate for a particular family will depend on the degree of care needed. Retirement communities, for elders who are self-sufficient, provide apartment-type housing and, often, recreation, social activities, and some health care. Congregate housing also requires some degree of self-sufficiency; residents live independently but may take meals in a communal area. Medical care usually is provided on a contract basis on the premises. Foster homes are an alternative for a small number of people who require constant care.

As Judy Jones found, nursing homes vary greatly in type and quality of care provided. Intermediate care facilities are for those who don't need constant attention. For those who do, skilled nursing facilities provide 24-hour supervision. Her mother's needs will predictably increase, and so will the costs. Government entitlements, such as Social Security and Medicaid, vary and are usually inadequate by themselves. Planning and saving for the senior years is essential to maintain a reasonable quality of life and avoid becoming a financial burden on the next generation.

Social Security Benefits Can Be Estimated

To receive a free statement of your earnings covered by Social Security and your estimated future benefits, all you need to do is fill out a form. This form may be obtained at any Social Security office. Information needed is your name, Social Security number, sex, last year's actual earnings, this year's estimated earnings, the age at which you plan to retire, and the estimated average yearly amount you think you will earn between now and when you plan to retire.

The form is very simple and takes about five minutes to complete, including reading the instructions, gathering the necessary facts, and filling out the form. If you do not have a Social Security office nearby, write to Department of Health and Human Services, Social Security Administration, 300 North Greene Street, Baltimore, MD 21201-1581.

Social Security continues to be the primary source of support for millions of Americans. If you have paid into it, you have certain retirement benefits. You should request a benefit estimate statement as a part of your planning.

Watch Out for Warning Signs of Financial Abuse

Frank and open communications and respect for the rights and needs of the elderly will solve most senior citizens' problems. Conservatorship should be used only as a last resort, after consulting with family and friends, to preserve a mentally incompetent individual's financial security.

Seniors often suffer physical and mental abuse at the hands of family caregivers who want to control their assets. Abuse often starts with fake affection. Most abusers start by trying to win the senior's trust. The level of intimacy gradually increases. As the senior becomes more and more infirm, the abuser assumes greater financial and personal responsibilities. Abusers often try to gain the senior's sympathy. They complain that life has treated them unfairly, placing them in dire financial straits. The stories vary, but the message is always the same: "I'm hurting, you're not, and I want you to give me money."

Relatives already named in a will can be especially insistent. They believe it's their right to ask for an advance on their inheritance. They often resort to blackmail, telling the senior that if money is not forthcoming, they'll stop giving care. Watch out for these signs of financial abuse: seniors who sign a power of attorney statement or draw a new will when they lack mental capacity; seniors who transfer property, including title to a house, when they lack mental competency; relatives who promise lifelong care in exchange for the senior's assets; withdrawals from bank accounts and other assets transfers.

Consider Giving Property to Your Heirs During Your Lifetime

About 20% of first-time home buyers rely on their parents to help with down payments. The parents usually provide half or more of the amount, which usually is 20% of the home's price. It's generally better to give rather than loan the money, because a large debt, even to parents, can jeopardize qualifying for a mortgage loan. Lending institutions usually permit such gifts if the prospective owners can contribute at least a fourth of the down payment. They may want to see a letter from the parents stating that they aren't asking for repayment.

Ruth and Dick Blocki found satisfaction in helping their children purchase their first homes. They contributed funds for their two daughters to make both down payments and installment payments.

"The best thing I can do is help my daughters pay off the damn mortgages," says Blocki, a retired Chicago businessman. "I'd rather see my kids enjoy my money while I'm alive. And the most fun I have is shopping with my grandkids."

But the Blockis' generosity didn't stop there. In 1984 they established college funds for each of their four granddaughters. So far, they have contributed more than $20,000, including $7,000 worth of tax-exempt Illinois college savings bonds.

The state of Illinois was the first to offer tax-free, general obligation, zero coupon bonds that accrue interest until a student is ready to start college. Illinois sold $328 million worth of the bonds in 1988, 20% of them to grandparents. Nineteen other states soon made similar offerings or established prepaid tuition plans, and others have indicated that they will follow suit.

There are various incentives for such gifts, besides grandparents' pleasure and the gratitude of their offspring. Gifts may be tax free now and help reduce estate tax liability later by removing assets from the estate. But it's important for grandparents who want to set up college funds to explore all the options and the tax implications of each. Setting up a trust fund requires the assistance of a knowledgeable attorney.

But one thing is certain—college costs have been increasing at a rapid rate, nearly 50% in the 1980s with the same trends in the '90s and beyond. If you're going to set up a college fund for your children or grandchildren, you should start as early as possible for the greatest yield.

GUARDIANSHIPS, CONSERVATORSHIPS, AND OTHER SPECIAL NEEDS

◆ ◆ ◆

If neither parent is able to take care of a minor child or incompetent senior citizen, a special need exists to appoint a guardian or conservator. A guardianship can have two different purposes: (1) to take custody and control over a person's property and (2) to take physical custody of a person. Over time, a distinction has come to be made between guardianships and conservatorships. Guardianships of estate property are generally referred to as conservatorships and guardianships of the person are referred to as guardianships. A conservatorship is a court-supervised legal proceeding in which a party is appointed to protect, or conserve, your property interest. This legal option is much more formal than the power of attorney, which is normally an unsupervised arrangement. The proceeding is initiated by a petition to the court asking for the appointment of a fiduciary, the conservator.

The use of general durable powers of attorney which survive disability have greatly replaced the need for conservatorships. However, if someone, such as one of your children, believes that you are unable to make or carry out important decisions concerning your financial affairs, or if some other statutory requirement exists, then that person may petition the court for the appointment of a conservator of your property. The appointment is made if the court is satisfied that the allegations of the petition are true and in conformance with state law. A guardianship, on the other hand, is typically used where a child is to be in the physical custody of someone other than a parent. This may happen when both parents are deceased or abandon the child or when a government agency takes the child from the parents and a court order terminates parental rights. There are also temporary guardianships for special purposes, such as school boundary requirements. You should always have a written designation of a guardian for your minor children in the event both parents are unable or unwilling to fulfill their parental responsibilities. If you don't, a state court will make the decision for your child if necessary. First choice should be the surviving parent, unless death, divorce, or other situations make that choice impossible or undesirable. Second choices should be loving members of your immediate family or loving friends. Ask your child who he or she would like to live with if you were in heaven. Your will is a perfect place to name one or more guardians for your minor children. In many states, you may also use a simple form such as the one that follows. Check with your lawyer to assure compliance with appropriate state law.

Instructions for Designation of Guardian Outside of Will

Most state laws allow you to name a Guardian of your minor children either through your Will or through another written instrument. Check your state law to assure full legal compliance with the laws of your jurisdiction.

DESIGNATION OF GUARDIAN OUTSIDE OF WILL SAMPLE

◆ ◆ ◆

I, _____, the natural or adoptive parent of the following children:

Name   *Date of Birth*

do designate that upon my death, then of, be appointed the Guardian of any minor child of mine including the above-named children and any children hereafter born to me or hereafter adopted by me.

Done this _____ day of _____, 19 .

_____

Durable Powers of Attorney Are Particularly Important for Older Folks

A power of attorney gives another person (the agent) the authority to conduct your business and financial affairs. If you execute a power of attorney, naming your son or daughter as agent, they have the authority to sign your name pursuant to the terms and conditions of the power of attorney. The authority can be limited to specific transactions, or can be general enough to grant authority to do anything you could do. A power of attorney is "durable" if it has a specific provision stating that the authority of your agent continues in spite of your subsequent disability or incapacity. A power of attorney is automatically revoked at death, and therefore cannot be used for testamentary dispositions.

Durable powers of attorney often avoid the need for a court-supervised conservatorship if you become disabled or incapacitated, such as mental incompetence. More often, a durable power of attorney is used for convenience. Children pay the bills and manage the affairs of the parents. One spouse signs the other spouse's name under the power of attorney to conduct business while one spouse is away on a trip. Powers of attorney may be misused. Therefore, you should select only an agent whom you completely trust. Powers of attorney may be revoked in writing.

A sample statutory power of attorney follows. This power of attorney provides for granting of various specific powers and includes space for special instructions. Power of attorney forms vary greatly. Use a form adapted to your needs and state law.

STATUTORY POWER OF ATTORNEY SAMPLE

❖ ❖ ❖

Notice: The powers granted by this document are broad and sweeping. They are explained in the Uniform Statutory Form Power of Attorney Act. If you have any questions about these powers, obtain competent legal advice. This document does not authorize anyone to make medical and other health-care decisions for you. You may revoke this power of attorney if you later wish to do so.

You may have other rights or powers under state law not contained in this form.

I, _____, of the County of _____, State of _____, appoint _____, of the County of _____, State of _____, as my agent (attorney-in-fact) to act for me in any lawful way with respect to the following initialed subjects:

To grant one or more of the following powers, initial the line in front of each power you are granting. To withhold a power, do not initial the line in front of it. You may, but need not, cross out each power withheld.

Initial

_____ (A) Real property transactions (when properly recorded).

_____ (B) Tangible personal property transactions.

_____ (C) Stock and bond transactions.

_____ (D) Commodity and option transactions.

_____ (E) Banking and other financial institution transactions.

_____ (F) Business operating transactions.

_____ (G) Insurance and annuity transactions.

_____ (H) Estate, trust, and other beneficiary transactions.

_____ (I) Claims and litigation.

_____ (J) Personal and family maintenance.

_____ (K) Benefits from social security, medicare, medicaid, or other governmental programs, or military service.

_____ (L) Retirement plan transactions.

_____ (M) Tax matters.

Special Instructions

On the following lines you may give special instructions limiting or extending the powers granted to your agent.

_____

_____

_____

Unless you direct otherwise above, this power of attorney is effective immediately and will continue until it is revoked.

This power of attorney will continue to be effective even though I become disabled, incapacitated, or incompetent.

(Strike and initial the preceding sentence if you do not want this power of attorney to continue if you become disabled, incapacitated, or incompetent.)

I agree that any third party who receives a copy of this document may act under it. Revocation of the power of attorney is not effective as to a third party until the third party learns of the revocation. I agree to indemnify the third party for any claims that arise against the third party because of reliance on this power of attorney.

Signed this _____ day of _____, 199 .

_____
Name

_____
Social Security Number

STATE OF _____)

                        : ss.

COUNTY OF _____)

This document was acknowledged before me on _____, 199__ by _____.

Witness my hand and official seal.

My commission expires: _____.

_____
Notary Public

Warning: Because the law regarding powers of attorney may vary in each state, this form should be considered a sample only. You should check with authorities in your state to determine specific laws and forms required to achieve your goals.

KEY POINTS TO REMEMBER:
SPECIAL NEEDS OF THE OLD AND THE YOUNG
❖ ❖ ❖

1. Plan for your parents' elder care and needs. Talk it over with them. Discuss options and project costs. Be realistic.

2. Investigate retirement, long-term care, and nursing home facilities. There are an increasing number of options available.

3. Investigate available insurance options. Health, hospital, disability, and nursing home insurance will become important variables in planning.

4. Consider extending a helping hand to nieces, nephews, cousins, neighbors, and even strangers to help their quality of life, further their education, or obtain meaningful employment.

5. Investigate all federal, state, and local government programs for the elderly, minors, disabled, and dependent individuals. Medicaid and Supplemental Security Income are only two of many available programs.

6. Designate guardians for your minor children in writing in case something should happen to you. Ask them whom they would like to live with. Who they trust? Consider who would be most responsible and loving.

7. Consider appointing a good money manager to manage minors' or incapacitated heirs' financial affairs. A bank trustee is an independent and reliable money manager.

8. Plan to avoid conservatorships. Seeking a court order appointing a conservator requires a court finding that the person is mentally incompetent, often a difficult burden of proof for the petitioner, and a mentally devastating experience for the elderly person. A conservatorship may be avoided by the use of a general durable power of attorney, appointing an agent to act for the individual, or by the funding of a revocable living trust naming an individual or corporate trustee to manage the assets.

9. Maintain honest and open communications. Respect for the rights and needs of the young and old will solve most problems.

Chapter 14

MEMORIES AND INSPIRATIONS LAST FOREVER

MEMORIES LEAVE MARKS: PLAN GOOD ONES

◆ ◆ ◆

One of the best gifts you can give your loved ones is also one of the least tangible—memories. And, as Carol Burnett found out, giving memories can be a gift to yourself as well.

In 1983, Burnett began a letter to her three daughters, Carrie, Jody, and Erin. Two years later, the letter had become a 350-plus page book, *One More Time,* published by Random House in 1986.

Burnett wrote about her earliest recollections of growing up in San Antonio, Texas, and Santa Monica, California, and of being raised by her grandmother, whom she called Nanny, and her mother, who was divorced from her dad.[1]

---

[1] Carol Burnett, *One More Time* (New York: Random House, 1986); the excerpts that follow are taken from pages 3–6 and 355–356 of the book. (Reprinted with permission.)

243

The book is full of anecdotes and revelations about her family and gives an account of how she came to recognize her comic gift and her vocation.

Burnett wrote her memoirs because she hoped her daughters would recognize parts of themselves in her story, "recognitions that…have everything to do with the same feelings that I think we all have in this world, no matter when we were born…feelings we should share as much as possible." But more than anything, she wanted them "to get to know Nanny and Mama and Daddy, since there's no other way now." Along the way, she made many discoveries about her parents, both of whom were alcoholics, and about herself.

"I never knew what a special person Daddy was until I started writing about him. They'd said he was so 'worthless.' No. He wasn't," she learned.

"Memory is a tricky thing," Burnett wrote. "I was never able to share that much. I closed myself in real early because it made me feel safe. I put a wall up.…I was able to let things out only by being somebody else."

But once Burnett started writing, "I wrote as much as I could whenever I could, and it took a lot longer than I expected. Not because I couldn't remember but because I remembered so much more."

"I wrote it for you," she told the girls, "but it turned out that I wrote it for me, too. I hope you'll do the same thing someday for yours…and for you."

Burnett has created many lasting gifts through her acting, recording, and writing. Someday the remainder of her wealth will be distributed to her heirs. All these gifts have made and will continue to make last marks which could be called "giftmarks."

Giftmarks: A New Way of Thinking

This book adds giftmarks to the many types of marks recognized in everyday life. Literature and conversation are full of references to landmarks, benchmarks, trail marks, bookmarks, beauty marks, and health marks. Marks of all kinds serve useful functions as a basis for comparison, identification, and reference.

Giftmarks are intended to be points of reference in your estate and inheritance plan. You have given and received giftmarks during your life. Consciously or subconsciously, each person leaves giftmarks. Some may be people-oriented, directed toward family, friends, strangers, or even enemies. Having children, practicing a religious faith, giving money away, giving advice to a friend, or even committing a heinous crime result in giftmarks.

Fame and fortune are nothing more than giftmarks. Movie stars leave giftmarks in their films and videos as they portray various characters. Rock stars and rap musicians fill their songs with messages, which may affect the actions of the listeners. Military officers in wartime leave lasting marks in our history books. Those who accumulate or inherit property leave giftmarks by the way they manage, use, and distribute their wealth. The Ford Foundation, established by the maker of Ford automobiles, is a vast charitable giftmark-making organization that tries to help, improve, and change our society and institutions. Most important, giftmarks are made by everyone daily in small ways, such as the grandmother who gives her favorite silver spoon to a special granddaughter.

Take control of your giftmarks. Make sure they are positive and achieve your goals. One meaningful way is by lifetime or inter vivos (living) gifts. By creating the mark while you are alive, you may design the gift and enjoy the results. If changes or fine-tuning are necessary, you are there as the producer and director. Living gifts may be highly public or anonymous. If publicity is generated, the donor often becomes recognized as a leader, which creates opportunities to leave additional giftmarks.

A universally recognized time to leave your giftmark is at life's end, called a testamentary gift. Most people think of a will as a testamentary document that pertains only to the family of the giver. It certainly does apply to the family, and may be used to reward or manipulate family members quite effectively. But testamentary gifts may have far greater spheres of influence. Giving is the greatest power an individual has to effect change. Testamentary wills are effective social tools. A will can express, and even enforce, your beliefs, goals, and values.

Trusts may be established during lifetime, and continue after death, be revocable and irrevocable, and achieve many other goals, such as avoiding probate, retaining privacy, extending benefits to future generations, retaining control, protecting assets from creditors, and reducing or eliminating taxes. Trusts are one of many giftmark tools.

Many marks may actually be charitable contributions, which are deductible for tax purposes. In fact, the tax savings achieved may often be a substantial portion of the total cost of the mark. Thus Uncle Sam becomes a willing participant in your decisions. Talk to a good tax advisor if you have questions.

OFFBEAT, FUNNY, AND INSPIRATIONAL INHERITANCE IDEAS
❖ ❖ ❖

The following inheritance ideas have been collected from individuals and sources as different as the suggested gifts themselves. Most were first reported in newspaper clippings, law journals, and books about wills. To speed up the collection process, some were collected by asking folks what special gift provisions they would like to see included in estate plans.

Inheritance should not be limited to money and property. A will or trust is an opportunity to express your philosophy, values, advice, sense of humor, satire, and yes, verbal revenge or a last word. Don't be too shy or embarrassed to tell the attorney preparing the documents to include special messages or conditions. Better yet, write out your message on a piece of paper and insist that it be included in your estate plan. Why not leave with a bang instead of a whimper?

The following are ideas: if you decide to include your own far-out idea in your inheritance plan, eliminate all ambiguity and uncertainty. Make sure your bequest is fixed and able to be stated as a definite sum of money or specific property at the date of death. Seek the advice of an attorney in drafting the specific language to implement your own special gifting ideas. If the attorney discourages your ideas, you are using the wrong attorney. Change to one who is creative enough to incorporate your ideas into a legally enforceable document.

GIFTMARK CHECKLIST

❖ ❖ ❖

1. Write a short letter, perhaps just a paragraph or two, expressing your philosophy or commenting on the property gifted. Include your favorite poem, quotation or song. Request that a copy be given to each beneficiary when he receives his gift.

2. Give family photographs and albums to the family members who would most appreciate them.

3. Give $10 to every person attending your funeral. The money is to be enclosed in an envelope together with instructions that the money be used to celebrate your life with food, drink, and celebration.

4. Give your estate to the U.S. government for maintaining the Statue of Liberty, in appreciation for the freedom and liberty afforded in this country to all citizens.

5. Give $1,000 to plant a memorial display of flowers in a location to be selected by your executor.

6. Give $1,000 to the park department to plant trees in a certain park in memory of your parents with an appropriate plaque.

7. Direct that a showing and silent auction of all your creative works be held before your funeral, so that your friends can see the best of what you were able to create. The proceeds from the auction shall be given to encourage art, and your remaining works shall be given to anyone who shows interest.

8. Give a six-pack of beer to each member of your local union, in the knowledge that some afternoon after 4:30, when the union rank and file are tired and weary and ready for a beer, they will drink one to you.

9. Give $1,000 to your favorite bar for public celebration and free drinks in your honor.

10. Give $1,000 to be used to purchase roasting turkeys to be given away the week before the Christmas after your death to poor people who profess a belief in a God.

11. Give real estate to your state, under the condition that the state accept the gift as a nature preserve for the use and enjoyment of the public. If the gift is not accepted within two years, direct that the property be sold and the proceeds distributed to school districts in your county to be used to enrich academic programs and encourage the study of conservation of natural resources.

12. Give family dinnerware, such as silverware and dishes, to the family members who enjoy entertaining and will use them.

13. Give your collection of hats to someone who will wear them.

14. Give $10 to someone who disappointed you and tell him or her why.

15. Give $1,000 to your best friend for putting up with you and to host a party in your honor.

16. Give $5,000 to your high school, with the interest to be used to purchase trophies and medals to be awarded each year to students who have not been recognized and need encouragement, known as the "Rocket Awards," to encourage each recipient to "take off."

17. To break a bad habit, give $1,000 to a good friend if the friend will sign an affidavit that he or she has not smoked for six months after receiving notice of this conditional gift.

18. To encourage a life-style, give $1,000 to your brother if he will sign an affidavit swearing that he has not consumed alcoholic beverages for six months after receiving notice of this conditional gift.

19. To help a known drug user, give $5,000 to the user if he will sign an affidavit swearing that he has not taken illegal drugs for six months after receiving notice of this conditional gift.

20. Give your artwork to people who expressed an interest in the specific pieces of art.

21. Give $1,000 to your school district, to be awarded to the first five students who have dropped out of high school, later received a high school diploma, and enrolled in a college or university program to show your appreciation and respect for the difficulty of putting life together again after making a mistake.

22. If you are a women's or minority rights advocate, give your entire estate in trust to be distributed to the first woman or specified minority who is elected governor of your state, to be used freely as the elected official determines. Wish him or her wisdom, understanding, good fortune, and the grace of God in the hope that he or she will be able to straighten out the mess that predecessors have made of the job up to this point. If no woman or specified minority qualifies for this trust within 21 years after your death, the entire balance of the trust estate shall be distributed to the political party that has the greatest number of women or specified minority members in the state legislature at that time.

23. Give $500 to your high school to be used as prizes for the best papers written on how to solve the coming energy shortages.

24. Give $10 to 100 different people who peacefully make some type of social statement against racial discrimination with a written directive to each person that the money be used to further the cause.

25. Give $25 to every person who attends your funeral. The money should be placed in an envelope, together with a note, indicating that the money is to be used to encourage a child's religious education.

26. Give $1,000 to any member of your family who climbs to the top of Pikes Peak within one year of your death.

27. Give your books to people who would appreciate them, and if there is no such person, sell them to a used bookstore so that they may be recycled and enjoyed.

28. To encourage a lazy friend to get off his duff and begin supporting himself, create a trust that will match dollars earned and reported for tax purposes by a beneficiary. Distribute $1 for every $20 earned up to a total annual distribution of $2,000. After five years, give the remaining trust assets to your children.

29. Leave your home to a church or social agency to be used as shelter for abused children. If the house cannot be used, the house should be sold and the proceeds used to purchase another shelter for the same purpose.

30. Create a trust to compensate someone for taking care of your pet for the rest of its life. Upon the death of your pet the balance in the trust should go to your favorite animal charity.

31. Give money to a symphony orchestra to play your favorite concerto or present a concert in your memory.

32. Leave funds for a New Orleans jazz band to walk behind your casket playing "When the Saints Go Marching In."

33. Leave money for a rock and roll band to cheer up your loved ones at a party one year after your funeral.

34. Leave your favorite fishing rod or gun to your favorite fishing or hunting companion.

35. Leave money to your hometown to set up a task force to improve traffic flow, and if the city does not accept and use it for that purpose, give the money to a school district to improve safety for children at school crossings.

36. Create a trust fund to provide a teddy bear for each minor child of every person with a child under age ten who applies for welfare in your county for a period of 10 years or until the funds are exhausted, whichever comes first. Any money after ten years should be used to buy and distribute teddy bears to all children under the age of 10, on a first-come basis.

37. Give money to a university, with one portion to be used in research to study the probable effects of nuclear war, and the other portion to publicize the results of that research.

38. Give $100 to each of three of your former school teachers in appreciation for the help and encouragement each gave to you. If they are not alive, give it to a school in their honor. Give $1 to teachers who did not understand you or were, in your opinion, poor educators.

39. Give $1,000 to the music department of your church, school or other organization to purchase music materials or encourage performance.

40. Leave money to have the book you wrote, which was turned down by each of the unenlightened and ignorant publishers to which you sent it, privately published.

41. Direct your personal representative to use up to $1,000 to purchase and distribute to all the doctors' attorneys in your city information on the poor and disadvantaged.

42. To encourage your busy children to spend a bit of time together to commiserate and listen to each other's stories, leave each child who spends at least the first four nights after your funeral in your home a one-week Caribbean cruise.

43. Give $1 to your son, a liberal Democrat (or vice versa), for each half dollar he donates to the Republican party, the affiliation of your choice.

44. Leave $1,000 to a city park and recreation department to provide a kite to each child in your hometown between the ages of 7 and 10 on April 1 of each year until the funds run out.

45. Give $2,000 to your YMCA to award $50 "good buddy" awards to recognize youth members who demonstrated an unusual effort to be a "good buddy" to someone else. These awards will carry your name on them. At least five must be awarded each year until the money has been exhausted. The volunteer board of directors of the YMCA will make the award decisions.

46. Give your real estate to the state division of wildlife as a wildlife habitat. Omit access to blue birds, sharp tail grouse, red tail fox, seasonal herds of elk, and any other wildlife. Prohibit hunting, fishing, and banking or tagging of birds or animals. Ban construction of recreational facilities, roads or trails. Allow wildlife officials who manage the off-limits property to enter only on foot or horseback or by aircraft. Prohibit motorized vehicles. Create another "Noah's Ark" for the perpetuation of species.

47. Give $5,000 to a charitable organization for the specific purpose of establishing awards to honor families who recycle trash.

48. Give $1,000 to your city's recreation department to offer $500 each to the boy and girl under 18 who make the most consecutive standard basketball free throws under supervised conditions during your city summer recreation program.

49. Give $50,000 to a college to establish scholarships. The scholarship awards shall be made by a panel of five different students each year selected at random from the student body and willing to serve. Only the income from the gift shall be awarded each year. Criteria for the awards shall be established by the students each year.

50. Take out a $100,000 whole life insurance policy on your life, and then give the policy, and any cash value that may accumulate, to your favorite charity or organization.

51. Give 100 roses to 100 different senior citizens in nursing homes on Christmas Eve.

52. Give $1,000 to the local Big Brother/Big Sister Program to provide surrogate parents to children in need of a substitute mother or father.

53. Give $1,000 to your YMCA to provide memberships to children who could not otherwise afford them.

54. Give $5,000 to your city to build bicycle paths and a memorial plaque naming at least one path in your honor. The paths will be dedicated to good health and the saving of energy.

55. Give $100 to one or more schools to award teachers, administrators, or coaches $25 engraved plaques for good work. Name the awards after yourself or a friend, to be limited to persons who have not been recognized before. Designate a student organization to make the selections.

High-Technology Communications

Many people prefer to express themselves to the next generation outside their estate plans, such as by letter, to be opened and read after death. Now, with new electronic developments, many are choosing to make video tapes, compact disks, or videos including both visual and audio, to express themselves and create memories.

LEGAL GUIDELINES FOR GIFT-GIVING

◆ ◆ ◆

There are fairly clear legal guidelines from court decisions determining what is enforceable in a will or trust. Good common sense will usually lead you to the right conclusion. Your attorney is your best source of advice on whether a provision you have in mind is enforceable. Request your attorney to draft the proper legal language with enforceable terms and conditions which will discourage or avoid challenge. The following are some, but not all, of the legal guidelines to consider:

1. *Public policy.* Courts have said some kinds of gifts are against public policy. For example, don't give half of your estate to your daughter only on the condition that she divorce the worthless jerk she married. Similarly, don't insist that your son remain single just to inherit.

2. *Illegal act.* Don't advocate anything patently illegal, such as distributing liquor to minors or contributing to legal or civil disobedience or insurrection.

3. *Vague, indefinite, or unclear.* Avoid ambiguous gifts. Don't say, "I leave the balance of my estate to the best-looking woman in Chicago." If that is your desire, establish a definite method for selecting that special woman, such as a beauty contest or

allowing your best friend the pleasure of choice. If you leave gifts to a federal, state or local government, specify the terms and conditions of the gift, or it will disappear into the general fund.

4. *Tax effective.* Include tax planning. Make sure the bequest meets all Internal Revenue Code requirements. Under the law, to be deductible, a charitable bequest must be fixed and able to be stated as a definite sum of money at the date of death. Dr. M's defective estate plan cost his estate a $2.1 million deduction. In his will, he gave his personal representatives the discretion to give people they felt were helpful to him during his lifetime up to 1% of his gross estate each, and the balance to charity. A court held that, since the number of people who could receive gifts was not limited in the will, the balance of his estate was not fixed at death. If the gift had included a clause limiting the number of individuals who could receive gifts, or a maximum dollar amount that could be gifted, the charitable deduction would have survived.

5. *Noncontestability clause.* Don't include a provision disinheriting any beneficiary who contests a will. It is a waste of time and effort. The courts uniformly refuse to enforce such a manipulative provision.

Literary Communications: Leaving a Will for Christmas

The following "Christmas Will" has been adapted from a will left to all mankind by a derelict named Charles Lounsberry. Lounsberry was once a lawyer, but died penniless in Chicago. The will, written in a legible hand, was found pocketed in his ragtag clothing and was so moving that it was read before the Cook County Probate Bar Association.

Charles Lounsberry's Christmas will reads as follows:

"I give to all good fathers and mothers in trust for their children, all good little words of praise and encouragement, all quaint pet names and endearments, and I charge such parents to use them generously, as the needs of their children shall require.

"I leave to children inclusively, but only for the term of childhood, all and every flower of the fields, and the blossoms of the woods with the right to play among them freely, according to the customs of children, warning them at the same time against thistles and thorns.

"And I devise to children the banks of the brooks and the golden sands beneath the water thereof, and the odors of the willows that dip therein, and the white clouds that float high over the giant trees.

"Long days to be merry in, and the night and the train of the Milky Way to wonder at, but subject nevertheless to the rights thereof given to lovers.

"I devise to children, jointly, all the useful idle fields and commons where ball may be played, all pleasant waters where one may swim, all snowclad hills where one may coast, and all the streams where one may fish or, when winter comes, where one may skate—to hold the same for the period of childhood.

"And all meadows with the clover blossoms and the butterflies thereon, the woods with their appurtenances, the squirrels and the birds and the echo of the stream's noises and all the distant places which may be visited together with the adventures there found.

"And I give to said children each his/her own place at the fireside at night with all the pictures that may be seen in the burning wood—to enjoy without let of hindrance or care.

"To lovers I devise their imaginary world, with whatever they may need, as the stars in the sky, the red roses by the wall, the blossoms of the hawthorn, sweet strains of music and aught else they may desire to figure to each other the lastingness of their love.

"To young women I gift all beauty and charm, with the love, warmth and understanding they must pass unselfishly to their children.

"To young men jointly, I devise and bequeath all boisterous and inspiring sport and rivalry, and I give to them the disdain of weakness and undaunted confidence in their own strength.

"I leave to children the power to make lasting friendships and of possessing companions, and to them exclusively I give all merry songs and light voices to sing with lusty voices.

"And to those who are no longer children or youth or lovers I leave memory and bequeath to them the columns of poems of Burns and Shakespeare and of other poets, if there be others, to the end that they may live the old days over again freely and fully without lithe or diminution."

"I joked about every prominent man of my time,
but I never met a man I didn't like."[2]

"When I die," said Will Rogers, "my epitaph or whatever you call those signs on gravestones is going to read: 'I joked about every prominent man of my time, but I never met a man I didn't like.' I'm so proud of that I can hardly wait to die so it can be carved. And when you come to my grave you will find me sitting there proudly reading it."

---

2 Paula McSpadden Love, *The Will Rogers Book* (Waco, TX: Texian Press, 1971), pp. 166–167.

KEY POINTS TO REMEMBER:
MEMORIES AND INSPIRATIONS
❖ ❖ ❖

1. Make specific gifts to specific people or organizations. Avoid vagueness, generalizations, and ambiguities.

2. If a gift is to be made for a charitable purpose, the most practical approach is to make the transfer to a specific charitable organization. There is an estate or gift tax deduction for bequests to qualified charities. The charitable deduction may not exceed the value of the transferred property required to be included in the gross estate.

3. Express your philosophy and give advice to the next generation. If your lawyer resists personalizing your will, change lawyers. With new, high-technology word-processing equipment, lawyers have forms ready to print at the press of a key, which maximizes efficiency, but often reduces estate planning documents to many pages of impersonal legalee.

4. Use high-technology and electronics to preserve memories and inspirations.

Epilogue

◆ ◆ ◆

A PROPOSAL TO SAVE TIME, MONEY, AND TAXES AND AVOID PROBATE

Alternative Estate Administration

How to avoid probate! Probate versus nonprobate! Newspaper and magazine articles headline the national debate. Best-selling books argue the issues. How to avoid probate by using the living trust is a hot topic playing to standing-room-only crowds at educational and promotional seminars across the country.

This national debate affects every American for one simple fundamental reason—each of you will die. When the time comes, most of you will own some tangible property that will be transferred to someone else.

The basic contestation is not wills versus living trusts. It is probate versus nonprobate.

The present common system of requiring probate in uncontested estate proceedings is outrageous. Why should a grieving wife be required to file a court action because her husband dies? Why should adult children be subject to judicial proceedings before they can receive their undisputed property? Why burden the overloaded and understaffed court system with unnecessary administrative work? The present probate system is antiquated, inefficient, and expensive to both taxpayers and users. The consumer probate revolt is directed at this outmoded system. Reform will save taxes and better serve the public.

A living trust is a very imperfect estate planning alternative to avoid probate. It is fraught with its own problems. Why should a husband and wife need to transfer property into a trust while they are alive for the sole purpose of avoiding probate? The paperwork is substantial and documents often complex. Property transfers require new deeds and titles and create unending questions by all who must deal with the trust. A living trust requires two transfers, one into the trust during life and one out of the trust at death. Living trusts create more work for you than the probate alternative. Your beneficiaries receive all the probate avoidance benefits. The Internal Revenue Service may treat the tax aspects of living trusts less favorably than probate.

American consumers are educated by the mass media. They are a wise lot and expect fair treatment. Legal services, like medical services, are a marketplace commodity. Users expect honest, prompt, competent services at reasonable prices. And they expect service advances and breakthroughs, as they experience in medicine and high technology. Why should they expect less? Legal services must change and improve, or be replaced by alternatives that achieve the same or better results.

Are wills and living trusts the only alternatives? Is the ultimate issue probate or nonprobate? The answer is no to both these questions. A new alternative is needed. Out with the old and in with the new. These national debates have served a useful purpose to identify the problems. Now advances and breakthroughs in legal services are demanded. If the courts, lawyers, accountants, bankers, trust officers, life insurance underwriters, and financial planners do not respond as revolutionaries ready for the revolt, they will be labeled reactionaries and replaced. Let the probate revolution begin.

IS PROBATE NECESSARY?

❖ ❖ ❖

In Germany, heirs are vested with possession and management of the estate and are also authorized to dispose of it. An executor may be named in a will, but he is not an executor in the American sense of the term and is not vested with property. Special judicial procedures, including the appointment of an estate manager (*Nachlasscerwalter*) and a limitations period for making claims, are available to resolve unpaid creditor claims.

France provides no procedure exactly corresponding to probate. Estates vest directly in the heirs (the French word *heritier* includes next of kin). Heirs may accept with "benefit of inventory," in which case a special proceeding is followed with the result that heirs are not charged with debts of the estate greater than their distributive share. Unless the heirs accept with "benefit of inventory," heirs are deemed to have accepted their inheritance unconditionally, in which case they bear estate liabilities indefinitely, and estate creditors may move against the assets of the individual heirs. If an executor is appointed, the executor has no power over immovables, which include real property, since the law assumes the inheritor can protect his own property by registering his interests as provided by law. There is no provision as to advertising for creditors.

Japan permits the appointment of an executor by will, by a person commissioned to do so in a will, or by family consent. There is no probate court, and executors generally are without court supervision. Administrators of estates, in the Anglo-American sense, are virtually unknown, since heirs usually assume control immediately of all estate property if someone dies without a will.

PROPOSED LAW THAT MAKES PROBATE UNNECESSARY
◆ ◆ ◆

There should be a law to encourage probate avoidance—a new law in each state that makes probate unnecessary except in contested cases. Reform is needed to make transfers of property after death easier, less costly, and less stressful. I propose long overdue and remarkably simple changes in the law to achieve reform of the entire probate process.

Attorneys and trust officers will defend the probate process by arguing that modern probate laws allow for many options and varied proceedings, such as formal and informal probate, supervised or unsupervised administration, and an alternative small estates process. These probate advocates of the status quo will plead that a good attorney can probate an estate with a minimum of paperwork and almost no court involvement.

But every attorney and trust officer must admit that probate usually requires an attorney be hired to file a judicial proceeding with the specific state court that has jurisdiction over probate matters. They must admit that a docket fee will be required to be paid to the court, that the attorney of record will appear in the judicial proceedings, that forms must be correctly completed and filed, that a fiduciary, such as executor or personal representative, must be empowered by the court to administer the estate, that a very large body of probate law must be known and followed, that the probate estate must remain open for a legally mandated minimum period of time, that the probate estate must be closed as provided by law, that the court will maintain a supervisory capacity during the entire estate administration, that court proceedings must be reopened if additional property is located after the probate is closed, that corporate fiduciaries charge more fees for probate transfers than for nonprobate transfers, and that attorneys charge more fees for probate services than for nonprobate services.

Although many states have adopted enlightened probate laws, and follow a form of the Uniform Probate Code, probate remains a mysterious legal process intimidating and costly to consumers. This remains the exclusive domain of lawyers. In some cases, lawyers perform important services, particularly when there are contested or undetermined issues, such as creditors' claims or determination of heirship. However, in the majority of cases, probate is nothing more than an administrative form process. The probate revolution is directed to an alternative for this routine paperwork. You can join the probate revolt and personally help change this American legal anachronism.

Alternative Dispute Resolution (ADR) Leads the Way for an Alternative to Probate

During the last ten years, there has been a consumer revolt in court litigation. Most civil trial litigation is too expensive and complex for the average American. It is fraught with expensive legal discovery and motion practices that run up attorneys' fees and cause delay. It may take one to three years to move from a filing to trial because of our congested court system. Our litigious society has caused our judges and court systems to be overburdened. Taxpayers pay more and more as the system expands to meet increased demands.

Finally, an alternative is available to judicial litigation. It is called alternative dispute resolution (ADR). ADR offers contesting parties an alternative to a public court trial. The parties may arbitrate or mediate disputes outside the court system. By agreement or court mandate, the parties meet and present their case in an informal setting with a minimum of technical pleadings and evidentiary rules. Privacy is at a maximum and costs at a minimum. The proceeding takes a fraction of the time and costs of a standard trial. The parties pay the nominal costs of the proceedings, and the taxpayers escape untouched.

This revolution in American jurisprudence is speeding up justice, saving taxes, and resolving disputes at a minimum of costs. It is time for similar changes in the probate system.

Alternative Estate Administration (AEA)—The Proposed Alternative to Probate

Alternative estate administration (AEA) should be to probate what alternative dispute resolution (ADR) has become to litigation. AEA will save consumer costs and time, reduce taxes used to support the judicial system, reduce court overload and unnecessary administrative overview, and move away from a mysterious lawyer-controlled process to a user-friendly new choice.

Alternative estate administration incorporates the use of a springing power of fiduciary. Some readers will say this is a new idea. Others will say it is a reworking of ideas already in existence. The concept should satisfy both those who enjoy new ideas and those who feel more comfortable using and reworking established practices.

The springing power of fiduciary is very simple. A fiduciary is the person named in the will to carry out the desires of the will maker, and is usually called an executor, executrix, or personal representative. A fiduciary has duties, responsibilities, and a high standard of performance responsibility well established in the law. A fiduciary requires powers to act, which are granted under the fiduciary powers acts of most states, and also in the will. Under a springing power of fiduciary, these powers spring into being at the death of the will maker.

The same goal of avoiding probate, court administration, and excessive fiduciary and attorneys' fees can be achieved by setting up a living trust. If such an expensive, paper-intensive alternative such as a living trust is well accepted, a direct inexpensive approach provided by AEA should be acceptable to all interest groups. There should be no reason why your state legislature should not approve of achieving directly what you can now achieve indirectly through a living trust.

Alternative Estate Administration (AEA)—Analogy to a General Durable Power of Attorney

A general durable power of attorney is a document, usually witnessed and acknowledged, authorizing the person named to act for the individual in all matters. A durable power of attorney survives the disability of the principal. If the authority granted in the power of attorney commences in the future only upon the occurrence of a specific event or contingency, such as disability, the power of attorney is known as a springing power. All powers of attorney are revoked and become unusable upon the death of the principal.

Prior to the existence of a general durable power of attorney, the state always took the position that the only way for an incapacitated person to be protected would be for the state, the courts, and several attorneys to step in and "protect" the incapacitated person from the vagaries of that person's closest and most trusted relatives or friends. Oftentimes what in fact occurred was that the court, the attorneys, and the various guardians ad litem and friends of the court took enough fees, such that there was not enough left over to worry about the vagaries of the incapacitated person's closest and most trusted friends and relatives. This finally became apparent and a durable power of attorney was born.

The springing power of fiduciary is a very logical next step in the process. In fact, in many respects, there is less risk in a springing power of fiduciary than there is in a general durable power of attorney. If under a general durable power of attorney the agent absconds with the funds, then the principal himself or herself may be left destitute as well as incapacitated. Thus the principal loses all his or her funds, and after the principal's death, the heirs and successors receive no inheritance. On the other hand, with the springing power of fiduciary in a will, even if this trusted agent absconds with the funds, the principal has no direct loss to his or her own well-being during his or her lifetime. The risk is to the designated beneficiaries, who typically are the same persons who are designated as the executor (fiduciary) in the will.

PROBATE, LIVING TRUST, AND ALTERNATIVE ESTATE ADMINISTRATION ASSET TRANSFER COMPARISONS

I support new laws to eliminate probate in testate cases and the need for living trusts to avoid probate. Neither presently available choice is user friendly or cost effective. One new proposal is Alternative Estate Administration (AEA) described in the Epilogue. AEA would eliminate probate estates and living trust estates in uncontested property transfers by will at death. You would empower your executor to transfer your assets at death. No court-empowered executor or privately-empowered trustee would be necessary. You would avoid the paperwork anguish and cost of a living trust. Your heirs and creditors would eliminate the expense and delays of probate while being better protected than a living trust alternative since the estate could be pushed into probate for protection, if needed. Routine paperwork would be removed from our overburdened, tax-supported probate courts. Today, simplified decedent estate transfer laws in France, Germany and Japan work effectively. Similar simplification in the United States is long overdue. You, your heirs and taxpayers all win in this legal reform game. Compare asset transfer methods in the accompanying chart.

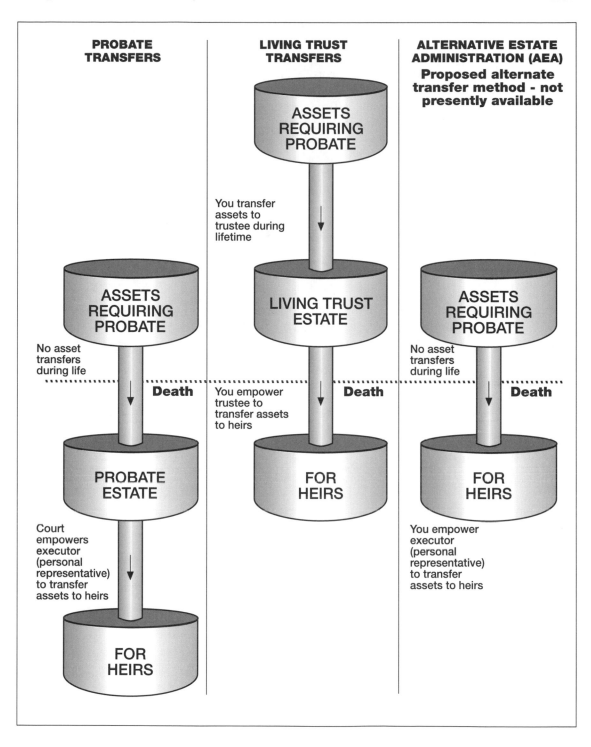

Alternative Estate Administration—Proposed Model Law

The Alternative Estate Administration Act (AEA Act) offers a new alternative to probate and nonprobate property transfers. The adoption of some form of alternative estate administration will not require changes in probate or nonprobate transfer law. It incorporates many advantages of both probate and living trusts, while avoiding the disadvantages of excessive paperwork, costs, time, and frustration. It is far too easy in this complex world to make every problem overly complicated. Consider this simple solution a beginning to reform the probate process by introducing AEA laws in every state legislature in our nation.

ALTERNATIVE ESTATE ADMINISTRATION PROPOSED LAW MODEL

❖ ❖ ❖

Short Title: This law shall be known and may be cited as the Alternative Estate Administration Act or AEA Act.

Purpose: To provide an alternative procedure to allow the administration of decedents' estates without invoking court jurisdiction where the decedent's will grants springing powers of fiduciary to the executor.

Definitions: Definitions shall be as set forth in the (state) Probate Code, unless modified or expanded by this AEA Act.

Executor AEA: An Executor AEA shall be any executor who has been granted springing powers of fiduciary as provided herein and elects Alternative Estate Administration (AEA).

Alternative Estate Administration (AEA)

(1) Any person who properly executes a valid will may delegate to any designated executor springing powers of fiduciary by specifically incorporating this law into the testator's will with specific reference to this AEA Act.

(2) Upon incorporation by reference, the designated executor shall automatically have the following powers to administer the estate upon and after the death of testator, and registering the proper Letters Affidavit: all powers conferred by the provisions of the (state) Fiduciaries Powers Act and all powers contained in the will. These powers shall spring into being upon the death of the testator and filing of Letters Affidavit without further action of any party, shall not require the filing of any probate proceedings, and shall not require, or cause to be invoked, the jurisdiction of any court.

(3) Upon electing administration under this AEA Act, the executor shall be designated Executor AEA and shall have all duties and liabilities of a fiduciary in the administration of the estate.

Electing Alternative Estate Administration by Execution of a Letters Affidavit

The designated executor shall elect alternative estate administration by

(1) Executing a Letters Affidavit which shall set forth:

    (a) Name and address of the affiant;

    (b) Decedent's date of death, age, and county and state of domicile at death;

    (c) A statement that no probate proceeding has been commenced in decedent's place of domicile or elsewhere;

    (d) Date of decedent's last will (and codicils) specifically incorporating AFA;

    (e) Specific court where the original last will (and codicils) of decedent has been lodged, and date lodged;

    (f) Affiant is unaware of any instrument revoking the will (and codicils) so lodged and believes the instrument is the decedent's last will and was validly executed; and

    (g) Affiant is twenty-one (21) years of age or older and has priority for appointment for executor under the will;

(2) Filing the Letters Affidavit in the court having probate jurisdiction.

Springing Power of Executor AEA

(1) After the lodging of decedent's last will (and codicils) and filing the Letters Affidavit, the court having probate jurisdiction shall stamp the letters affidavit, and any copies thereof, "Filed," which stamp shall authorize the Executor AEA to exercise all powers conferred by the provision of the (state) Fiduciaries Powers Act and the will.

(2) All third parties may rely upon the letters affidavit, the Executor AEA submits personally to the jurisdiction of the court in any proceeding relative to the will that may be initiated by any party.

(3) By filing the Letters Affidavit, the Executor AEA submits personally to the jurisdiction of the court in any proceeding relative to the will that may be initiated by any party.

(4) The Executor AEA shall be held to the same fiduciary standards and liabilities as an executor appointed pursuant to the (state) probate code.

Invoking Probate Jurisdiction

Any interested person claiming any right or allowance, or requesting court action or review, concerning the will or estate administration, as provided in the (state) probate code, may file an application or petition for probate of the will in the court having probate jurisdiction, requesting that the springing powers of the personal representative be terminated. Upon the filing of such application or petition, the court shall automatically and forthwith enter an order terminating such springing powers and order the estate be administered pursuant to the (state) probate code. The Executor AEA shall be given notice of such termination of springing powers. The probate proceeding shall relate back to the date of death. The Executor shall thereafter comply with all probate laws, rules, and regulations as if no Alternate Estate Administration had occurred. All actions taken by the Executor AEA shall be binding upon the estate and may be relied upon by third parties for all purposes.

Creditors' Claims

Any creditor or other claimant desiring to present a claim against the estate must invoke probate jurisdiction as provided herein within six months of decedent's death or be forever barred from bringing such claim against the estate.

No Appropriation

The General Assembly has determined that this act can be implemented within existing appropriations, and therefore no separate appropriation of state monies is necessary to carry out the purposes of this act.

Safety Clause

The General Assembly hereby finds, determines and declares that this Act is necessary for the immediate preservation of the public peace, health, and safety.

LAWYERS, JUDGES AND LEGISLATORS SHOULD ACCEPT THE CHALLENGE TO REFORM ESTATE ADMINISTRATION LAWS

❖ ❖ ❖

This AEA Model Act is intended only as a summary form beginning. Lawyers more intelligent than I will develop better and detailed estate planning administration alternatives. I encourage and cheer them on. Pride of authorship should not be an issue. It's the consumer's turn to control the estate transfer process.

I call for a revolt and revolution in the laws and process of estate administration. The need is desperate from state to state. Change must occur to make inheritance a user-friendly process instead of an arcane dreadful experience. You can become a part of this change by the self-help promotion of some form of Alternative Estate Administration (AEA) to your family, friends, civic clubs, political groups, and state legislators. Become a lobbyist for change.

Do it now.

DIGEST OF LEGAL AND TAX TERMINOLOGY

The following definitions and explanations are designed to be brief and helpful. You will find more details about these words and phrases throughout the book. The listing is alphabetical. The goal is a fast and easy digest of terms.

Anatomical Gift—A gift of one or more of your organs during your life or upon your death. Use forms approved in your state.

Annual Exclusion—The amount of property, valued up to $10,000 per year plus cost of living adjustments, you are permitted to give away to any other person annually without incurring any gift tax or filing a gift tax return. There is no limit on the number of people to whom these gifts can be made in a year. To qualify for this exclusion, the gift must be of a present interest, meaning that the beneficiary can enjoy the gift immediately. This exclusion can be doubled per person annually if you are married and your spouse joins in the gift. This is called gift splitting.

Applicable Credit Amount—The Applicable Credit is the amount of the unified estate and gift tax credit available as a direct credit against gift or estate taxes due. See "Applicable Exclusion Schedule" on page 273.

Applicable Exclusion—The actual asset value of the Unified Credit in taxable estates or taxable gifts. See "Applicable Exclusion Schedule" on page 273.

Appointment of Guardian—A guardian is a person given the responsibility to care for minor children or others who require special care. The term is also used in connection with the person appointed to manage assets for minors or those requiring special care. If you have minor children or any dependent who is incapable of taking care of himself, you should by the appropriate legal document under your state law appoint a guardian to take care of such person and to manage his assets.

Attorney at Law—A person who is legally qualified and authorized to represent and act for clients in legal proceedings; to be distinguished from attorney in fact.

Attorney in Fact—A person who acting as agent is given written authorization by another person to transact business for him out of court; to be distinguished from attorney at law.

Beneficiary—A person who is named to receive benefits.

Beneficiary Designations—Forms to transfer life insurance, pension, profit-sharing, 401(k), IRA, and annuity survivor and death benefits and other pay-on-death proceeds to your designated beneficiaries at your death. Must be in writing, usually on forms provided by the benefit administrator.

Bypass Trust—A trust designed not to qualify for the unlimited estate tax marital deduction. It takes advantage of your lifetime applicable exclusion. This trust is called a bypass trust because it bypasses the surviving spouse's taxable estate and is not subject to estate taxes. The trust is also technically referred to as an exemption equivalent trust or credit shelter trust as well as a family trust. It may sprinkle benefits to a spouse, your children and other beneficiaries. Ultimately, it establishes the conditions and beneficiaries for final distribution. The bypass trust is the most universally used method of saving estate taxes in family situations.

Charitable Gift—A gift to a legal charity. The gift is typically made to an organization that meets specific requirements so that the gift will be deductible for income and estate tax purposes. There are many charitable gift alternatives that create varying tax advantages.

Charitable Trust—A charitable trust is created for the benefit of a legal charity. You may create many different types of charitable trust, each with differing characteristics and results. See Chapter 5 for explanations and illustrations.

Community Property—A way of owning property under the law of the eight original community property states of Arizona, California, Idaho, Louisiana, Nevada, New Mexico, Texas, and Washington. Under community property law, when a married couple acquires property, each spouse will be considered to own a one-half interest in the asset.

Disclaimer—Any beneficiary may refuse to accept property he or she is entitled to receive. The property will then be transferred to the person next in line as provided by a will, trust, other instrument, or state law. The disclaimer often must be completed within nine months of death. Disclaimer is also called renunciation.

Durable Power of Attorney—A power of attorney that continues to remain in effect if you become disabled or that comes into existence after you become disabled.

Dynasty Trust—An irrevocable trust designed to provide benefits to successive generations without initial payment of gift, estate, or generation-skipping taxes (GSTs). The trust may last for as long as state perpetuities law allows, which in Idaho, South Dakota, and Wisconsin may be forever. Funding is designed to take advantage of applicable exclusion amount and the $1,000,000 plus adjustments GST exemption. Eventually, as the trust property vests in final beneficiaries, transfer taxes may be payable at rates as high as 55% federal, plus possible state tax. Principal and income may be distributed or accumulated for successive generations of beneficiaries. Trust income taxes may discourage accumulation. Complex planning tool to protect as much as you can for as long as you can.

Estate Planner—This term is used in the book to refer to anyone who is educated, trained, and experienced in estate planning of both your legal estate (ownership and transfer of your property under state law) and your taxable estate (income, gift, estate, and generation-skipping taxes which may apply to your estate). These planners are most often attorneys, accountants, trust officers, life insurance agents, and financial planners.

Estate Tax (Federal)—The transfer tax that the federal government assesses on a person's right to transfer assets at the time of death. The tax applies to taxable estates worth more than the applicable exclusion and the tax rate goes up to 55%.

Executor—A person designated to manage an estate including gathering assets, paying expenses and taxes, and making distributions to beneficiaries. The executor is often called a personal representative. If there is no will, the executor may be called an administrator. There are variations to terms depending on masculine or feminine form.

Family Partnerships, Corporations, and Limited Liability Companies—Business organizations owned by family members. Control of management and operation is usually retained by a parent, but the economic benefits are often transferred to children through a series of gifts to reduce the value of the parent's taxable estate. These organizations can be used to operate family businesses or hold assets, such as real estate.

Partnerships may be either general or limited. Limited partnerships may name the parent as general partners with full control and risk, and the children as limited partners with no control and limited risk. *Corporations* may elect under the Internal Revenue Code to be taxed as a C corporation, with full tax exposure, or as an S corporation, under which there is no tax at the corporate level. The *limited liability company (LLC)* is a form of entity that offers advantages and benefits not otherwise obtainable when operating as an S corporation or partnership. The LLC combines the S corporation characteristic of limited liability for all investors with the income flow through attributes of a partnership. Because the LLC form of entity is relatively new, its use involves new laws. Limited liability companies are destined to become very important business and estate planning entities. All family businesses should have written agreements concerning ownership, sale, and management continuation under specific situations including death.

Fiduciary—A person in a position of trust and responsibility, such as the executor of a will, trustee of a trust, or agent under power of attorney.

Generation-Skipping Transfer (GST) Tax—A transfer tax generally assessed on gifts in excess of $1 million plus cost of living adjustments to grandchildren, great-grandchildren, and others at least two generations below the individual making the gift. It is a flat tax computed with reference to the maximum federal estate tax applicable at the time of transfer, which is 55%. There may also be a state generation-skipping transfer tax, which varies.

Gift Tax (Federal)—A transfer tax that is assessed by the federal government when the value of a gift exceeds both the annual exclusion and the applicable exclusion amount. Tax rates are the same as estate tax. There may also be a state gift tax, which varies and is not considered in Sixty-Minute Estate Plans™.

Grantor Retained Income Trust (GRIT), Grantor Retained Annuity Trust (GRAT), and Grantor Retained Unitrust (GRUT)—These are lifetime transfers that may save taxes, avoid probate, and benefit your heirs. The most common is the GRIT. The strategy consists of creating an irrevocable trust naming your beneficiaries as remaindermen to receive the principal. You receive the income or benefit for a period of years. Length of the period depends on specific tax laws and your goals, but often is about ten years. If you die before the specified period expires, the trust value may be included in the estate, but often at a less-than-present-dollar value. If you outlive the period, the income or benefit stops and the gift is complete and excluded from your estate. GRITs are typically used for transferring high-value residences, vacation property, or valuable art. Other irrevocable lifetime trusts that include features that permit you to enjoy some use of the transferred assets, avoid probate, and save estate taxes are grantor retained annuity trusts (GRATs) and grantor retained unitrusts (GRUTs).

Gross Estate—The total value of your assets owned at death, or that are included in your estate, before debts, taxes, and other expenses or liabilities have been deducted. For estate tax purposes, the value is determined at the date of your death or on an alternate valuation date six months after death.

Heir—One who receives the property of a deceased person and especially by operation of law or by virtue of a will or trust. In this book, the word is used in the general sense to indicate all beneficiaries of your estate.

Irrevocable Life Insurance Trust—A trust used to hold life insurance policies. It cannot be materially changed or terminated. If properly designed, the life insurance proceeds payable upon death will not be part of your probate estate or be subject to estate taxes. This is a good method for establishing a fund to pay estate taxes and provide liquidity for an estate.

Irrevocable Trust—A trust that cannot be changed. You must make gifts irrevocably outright or in trust to remove them from your estate.

Joint Tenancy with Rights of Survivorship—A legal method of owning property in joint names, with two or more people, each having an automatic ownership right to the property after the death of one owner. This method of owning property avoids probate, but may often produce unintended legal results and undesirable tax disadvantages.

Legal Estate—A term used in this book to refer to all your interest in property, how these interests are titled and how they will transfer at death under applicable state law. Your estate plan should determine how each property interest will transfer at your death.

Letters of Instruction—Informal letters or documents that you can prepare without professional help to express affection, give advice, describe your philosophy, assist your survivors to inventory and collect your assets and comply with funeral and burial instructions, and so on. Not legally binding.

Living Trust—A trust created during your lifetime. It is revocable, which means it can be amended or terminated anytime while you are competent and is legally referred to as a revocable inter vivos trust. The trust becomes irrevocable upon your death. A living trust is used primarily to avoid probate and manage property. It does not save taxes.

Living Will—This is not a will. It is a document that specifies whether life-sustaining measures should be undertaken to preserve life when one is not expected to recover. Living wills are limited. A medical durable power of attorney for health care covers a broader range of health care decisions.

Marital Deduction—The unlimited amount of assets that can be transferred from one spouse to another during life or at death of the first spouse without incurring any gift or estate tax costs.

Medical Durable Power of Attorney for Health Care—A power of attorney that authorizes someone to make medical decisions on your behalf if you are unable to do so.

Minor's Trust—This irrevocable trust is often referred to as the 2503(c) trust, in reference to the relevant section of the Internal Revenue Code. The trust may be useful in transferring appreciating assets from your estate or making gifts to minors while retaining control. Income and principal may be accumulated or distributed, but in any event, the trust must terminate and all trust assets distributed to the child upon reaching age 21, unless the child voluntarily consents to allowing the trust to continue. Funding may be by the use of the gift tax annual exclusion or the lifetime applicable exclusion amount. For example, if you have four children, each parent could gift $10,000 plus adjustments to each child, which would allow a total gift of $80,000 plus adjustments per year. Tax law attributes the income of a gift trust for children under the age of 14 to the parents in accordance with the kiddie tax enacted in 1986. Gifting forfeits a stepped-up valuation on the gifted assets upon your death.

Net Taxable Estate—The gross estate reduced by allowable deductions, credits, and charitable contributions.

Nuptial Agreement—An agreement made between two persons who are married, or who are about to marry, which specifies the rights of each spouse in property in the event of marriage dissolution or death. These agreements are often used in second marriage situations and can be helpful to ensure that children of prior marriages will enjoy a share of the estate of their parent upon death.

Pour-Over Will—A will that transfers property owned by you at your death to a trust. There must be a previously existing trust to receive these assets. The will "pours over" assets to the trust by use of the probate transfer process. A pour-over will should be used with a living trust to sweep up any assets that may not have been transferred to the trust during your lifetime.

Power of Attorney—A document that authorizes another person to act for you and may take various forms. The person to whom the power is given is called an "attorney in fact." If the attorney in fact is authorized to act in all matters, he or she has a "general power of attorney"; if the attorney has the authority to act only in limited matters, he or she has a "special power of attorney." A power of attorney terminates at death. A power of attorney will also terminate upon disability, unless it is a "durable power of attorney." A durable power of attorney remains effective after disability. A power of attorney may also become effective only upon the occurrence of a specific event, such as disability, in which case the power of attorney is known as a "springing power."

Probate and Intestate Administration—Probate is a court proceeding in which a determination is made that the will submitted to the court is the correct will, assets are inventoried, notice is published inviting creditors to make claims, legitimate creditors are paid, and the balance is distributed to the persons named in the will. Only property that is owned by a person at the time of his or her death goes through the probate process. Administration is a court proceeding to determine how property should be distributed when one dies without a will. The process is similar to probate, except that no will is involved. After inventorying the assets, inviting creditors to make claims, and paying claims of legitimate creditors, the property is distributed to those entitled to it. When one dies without a will, the laws of the state regarding "intestacy" (i.e., the laws of "descent and distribution") specify the "heirs" or the persons entitled to receive the property and the proportions to which they are entitled.

Qualified Domestic Trust (QDOT)—A variation of the QTIP trust that must be used (along with the QTIP trust) when one spouse is a noncitizen of the United States. The QDOT trust requires that if the surviving spouse is a noncitizen of the United States, the trustee (or co-trustee) must be a citizen of the United States in order for the QTIP trust to qualify as a vehicle for deferring estate taxes. Remember, if the noncitizen surviving spouse chooses to elect the QTIP trust and defer the payment of estate taxes, then the trustee (or co-trustee) must be a citizen of the United States unless specific authority is received to waive this requirement. The citizen trustee (or co-trustee) has the responsibility to ensure ultimately that the appropriate tax is paid upon the death of the surviving spouse. The choice of appointing a citizen trustee (or co-trustee) and electing to use the QDOT trust or paying the estate taxes need not be made until the death of the first spouse.

QSST (Qualified Subchapter S Trust)—Tax laws limit shareholders of an S Corporation. An S corporation election terminates if stock is acquired by a nonqualified shareholder. If the trust qualifies as a Subchapter S Trust (QSST) and a timely election is filed with the Internal Revenue Service, it can hold stock in an S corporation without the corporation being disqualified. A QSST is required to distribute all income currently to one individual, who must be the sole beneficiary, and a U.S. citizen or resident. Check with your tax planner for more qualifying conditions.

Qualified Terminal Interest Property (QTIP) Trust—A trust that requires a surviving spouse to receive all income from the trust at least annually, but which ultimately transfers property to persons designated by the deceased. The trust qualifies for the unlimited marital deduction. Trust assets are included in the taxable estate of the second spouse to die.

Separate Property Agreement—An agreement made by a married couple, typically in a community property state that specifies which assets constitute the separate property of each spouse. *See* Community property.

Simple Will—A will that transfers property owned by you at your death by use of the probate transfer process.

Sixty-Minute Estate Plan™—An estate plan designed for you, in accordance with the illustrations and directions included in this book.

Spousal Transfer Documents—Documents that transfer ownership of assets from one spouse to another. The purpose of the transfer is to assure each spouse will have sufficient assets in his or her estate to take advantage of the $600,000 exemption equivalent.

Sprinkling Trusts—Trust in which the income or principal is distributed among the members of a designated group in amounts and proportions as may be determined in the discretion of the trustee.

Standby Trust—An unfunded inter vivos trust (living trust) usually executed in conjunction with a durable power of attorney, to which property may be subsequently transferred.

State Estate, Inheritance, and Gift Tax—The transfer tax, if any, that each state government assesses on property transferred during life or at the time of death. Varies from state to state. Because of federal tax credits, and differing state laws, these taxes are small in comparison to the federal estate tax. For purposes of simplification, these taxes are not considered in Sixty-Minute Estate Plans™.

Step-up in Basis—Basis is a term used for federal income tax purposes. Basis, or "cost basis" as it is sometimes referred to, is the amount that is generally used to compute the taxable gain for federal income tax purposes on the sale of property. Assets that are in the estate of a deceased person, whether the estate pays federal estate taxes or not, take as their cost basis for federal income tax purposes the fair market value of the assets at date of death, or six months after date of death, whichever evaluation date is elected. This step-up in basis means that the appreciation of assets in the estate is not subject to federal income tax. Planning should always include taking maximum advantage of this tax-reducing opportunity.

Taxable Estate—This term is used in this book to refer to that portion of your estate which may be impacted by federal income, gift, estate, and generation-skipping taxes. Your estate plan should include decisions on how to defer, reduce, or avoid all these taxes.

Testamentary Trust—A trust that becomes effective upon your death. The trust provisions are typically contained in your will.

Trust—A trust is created when one holds property for the benefit of another. The one creating the trust is the "trustmaker," "trustor," "grantor," or "settlor." The person holding the property is called a "trustee." The one for whose benefit the property is held is the "beneficiary." The trustee holds "legal title" to the property and the beneficiary holds "equitable" or "beneficial" title to the property. The document establishing the relation among the parties is the "trust" or the "trust agreement." The trust agreement specifies the powers and duties of the trustee, the rights of the beneficiaries, and any rights retained by the settlor. A trust that becomes effective during the settlor's life is an "inter vivos trust." A trust that becomes effective upon the settlor's death is a "testamentary trust." A trust that can be terminated or modified by the settlor is a "revocable trust." A trust that cannot be terminated or modified by the settlor is an "irrevocable trust." A trust can be used for many purposes such as providing support for spouses and children, protecting assets from creditors, and avoiding probate.

Trustee—The person (fiduciary) who manages and administers a trust.

Unified Estate and Gift Tax Credit—A Unified Estate and Gift Tax Credit effectively exempts from federal estate and gift taxes the applicable exclusion amount. The applicable exclusion amount is the actual market value of the property transferred. The credit equivalent is equal to the applicable exclusion amount.

APPLICABLE EXCLUSION SCHEDULE

Year	Unified Credit	Applicable Exclusion
1997	$192,800	$600,000
1998	$202,050	$625,000
1999	$211,300	$650,000
2000/2001	$220,550	$675,000
2002/2003	$229,800	$700,000
2004	$287,300	$850,000
2005	$326,300	$950,000
2005 and after	$345,800	$1,000,000

Uniform Gifts (Transfers) to Minors Act—A simple way of holding property for the benefit of another, similar to a trust, governed by state law. Simpler and cheaper to establish and administer than trusts, but very inflexible with mandatory age distribution requirements.

Will—A will is a document that transfers property at a person's death to designated persons. A will becomes effective only upon the death of its maker. Until death or incompetency of the maker, the will can be modified or revoked. A will affects only property owned by a person at his or her death which does not transfer automatically to another. For example, property owned in joint tenancy with another automatically passes to the joint tenant, and insurance proceeds automatically pass to the designated beneficiary. A person making a will is called a "testator" (masculine) or "testatrix" (feminine). Persons entitled to the benefits of the will are called "beneficiaries." The person in charge of administering the will is the "executor" or "personal representative." A person who dies, after having made a will, is said to have died "testate." A person dying without a will is said to have died "intestate." A will can be used not only for distributing property to beneficiaries, but also to appoint persons responsible for managing the estate and taking care of children.

LIFE EXPECTANCY TABLE

Use this table to calculate the average life expectancy of a person your age. Does your estate plan take into consideration your remaining life expectancy? A good plan will serve you and your heirs.

	All races				All races		
Age	**Both sexes**	**Male**	**Female**	**Age**	**Both sexes**	**Male**	**Female**
0	75.5	72.2	78.8	31	46.4	43.4	49.2
1	75.2	71.8	78.4	32	45.5	42.5	48.2
2	74.2	70.9	77.5	33	44.5	41.6	47.3
3	73.3	69.9	76.5	34	43.6	40.7	46.3
4	72.3	68.9	75.5	35	42.7	39.8	45.4
5	71.3	68.0	74.6	36	41.8	38.9	44.4
6	70.3	67.0	73.6	37	40.8	38.0	43.4
7	69.3	66.0	72.6	38	39.9	37.1	42.5
8	68.4	65.0	71.6	39	39.0	36.2	41.6
9	67.4	64.0	70.6	40	38.1	35.4	40.6
10	66.4	63.0	69.6	41	37.2	34.5	39.7
11	65.4	62.0	68.6	42	36.3	33.6	38.7
12	64.4	61.1	67.6	43	35.4	32.7	37.8
13	63.4	60.1	66.7	44	34.5	31.8	36.9
14	62.4	59.1	65.7	45	33.6	31.0	35.9
15	61.5	58.1	64.7	46	32.7	30.1	35.0
16	60.5	57.2	63.7	47	31.8	29.2	34.1
17	59.5	56.2	62.7	48	30.9	28.4	33.2
18	58.6	55.3	61.8	49	30.0	27.5	32.3
19	57.7	54.4	60.8	50	29.2	26.7	31.4
20	56.7	53.5	59.8	51	28.3	25.8	30.5
21	55.8	52.6	58.9	52	27.4	25.0	29.6
22	54.8	51.6	57.9	53	26.6	24.2	28.7
23	53.9	50.7	56.9	54	25.7	23.4	27.8
24	52.9	49.8	55.9	55	24.9	22.6	27.0
25	52.0	48.9	55.0	56	24.1	21.8	26.1
26	51.1	48.0	54.0	57	23.3	21.0	25.3
27	50.1	47.1	53.0	58	22.5	20.2	24.4
28	49.2	46.1	52.1	59	21.7	19.5	23.6
29	48.3	45.2	51.1	60	20.9	18.8	22.8
30	47.3	44.3	50.1	61	20.2	18.0	22.0

(continue on next page)

Age	All races Both sexes	Male	Female
62. . . . . 19.5		17.3	21.2
63. . . . . 18.7		16.6	20.4
64. . . . . 18.0		16.0	19.7
65. . . . . 17.3		15.3	18.9
66. . . . . 16.6		14.7	18.2
67. . . . . 15.9		14.0	17.4
68. . . . . 15.3		13.4	16.7
69. . . . . 14.6		12.8	16.0
70. . . . . 14.0		12.2	15.3
71. . . . . 13.3		11.6	14.6
72. . . . . 12.7		11.1	13.9
73. . . . . 12.1		10.5	13.2
74. . . . . 11.5		10.0	12.6
75. . . . . 10.9		9.5	11.9
76. . . . . 10.4		9.0	11.3
77. . . . . 9.8		8.5	10.7
78. . . . . 9.3		8.0	10.1
79. . . . . 8.8		7.5	9.5
80. . . . . 8.3		7.1	8.9
81. . . . . 7.8		6.7	8.4
82. . . . . 7.3		6.2	7.8
83. . . . . 6.8		5.9	7.3
84. . . . . 6.4		5.5	6.8
85. . . . . 6.0		5.2	6.4

Vital Statistics of the United States, 1993

INDEX

NOTES

NOTES